LEARNING FROM LEGENDS

JOHN EALES

© Mettle Media Holdings Pty Limited 2006

Fairfax Books® is a registered trademark of John Fairfax Publications Pty Ltd.

Publisher John Fairfax Publications Pty Ltd.
201 Sussex Street, Sydney, NSW, 2000

Cover design Peter Schofield
Internal page design Peter Schofield and Fiona James
Photo research Paul McLean
Pre-press The *Age* imaging department

Managing Editor, Fairfax Books Michael Johnston (02) 9282 2375
Product Manager, Fairfax Books Sophie Leach (02) 9282 3582
Publishing Manager, Fairfax Books Stephen Berry (03) 9601 2232
General Manager, Fairfax Books Lauren Callister (02) 9282 3904
Group General Manager, Fairfax Enterprises Kevin Stokes

For custom printed copies of *Learning from Legends*, please contact Fairfax Books on (02) 9282 3679.
To order selected images from this title go to www.fairfaxphotos.com

Fairfaxphotos

Printed by: McPherson's Printing Group

ISBN: 1 921190 46 9

LEARNING
FROM
LEGENDS

JOHN EALES

To my father Jack, who taught me the seriousness of sport
and then taught me to not take it too seriously.

FOREWORD: LEARNING FROM LEGENDS

There is nothing that brings Australians together as a nation quite like our love of sport. It is a source of great enjoyment for so many of us, either as participants or spectators. As a nation, we harbour a healthy competitive spirit and value sportsmanship and fair play. In this way, sport unifies the community. It provides us with common ground, through shared goals and the pride we take in achievement. It is very much at the centre of Australian life – a part of the cultural fabric of the nation.

We devote a significant amount of time and energy to sport. It is part of the consciousness and the daily lives of Australians and one reason why Australia's lifestyle has become the envy of the world.

Undoubtedly, our elite sportsmen and women are leaders and role models. Their inspiration to young people is an important element of who they are and what they represent. They are living examples of the rewards that come from taking on personal responsibility, working together and having a go.

They also demonstrate that leadership means many different things to different people. Tenacity, determination to succeed, skill, energy, the ability to inspire and a sense of history are just some of the traits that various leaders show.

There is no easier task in the world than humbly coping with victory, but it is our response to defeat that reveals a person's leadership and moral fibre, together with their ability to learn and move on with honour.

In compiling the material for this book, John Eales has interviewed a number of people associated with sport, many of whom have also been accorded the status of legend. *Learning from Legends* contains some fascinating insights into leadership and I have no doubt that it will provide inspiration to all who read it.

John Howard

John Howard, Prime Minister of Australia

CONTENTS

INTRODUCTION BY **JOHN EALES**

For however long I live I will never repay the debt I owe sport. Outside family, sport has been the greatest influence on my life and as I look back five years post retirement, I am only more convinced of this fact.

Australia is a sports-mad nation. We have an abundance of playing fields with a consistent climate and enthusiasm for a game beyond most. Throw in an exuberant Prime Minister, good funding and a great deal of success and you begin to understand that sport is pretty important south of the Arafura Sea. If someone fronts up against us, we'll front up against them, on the court, in the pool, on the field, in the air… it doesn't matter, bring it on.

Sport is about the experiences, the honour, and the opportunity but above all else it is about the people; those you compete with, those you compete against, and all those others who walk with you along the journey.

Sport breaks down barriers that politics cannot, that race cannot, and that religion cannot. Northern Ireland and the Republic of Ireland play rugby in the one Irish jersey. North Korea and South Korea march together at the Olympic opening ceremony. The Rugby World Cup in South Africa united a nation divided. In Australia it is no different. Sport is the ultimate level playing field, where the garbo lines up with the gastroenterologist and the labouror with the lawyer.

Though some will deny its carriage as a learning vehicle, I value the sports/learning metaphor immensely; not blindly as an ex-sportsperson conflicted in his view but because I believe the same fundamentals of success in one arena may apply just as well in another. Just as many lessons from the corporate arena, or from the arts, or the sciences, or even from the comedians may apply to sport, sport itself can teach. It's irrelevant from where the lesson arises: success teaches success.

Early in my career I discovered that if you follow the path of the successful it can lead you on a wonderful and successful journey of your own. This is called role modeling, and if there is one short cut in life it is through role modeling. Our first role models are our parents, then our teachers, and then, like it or not, the next are likely to be the sportspeople, rockstars and tv personalities that populate the media and win the hearts and minds of our young.

In Australia a child is more likely to be influenced by Grant Hackett than the Prime Minister. Whilst this is the case we must be proactive in identifying and promoting the most valuable lessons these people can teach.

This book should be read in the spirit of openness, in the spirit of learning, and with the spirit of humility. It's not to say that Steve Waugh has all the answers to life's quandaries or that Grant Hackett's strategy for Gold in Athens would work for a top CEO in mining. But then again, who's to say it wouldn't. If you close your mind to external thoughts you run the risk of being ignorant and ignorant people will never learn.

Many people think they know it all – that because they have been part of an environment for a long time they have seen it all – but some of life's most valuable lessons strike when you least expect it.

Take as an example when a young sportsperson makes their debut, an air of expectancy pervades the team. What will this person contribute? How are they different? What can I learn from them?

Over the next week you may learn more from your new team member, who has never played a test, than you would learn from the person playing their 100th test…that is, if you are prepared to listen.

Within the pages of this book are the leadership and performance stories and lessons from some of Australia's most successful and prominent sportspeople; players, coaches, commentators, and administrators. How did they achieve in their ultimate moment, their Stephen Bradbury moment, their Andy Warhol 15 minutes of fame, the moment that defines their career as much as any aggregate, average, or statistic. What did they learn from their greatest mistakes? Why are they a legend?

In compiling this list of legends, I admit to bias. However, everyone on this list has not only inspired me, but many others at home and around the world. Inspiration though wasn't the only criteria. They must have been legendary in their performance, but more specifically in their leadership. This is not a book simply about legendary performance - it is about legendary leadership performance. So interviewing these legends has been fascinating. Just as they each share common ground in how they made it to the top of their field, so each has a unique way of articulating how they did so. It is through these common elements and their unique stories that we learn.

For a start, great leaders have mentors. People that believe in them, aid and inspire them along their journey, push back at them when they need it, nurture them as required. Most of us have more than one. All the legends in these pages have been inspired by significant others. Sometimes it was their coach, sometimes their captain, almost always their family. Sometimes they have been there for the whole journey and sometimes just for a part of it. Regardless, they have been influential. Some of mine are in this book, I have been fortunate.

When I drove into the gates of the Brothers Rugby Club at Crosby Park for the start of under 19s pre-season training, the first person to shake my hand and greet me was a small elderly gentleman by the name of Merv Hazell. Now Merv was typical of so many figures in sport all around the world, his job was to sign-on all the young players that came to the club. Once you met Merv you were a Brother's man for life. Upon that first meeting, as he let go of my hand, he looked me in the eye and said, "Now, I've signed-on every international at this club since 1965 and I think you're going to be the next." Can you begin to imagine a young man's pride?

I could hardly contain myself until after training and whilst having a drink in the clubhouse with my mates, I confided Merv's words. The response I got was not as expected…they laughed at me. "Merv says that to everyone you idiot." The joke was on me…for a while anyway. Regardless, I had someone that believed in me…and I liked it…it gave me confidence. I had a mentor.

Mentors can only take you so far though, as success depends upon a persons own character, and among the legends consistency emerges around the qualities of integrity, humility and balance. A Person with high integrity is trustworthy, they keep their commitments to coaches and teammates and, importantly, they behave ethically and act on principles rather than on self interest.

I asked each legend a few common questions and to one I almost invariably received the same response. "What wouldn't you do in the name of victory?" "I wouldn't cheat." Not all were angels – they admitted that – but while playing tough and playing on the edge were expected and accepted, playing unfairly was not. This sense of fair play is also reflected in the legends unequivocal stance on performance enhancing drugs in sport. Zero tolerance was the mandate.

Equally, humility was common among the group and so perfectly represented by a quote about Ron Barassi where it was said, "The greatest thing about Ron Barassi is that he doesn't realise he is Ron Barassi." This is just as applicable to any number of those within these pages…not that they would say it themselves of course, as there is no room in the modest persons kit to praise themselves for their own humility.

Humility is the willingness to acknowledge that you have more to learn and the understanding that other people and sometimes good fortune have played a part in your success. Over the years great sportspeople such as Muhammad Ali haven't been poster-boys for humility, bandying such comments as, "I am the greatest," to his adoring public. However, even the greatest in ill health are eventually put in their place, as he acknowledges that God gave him Parkinson's to show him who really is the greatest.

Just as humility is not to be confused with meekness, confidence must not to be confused with arrogance. The difference between arrogance and confidence is essentially respect; respect for yourself, respect for your teammates, respect for the system, and respect for your opposition. People need confidence to succeed, the best may even be super confident, but they must be humble at the same time. Arrogant leaders do not respect their opposition. Arrogant leaders do not respect their own teammates. Arrogant leaders will not lead sustainable success.

Life is about balance. A simple concept, but hard to achieve. Balance is about having interests outside your main focus while also having a healthy level of self respect. Each of the legends were both balanced and unbalanced. Balanced when it came to preparing for performance, but sometimes unbalanced in the singular pursuit of their goal. As John Bertrand says, "Content people don't make world champions."

Off the field, the legends understand their responsibility to society, acknowledging that while they mightn't have chosen to be a role model, they are. They feel responsible for protecting the reputation of their sport, the sponsors that support it, and the fans. The media sometimes label them ornaments to their games, the parents simply thank them.

Sir Donald Bradman summed it up best by reminding players they are the custodians of the game, and as such, it is their job to leave the game in a better state when they finish with it, than what it was in when they began.

I love that sentiment because it assigns personal responsibility for each and every individual to make a difference through their contribution and it does not differentiate between contribution on the field and contribution off the field as they are not mutually exclusive.

To make a difference requires discipline. The word discipline easily conjures up images of schoolmasters, canes and Tom Brown's School Days. While that may have been the way in the old school yard, in high performance terms, discipline is the merest of requirements for success, and its definition is so much broader.

The essence of discipline is the ability to maintain your personal and your team's standards, to maximize results. Disciplined competitors are so in many facets of their lives. They are able to manage their behavior appropriately by controlling their impulses, and emotions such as anger, boredom, frustration and elation. This ability in turn allows them to focus on their training and competition rigorously.

One discipline consistent across great teams and among great leaders is the ability to communicate clearly, concisely and consistently. You must know your story, tell it well, and tell it often. It is also important to appreciate that communication doesn't just occur through what you say, it also occurs through your behaviour, through the systems (like the remuneration or reward systems) that operate in your environment, and through the symbolism (like the importance of the colours of the jersey or the cap you wear).

As the saying goes, "I can't hear what you say, who you are is too loud."

Central to communicating with people and therefore to leading people is knowing the people you lead. Leaders must first realise that everyone is different and then understand how they are different in order to extract the best out of them. Even in the united world of team sport, every athlete is different.

Great sporting leaders are fastidious about their preparation. Preparation in a team environment is about being tactically adept, coach-able and fitting into the team environment. Competitors that are tactically adept are sometimes called 'game-smart'. They quickly understand game plans and tactics, and through their intrinsic feel for the game, translate the theory into practice. Often they adapt tactics on the run and sometimes, over a period of time, redefine how their sport is played.

In sport people continually work on their skills long after they are selected, whereas In business, once you have undertaken your initial on-the-job training, it is often taken for granted that you continue to develop your skills. Sport does not take this chance and the best competitors are rarely satisfied.

Fitting into the team environment is also a consistent trait across this group. At times an individual must subjugate their personal ambition for the sake of the team. This requires a person to be the best player they can, for the team, and not worry about being the best player, in the team. That will look after itself…although most people in this book have been both.

There is one more important distinction between good leaders and great leaders. Great leaders understand the difference between passion and execution. Far too often I have been in losing teams, however, we never lost because we lacked passion. We were accused of lacking passion, and we probably looked to lack passion, but we never lacked passion.

The myth of passion is one of the greatest myths of sport. After a poor performance it a cliché for reporters to accuse a team of lacking passion. I would never deny our team's poor performances – fans and media alike know one when they see one and are entitled to challenge you on it - but please don't accuse us of lacking passion as there is no greater indictment on a person's character, and no greater insult, than to intimate they don't care. A poor performance is usually more accurately explained due to a lack of ability, in the skills of the game, to adapt to the conditions, to outwit the opposition, and to execute on the day, rather than a lack of passion

The ultimate goal of a team or an individual must be composure. Composure is about performing under pressure, it is about performing under no pressure, it is about consistency no matter what the external environment. Composure is calculated and it takes time. A captain cannot announce one morning that from now on our team will be composed. Composure is the product of dedicated planning and hard work, and only manifests itself in a team environment of faith – a faith grounded by a belief in yourself, in those around you, and in the system you operate within.

So success in sport is similar to success in life. Every legend in this book has been through good times and through bad. Where they differ from the average person, however, is in how they have reacted to their performances. They were rarely satisfied with their great performances, but equally, they weren't disheartened or destroyed by their bad ones.

Ultimately success is a journey not a destiny, and usually a long journey at that. Simon Burgess, a double world champion, and a member of the lightweight coxless four rowing crew that won silver in both Sydney and Athens paints the winner's journey in a metaphor of a 2000m rowing race:

At the start line, it is about having a clear head, a strong resolve and purpose, so that if someone asks the six competitors the question, Who wants to win the race? 6 crews put their hands up.

At the 500 metre mark, where things are a bit harder, the gut is burning, there are less voices of encouragement from within, and there is a separation between crews, the question is asked again, Who wants to win the race? A couple less hands go up in the air.

At the 1000m mark, the legs are burning too, one crew has picked up their pace - they only have half the race to go, another has dropped back beyond redemption - they are only half way along the journey, the voices of encouragement are fading, and the question is asked again, Who wants to win the race? What is your response? Is the glass half empty or half full? Are you looking forwards or backwards?

At the 1500m mark, your arms have little to give, your lungs are screaming for any scrap of air, your mouth is dry, forget about your legs - you can't feel them anymore, and the only voice you hear is the negative one inside your head. Who wants to win the race? Now only one or two are left in the hunt. Is it you?

At 2000 metres there is only one winner in a rowing race, only one crew with their hands in the air saluting victory…Is your hand in the air?

Every one of our legends learnt to keep their hands in the air until the end of the race – every one of them learnt how to win.

Life is like a rowing race with one vital distinction. In a rowing race there can be just one winner; in life everyone can win.

Every contributor to this book has pioneered in their field, or has taken an average team and contributed towards making them a great team, has maintained a great team's performance, has inspired their team, has inspired a nation, has shown great courage, has shown uncommon perseverance, has laughed, has cried, has failed, and has succeeded.

But long after the pain is forgotten, all the legends in this book remain winners, and not just for the results that we cheered. They are winners for the manner in which they won, for the journey they took, for the mistakes they made, and for the lessons they have taught us and for those they continue to teach.

RON **BARASSI**

"The best definition of professionalism is, 'working towards a complete eradication of error'. That's what professional is about."

RON BARASSI *Former AFL Player and Coach*

Vision: Ron Barassi watches the last training session before the final game played by Carlton at Optus Oval, 2005.

Photo: Vince Caligiuri

I can't believe I am sitting with Ron Barassi. I mean, Barassi is one of those household names that transcends Australian sport, and he seems to have been around for so much longer than he actually has. Or, at least, so much longer than his 70 years would suggest. I remember my surprise when I discovered he wasn't dead. When I was only 10 years old he was such a legendary figure and people spoke about him with such reverence that I just … well, I just assumed. Sitting here now, I don't even know what to call him. Should I call him "Sir" or "The Ron"?

"How are you, Mr Barassi?"

"Very well, thanks," he says, before continuing. "You know I spoke at two rugby luncheons here in Melbourne during the World Cup."

Great, I thought, common ground.

"I opened both with, 'I think rugby union is un-Australian' and there was deathly silence." *I'm sure.*

"Then I said, 'They're un-Australian because they won't allow Aussie rules in the door of those Sydney Public Schools'. It got a good reaction, and it did get their attention." It still does, Ronny, it still does.

Ron's biggest influence in life was his mother Elza. His father, Ron senior, days after playing with the Melbourne Demons in their premiership-winning

INFLUENTIAL PEOPLE
- Norm Smith, *Melbourne player and coach*
- Elza Ray, *mother*
- John Kennedy, *Hawthorn player and coach*

PLAYING CAREER
- 254 games
- 330 goals
- 6 premierships
- Melbourne (1953-1964) 204 games, 295 goals, captain 1960-1964, best and fairest 1961, 1964
- Carlton (1965-1969) 50 games, 35 goals
- Premierships Melbourne – 1955, 1956, 1957, 1959, 1960, 1964
- All Australian 1956, 1958, 1961

team of 1940, sailed off to war, to Tobruk. He never came back. He was the first VFL footballer killed in World War II. Ron jnr was five years old.

Elza worked, and then she worked and then she worked some more. She was the breadwinner and, with the only bread to win being in the city, she spent a lot of time away. Barassi stayed with his grandfather and aunt in the country, but his mother's influence prevailed. At Christmas time, however, his mother would take Ron and his aunt for a holiday down to Eastern Beach at Geelong. One year, when he was 10, he got himself into a bit of trouble with a few other boys on the beach. He called one of them a bastard. He doesn't remember whether it was a more sing-a-longish "You silly bastard" or a harsher "You bastard", but they definitely took offence.

"They wanted a punch-up and because there were three of them I started backing off. Mum comes along just at that moment. She comes and pushes them aside and grabs hold of me and says, 'We're going home. If your father was alive today he'd be ashamed of you.' "

Ron didn't think his mother had heard what he said so he jumped in immediately protesting that there were three of them against him. She stopped him short and hissed, "Don't ever back down!"

"She didn't know what I had said. She was just crook at me for backing down. She was a feisty, gorgeous person, very popular, very honest, direct, loving and caring. She was my big influence." Elza had a big influence in setting Ron up with legendary Melbourne coach Norm Smith. She worked with Norm's wife in one of her jobs. Ron was just about to turn 17 and, having just remarried, she was about to move to Tasmania, so they set up a bungalow in Norm's backyard where the boy would stay.

Norm was a great mentor, but he didn't make life easy for Ron. He had a saying, "Have favourites because you're human and you do have favourites, but don't play favourites." Playing favourites is a whole different scenario to having favourites. This wisdom made it easier for Ron to drop players when he became coach, but it didn't make it any easier for him in Norm Smith's backyard. "Norm was an absolute straight shooter; he didn't mince words, he was hard, very tough and liked vigorous football and all of that, but not dirty football. He wasn't into that at all."

"I don't know why I did it; the umpire was only 10 metres away and he saw everything. He just looked at me and said, 'Ron, the finals are in two weeks' and said nothing else."

When Ron was first chosen for a game in the senior side he learnt about it in the paper. "That's how strict Norm was on ethics. He'd say, 'Well, I hadn't told anyone else, I don't ring up anyone else about the game, so why would I do it for Ron.' In fact, I've heard it said at the club that he probably made it even harder for me than perhaps he should have. Some thought that I should have gone in a week or two earlier than I did."

In that first season, Ron played three full games and had three on the bench, so he really had to battle for his place, and it was no easier the next season. In one game, Ron, playing full forward and not yet fully established in the team, heard the taunts of the crowd. "You're only getting a game because your father played with Melbourne." It hurt, but as always Norm's words were the tonic, "Never trust a crowd, Ron. They're lovely and they support you, but when they're in a group and the mob feeling sets in, they can't be trusted."

One afternoon he was incensed at the crowd's reaction to his opponent and idol, the great John Kennedy of Hawthorn. After Kennedy took his first overhead mark, the crowd gave him the "Bronx cheer". Ron ran towards the stands waving

Learn from your mistakes: Ron in his coaching days at North Melbourne.

The wrong place ...

"I said to a fellow called Keith Greig, a terrific player for North Melbourne, 'Keith, if you weren't good at football you'd still be just a shit plumber.' As soon as it came out of my mouth, I thought, 'This is wrong, I don't think that way at all, I hate that sort of stuff.' But it was out and I couldn't do anything about it. He played a lot better and we did win the match, but I wanted to apologise to him. The next Sunday morning I was going to pull him aside and I was going to apologise to him in front of the whole squad. But he got my eye before he went out to train and said, 'Coach, can I have a word with you?' So we went to the coach's room and he expressed his disappointment in what I'd said. I said 'Look, I've got no excuse, you caught me red-handed.' I said that to him and I went out and apologised. I think a leader should apologise when they're wrong. However, if they find themselves doing that a lot, they won't be leaders for very long. And nor should they be. Leaders can't afford to be wrong a lot."

his arms, irate at the disrespect. It didn't matter that Kennedy was the opposition; he should have been celebrated, not slated.

Sportsmanship became a hallmark of Ron's career as a player and as a captain, winning six premierships with the Melbourne Demons, then turning to coaching first as captain-coach of Carlton and then at North Melbourne, Melbourne and the Sydney Swans. He was a tough player, but not dirty. "I used to like being aggressive, it was part of the thrill of our game, laying a good tackle on or hitting somebody with a hip and shoulder, but I wouldn't condone anything untoward.

"The one such hit I did on a bloke didn't hurt him, it was in his stomach. I don't know why I did it; the umpire was only 10 metres away and he saw everything. He just looked at me and said, 'Ron, the finals are in two weeks' and said nothing else."

As coach, Ron had no tolerance for the biff ... well, maybe just once. In charge of North Melbourne in the grand final he ordered one of his team to go after a Hawthorn player who had been doing "unpleasant" things to them previously. "I'm not very proud of that, usually I would never have a bar of that sort of thing. In fact, I was one of the first people who spoke out against that sort of stuff in the suburbs and in country football. It is absolutely disgraceful. In the end, Hawthorn got wind of it and he wasn't even in the ruck for the opening bounce. If you do that, then sensible people are not going to come and play our sport."

And that was important for Ron. He always had visions of a national game. And he backed his vision with action, coaching the struggling Sydney Swans in the early '90s. The year after he left in '96 they made the grand final and, 10 years later, they won it. Within that same decade, the Brisbane Lions, once the "Bad News Bears", won three grand finals in a row. Ron's dream is reality.

It is said the greatest thing about Ron Barassi is that he doesn't know he's

Ron Barassi. And it is true. For him, humility is a quality above all others, and he is intolerant of anyone who is arrogant. "The opposite of humility isn't appreciated in Australia. It's no more than fortune that you are good-looking, tall, strong, intelligent, gifted. You are just arsey. Norm Smith used to say, 'Success isn't what you achieve, it's what you should achieve with what you have.' We understand that disability is bad luck, but we don't understand that natural ability is good luck. If you have a good run and you are healthy, fit and intelligent, then you're lucky – so revel in it, but be humble because you have someone on your side. I don't know if you believe in God or not, it could be nature, it could be whatever! But it's not only you."

Humility ensured he was always aware of those around him, and it was a great reminder that he couldn't do everything himself. It also allowed him to accept disappointments, including being dropped just two weeks before the 1968 finals series when captain-coach of Carlton. "I didn't take part in the finals, and they were right; I didn't want to surround myself with 'yes' men. I was getting near the end and I didn't feel betrayed, but I got over it quickly because I had to focus on the final series as the coach. We went through the finals and won the premiership. Then I said to myself, 'I'll prove to these bastards' and I trained like a maniac through the summer. I was as fit as ever, but after two practice matches I knew they were right. I'd lost my reflexes, which I relied upon a lot in my role."

It is no coincidence that for the opening of the 2006 Melbourne Commonwealth Games Ron was chosen to walk on water. In Melbourne's tribal AFL community, no one baulked. It was totally appropriate. Just as he transcends Australian sport, he also transcends his own sport, in some ways a greater accomplishment.

Ron may have been a brilliant footballer, he may even have been the greatest, but you won't get that from him. He's been too well brought up for that. So well brought up that those Sydney public schools may have allowed him in, but only to play rugby. And he no doubt would have been good at that, too.

LAWS OF LEADERSHIP

- Be defined by your values

- Learn from your mistakes

- Lead by example

- Make the most of your ability and your opportunities

- Be committed

- Know the importance of the history of the game

- Know your expectations

- Be your own man, but mindful of people around you

PETER **BARTELS**

"Managers push, leaders pull. Managers command, leaders inspire."

PETER BARTELS *Australian Sports Commission Chairman*

Thinker: Peter Bartels, 1993.

Photo: Julian Kingma

He didn't realise it at the time, but each day as the 12-year-old Peter Bartels rode the 24 kilometres through the streets of Glen Waverly to Box Hill Grammar (now Kingswood College), he was earning an education, learning so much more than he ever did in the classroom. The journey started as a means to an end, a necessity born out of not living on the bus route to school, and through the unattractiveness of the alternative. One train and two buses each way was not an option.

These bike rides turned into training sessions for life. All of a sudden, Peter found himself wanting to pass the guy in front, marking off the milestones along the way and taking note of the time. Was he ahead or behind? It was important. Every landmark was the start of a new race, every rider – most of them older – someone he had to pass. There were no distractions, nobody was going to get in his way.

"I was just a kid, but I had this competitive spirit; I saw it as competition and I decided that I really wanted to win so I used to practise how I would finish my events. Inadvertently, I started interval training before anyone told me what it was. Each corner or each new set of traffic lights I saw as a start. I became a standing-start expert and a gold medallist for a time trial, which is all about standing and starting. In a one-kilometre time trial, the best time

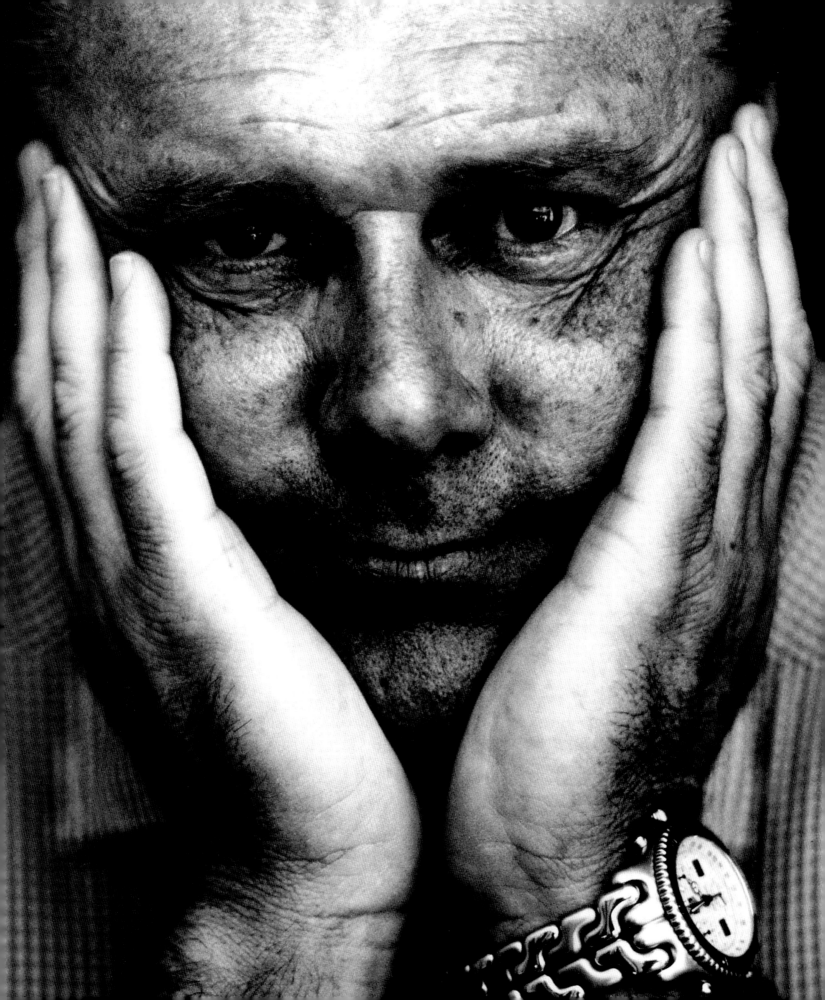

INFLUENTIAL PEOPLE

- Bruce Hendy, *early business career mentor*
- Tas, *father*
- John Elliott
- Sid Patterson, *cyclist*
- Herb Elliott
- Sir Donald Bradman
- John Landy
- Neale Fraser
- Ron Barassi

triallists in the world don't ride it as one kilometre; they ride it as four laps of a 250-metre track. They worry about the first lap, the second lap, the third lap, and just hope they can survive the fourth lap. In an odd way, I had done that thousands of times on the road between each set of traffic lights and getting up the hills."

The adrenaline-charged competitive nature of the world of cycling breeds them tough. There is no tolerance of weakness, and this is reflected in Peter's brashness – confidence for him reigns supreme. Although, for someone so competitive, Peter was raised on a foundation of homespun values. His early cycling influences were men such as his father Tas and his uncle Tassie Johnson, both competitive and both good men. Tassie represented Australia at the 1936 Berlin Olympics and the 1938 Empire Games in Sydney. Later that year, he turned professional and won every major track championship and wheel race.

Peter's father instilled in him the importance of behaving with integrity and of living consistently by your values. When he was about 15, his father decided it was time that he understood what was right and what was wrong. He sat him down and laid it out. "So here are the rules," he said. "If you come home and over the kitchen table can tell your mother and I what you've been doing, then it's probably right. If you can't, it's probably wrong."

Peter saw it as good advice, living it and even practising it in his boardrooms of the future. It was such simple advice, but combined with his competitive instincts it guided him through life.

On the track, his ultimate glory came at the '62 Empire Games in Perth. Two years earlier, set as the form rider heading into the Rome Olympics, he had an accident, damaging his wrist so that he couldn't compete. It ignited the tinder in his belly for which the only salve would be victory in Perth.

Winning was important to Peter: "I never kept prizes other than first prizes because everything other than winning for me was a mistake. I never wanted my trophy cabinet to be a reminder of errors."

And it was constantly drilled into him: "I had a coach, the towering Billy Guyatt, who, whenever he put me on my bike would tap me on the helmet and say, 'Son, this'll hurt a lot less if you win.' "

"So it's not surprising that sportspeople have emerged as the new heroes and heroines. Sport has a new role to play and new values ..."

A singular focus and ambition to win the gold in Perth crowned and completed his sporting career. "You can have balance in your life, but there are moments when you are totally unbalanced or you'd never get there." Peter knew what he wanted and simply decided to do it – whatever it took.

Business then beckoned as he focused on getting a job. "If I could be that good at sport with all of the skills that I'd developed, surely it wouldn't be too hard to be that good in the business world."

Cycling is an individual sport, but it taught Peter important lessons that he transferred to his corporate life. He became the CEO of both Foster's and Coles Myer, at the time two top-10 publicly listed companies in Australia. Currently, he sits as chairman of the Australian Sports Commission. In a big endorsement of his ability, transport mogul Lindsay Fox once hailed him as the best CEO in Australia, possibly the world.

Sport taught Peter to make decisions and it gave him instant feedback on those decisions. It was simple with cycling – decisions had to be made in

Crowning glory: Coach Joe Buckley cheers Peter to victory at the Empire Games in Perth, 1962.

PETER BARTELS' 10 BUSINESS COMMANDMENTS

1. **Focus on the key issues for survival.** In other words, don't be distracted by external issues. Keep your eyes clearly on the main game.

2. **Make budget.** Like any good household manager, set yourself a realistic budget and stick to it.

3. **Never run short of cash.** Cash flow is the lifeblood of an organisation. If I were offered the choice between an asset-rich company or one with strong cash flow, I'd take the cash any day.

4. **Change strategic direction with caution.** Don't be hasty to change direction. Sticking to your knitting is usually the best option. You have built up the expertise and the experience in that area – entering a completely new business may not be as attractive as it seems.

5. **Preserve market share.** You can build on market share as you can with nothing else – economies of scale, market influence, supplier relations, etc.

an instant, and they had immediate impact over your performance as well as your safety. Sport also helped spawn his key philosophy on running a business – the three Ss: Strategy, Structure and Staff. "Firstly, the best businesses in the world start with a strategy. They think about the strategic direction of what they're trying to achieve. Then they think about what structure is required. Then you need staff to do it."

Peter has been chairman of the ASC for nine years. His influence has been significant, particularly in broader agendas such as merging the interests of the state and federal governments across the portfolios of sport, health and education. The Active After-Schools Communities Program, for instance, aims to encourage a more healthy and active nation to help decrease childhood obesity.

"Sport does things to unite that no government has been able to do." The program keeps active about 130,000 children at 2580 sites. "This program has been exceedingly successful, thanks largely to the outstanding work of Mark Peters and his team at the Australian Sports Commission."

Peter believes that for Australia the leadership of the Australian Sports Commission goes far beyond just sport. "It's puzzling for young Australians today to find leadership, and I believe sportspeople are emerging as the new Anzacs.

"The Australian character was built in the early 1900s, and through World War I and World War II, and we still represent the same values today. People worked hard, they were driven by a sense of achievement, they were driven by purpose, and when the diggers went to war everyone wanted a digger beside them. It was, 'We'll have a go, we'll ask later, we'll fight first and we'll worry about it later.' Progressively, that's the ethos that Australia has developed, but young Australians are puzzled as to how to find that.

"It's harder these days for people to understand the purpose of war, so sport has become the new combat zone for Australians. Australians, whether they are rugby teams, football teams, cyclists, swimmers or whatever go overseas and they battle for their country's pride because they're wearing the Australian crest. And Australians love it because they see us challenging the world from a small population and they see us espousing those digger values.

"In the world today people are puzzled: who do they follow? They're not closely connected with the church. Families are not closely connected. People are not aggressive in universities today as compared to universities in the '60s. So it's not surprising that sportspeople have emerged as the new heroes and heroines. Sport has a new role to play and new values, and hence the role of the Australian Sports Commission."

Which is why Peter believes through the Australian Sports Commission the Government must take over from our diggers and take a key role in making sport the new role model for Australians.

"The diggers formed the Australian character in the eyes of the world, and we have it now for better or for worse, and if you go overseas representing Australia you are expected to have those Aussie fighting qualities: you're supposed to go until you drop, you don't take no for an answer, you're supposed to be resilient, you're supposed to be tough, and you're supposed to be able to do it in all forms of adversity."

And it is through striking people at their core motivation and through their core ambition and drive that Peter knows they will achieve ultimate success.

"Clarence Francis, the former head of General Foods in the USA, sums it up best for me when he says, 'You can buy a person's time; you can buy his physical presence in a given place; you can even buy a measured number of his skilled muscular motions per hour. But you cannot buy enthusiasm. You cannot buy initiative. You cannot buy the devotion of hearts, minds and souls. You have to earn those things.' "

PETER BARTELS' 10 BUSINESS COMMANDMENTS

6. **Maintain product integrity.** Customers today demand quality and consistency. If you don't deliver, you will lose them.

7. **Maintain the warmth of the organisation.** If your staff, suppliers and customers don't feel comfortable with your company, you can't expect their full support.

8. **Revel in outstanding performance.** Acknowledge it, celebrate it and reward it.

9. **Ensure communications are two-way.**

10. **Analyse the facts and then take action.** Research, analyse and assess – carefully. Taking decisive action is often risky, particularly if the stakes are high. Maximise your chances by being properly prepared. And when you're confident you have the facts, move quickly, ahead of the competition.

LAYNE **BEACHLEY**

"I try to remind people I wasn't born a world champion. I wasn't born a leader, I wasn't born a role model, but what got me there was my attitude, my never-say-die attitude, my love, my passion, my desires, my focus, my desire to be a world champion is what got me to be a world champion."

LAYNE BEACHLEY *Surfing World Champion*

Champ: Layne at Manly Beach, 2004.
Photo: Marco del Grande

"It was 2001 in Hawaii and I had been venturing into towing surfing, which means that you are towed into waves by a jet ski because you can't physically paddle fast enough to ride waves that big. On this day, we knew we were going to be blessed with the biggest swell in a very long time, and we knew the swell was going to reach over 30 foot.

"I really wanted to surf that day. So to be ready for this experience, a potential battering, I mentally prepared for the worst possible wipe-out, which could be close to drowning. I prepared myself to be shoved so deep underwater that I'd be completely disorientated; I may even have no oxygen left in my lungs and I was going to have to be able to relax and know that I could get myself back to the surface again. We do wear life jackets that are quite thin, but at least they're buoyant. At times when I've been pushed so deep I've just had to grab hold of the collar of the life jacket and see which way my head goes, and if it's up then that's the way I'll start swimming. These are the circumstances that you willingly put yourself under … well, I do anyway.

"We woke up that morning, the swell had indeed come and the conditions were beautiful and we were ready to hit it. My boyfriend at the time was my towing partner. He was in Florida and I was in Hawaii, and he was ringing me every 10 minutes, saying, 'You are not ready, you cannot go.' I ended up just

INFLUENTIAL PEOPLE

- Neil, *father*
- Barton Lynch
- Tom Carroll
- Martin Potter
- Wendy Botha
- Pam Burridge
- Rob Bain
- Stuart Entwistle
- Justin Cook

"My feelings of self-worth come from the friends I have around me, the passion and the fire I have in my heart to do what I'm doing."

turning the phone off and not listening to him. I got on the jet ski and went out with his current tow partner. Unfortunately, the channel we usually go through was closing out, and because the waves were so big, it wasn't deep enough to hold them, so we had to time it really well to get up through the break, jumping 10-foot waves in the process.

"When we arrived at the surf spot, we cruised around it for a little while as my heart was pounding and I was full of adrenaline and full of fear. But the adrenaline was overriding the fear. I just breathed and relaxed, and affirmed myself, 'I'm ready for this. I know I can do it. I'm ready to drown if I have to.'

"He said, 'You're first.' And I went, 'Yeah … ladies first.' I jumped off the back of the machine and slid my feet into the straps on my board. We motored around and it warmed up my legs. At this point we have hand signals between each other, because I'm 35 feet back from the machine and he's got the sound of the engine to listen to and can't hear me. So we motion to each other things like, 'this one' or 'the second one' or 'go around again.'

"All of a sudden, due to the size of the wave, the horizon turned black. And I was ready to catch it. I just went, 'THIS ONE! THIS ONE!' And he's like, 'Are you sure?' I'm like, 'YES! YES! YES! I WANT THIS ONE!'

"I remember letting go of the rope and, because of the speed I was travelling, I knew it was the biggest wave I'd caught in my life. I was going at about 40 kilometres an hour on my feet – thank God my board was really big and heavy and my feet were strapped in. Anyway, I let go of the rope and I remember I was going faster than the wave itself and had to slow down to the speed of it – it actually felt like I was going backwards. Then the wave hit the reef and stood up. That's when I started going down it, and it was like a roller-coaster, and I got to the bottom and I was going, 'I'm just free-standing.' It was the whole positive affirmation thing. Instead of 'Don't Fall' I always went with 'Stay Standing'.

"I got to the bottom and came up, and as I was coming back up the face of the wave I realised that this thing was massive; they called it a 30-foot wave, which stands at 50 foot high. Imagine standing at the bottom of a five-storey building and you'll get an idea as to how much water was above me. And as I was coming up and I looked behind me I saw the barrel was as wide as it was high. You could have driven a bus behind me. I just looked at it and went 'ah,

crap!' and just hauled arse. All I was thinking was, 'Just make the channel, just make the channel.' And I got to the channel. And I just screamed in elation because that's what I'd prepared myself for. That was the experience I wanted.

"It was all because I was so relaxed and so in the moment, and I haven't felt that kind of presence for a long time. I was in a death-defying situation, and my attention turned immediately to the present moment; I had never been aware of how present you could possibly become. That presence, that excitement, that adrenaline, that fear, all melded into one of the ultimate experiences of my life … And I never got my hair wet."

In surfing, the wave is both your friend and your foe. Victory is against your competitor working with the wave, but it is also against the wave as well. A bigger, stronger wave will present greater opportunity, but it will do so with a much greater degree of difficulty. It requires a balance of respect and fear – just enough fear to respect the wave and the opportunity it presents.

"Surfing is a sport where you never truly feel you have made it because

Outside the comfort zone: Layne prepares for competition at Manly, 1997.
Photo: Tim Clayton

29

CAREER STATS

- Professional surfer 1989-
- World champion 1998, 1999, 2000, 2001, 2002, 2003
- ASP World Championship Tour victories 29

you never truly master the inconsistency and uncontrollable elements of Mother Nature. Life in general can be intimidating and threatening; surfing is the same. One of the very valuable things it has taught me is to relinquish control. You are up against Mother Nature, and you can neither predict her nor control her. You must submit yourself to her control and be malleable and adaptable to what you come up against. "

To ride the Big Wave, Layne displayed many of the great qualities that have made her an inspirational leader in sport and in life. She leads through her surfing, her Layne Beachley Aim For the Stars Foundation, and her life, and she has inspired men, women and children from all areas of society. Her leadership revolves around passion, focus, fighting spirit, relationships, communication and a comfort with, and love of, herself. All of these qualities enabled her to ride the Big Wave.

In her early days on the tour, Layne felt shackled, having to build up from buckling under the pressure and coming dead last in her first event to her breakthrough tour victory in the Diet Coke Classic at Narrabeen in 1993. After years of leaving her sweat in the ocean, on the sand hills and in the gym, she had finally won. For her it was an epiphany, reclaiming a long-lost belief in herself that she could actually win a world title. "I remember coming out of the water crying because it was such an awesome relief to finally win an event. At the age of 16, I had been staking claim that I would be a world champion so this silenced the critics for a while, one week before my 21st birthday."

Her strong self-belief was nurtured in the male-dominated surfing culture of Sydney's Northern Beaches, at Manly. It was in those waves that little Layne steadfastly fought for her spot and her opportunity in the game. There was only one rule in the territorial waters: "Don't go north of the stormwater pipes." It wasn't her territory, and it was the only rule she respected.

Surfing was always a priority, although at one point she flirted with the idea of becoming a tennis pro or a stockbroker. Interest and opportunity thwarted the former, and a week's work experience turned her off the latter. But her interest in surfing never wavered and, while the environment at Manly was at times heated, it provided her with exposure to some of the best surfers in the world. Layne gleaned the lessons off the people she most admired, surfers such as Pam Burridge, Tom Carroll, Barton Lynch and the like. Pam in particular took Layne under her wing, advising her on tactics, equipment and competition. Barton advised her on handling the media, and on it went.

The only thing that competed with Layne's thirst for knowledge and improvement was her desire to be at peace with herself. Although fiercely competitive, her victories and titles are not where she derives her self-esteem. "It takes a lot for a human being to love themselves. It takes a lot for someone that pushes themselves so hard to be forgiving. I know that as a world champion there's a very fine line between being too hard on yourself and not taking things too personally. My feelings of self-worth come from the friends I have around me, the passion and fire I have in my heart to do what I am doing, and the acceptance of my experiences. Essentially, I've allowed myself to be me"

An important part of being herself was surfing within her natural rhythm. In 1997, Layne was frustrated that her surfing had plateaued. Watching herself on video, she knew she was surfing ugly compared with her competitors. She was disjointed and had no flow. She turned to Steve Forman. Again, she had to let go to grow. "He took me back to the fundamentals of surfing and slowed me down to speed me up. It was like I was joining the dots when I was surfing with no fluidity through my turns. Surfing is all about flow and motion and being adaptable and fluid with the ocean. He slowed me down and taught me how to flow with the wave. The next year I won my first world surfing title with a lot less effort and having a lot more fun."

In a sport where the competitors haven't traditionally been either the greatest role models or taken themselves seriously, Layne has broken the mould. World champion male surfer Kelly Slater said of Layne: "There's a lot of girls out there that have just as much ability as Layne, but none of them have the focus or the heart or the desire or the passion that she does."

"I try to remind people I wasn't born a world champion, I wasn't born a leader and I wasn't born a role model. What got me there was my never-say-die attitude, my love, my passion, my focus and my desire to be a world champion. Equally, it has been my ability to let myself be me and to have people around me that also allow that. When you find that very supportive, understanding, loving network of people, hold on to them and don't take them for granted.

"At the end of the day, you can become so controlled and you can become such a dummy that you lose sight of what you really want; you lose sight of who you really are, and if you get to somewhere without that then you haven't really made it at all."

LAWS OF LEADERSHIP

- Stay outside the comfort zones, it's the only time you learn

- The only thing I can control is me and my mental state

- Respect the wave, your competitor, yourself

- Leadership revolves around passion, focus, fighting spirit, relationships, communication

- Leaders are doers not sayers – we don't sit on our hands

- Acknowledge success

- Mistakes are just learning experiences

- Control your emotions

- Focus on yourself, not those around you

JOHN **BERTRAND**

"Our premise was to run a vision-driven model, and the vision for us was to become so good that even with the worst luck we'd still be successful."

JOHN BERTRAND *America's Cup Winning Captain*

John Bertrand has a maxim: "Content people don't make world champions." And while his theory is founded on the unrepresentative sample of just one – himself – his is a very important perspective in Australian sport. In early adulthood, John was a driven man. He had enormous ambition, but he lacked contentment, and it showed.

One of his early employers was a sail-making company in San Diego called North Sails, a business started by Olympic gold medallist and scientist Lowell North. On one conference with the company, all franchisees from around the world spoke with a psychiatrist whose job it was to analyse the characters in the group. At the end of their time together, the psychiatrist said to John, "John, I hope you find happiness. I'm concerned for you." John didn't quite understand, but the thought stuck with him for a long time.

Growing up, he loved sport but hated competition. At 10, before competing in local track and field events he would be sick from the nerves. Even the smell of the freshly cut grass at the track disturbed him. He didn't like racing boats, either, but loved the water and sailing and just watching the bubbles go by. School lessons would pass with little mind to maths or English, but with many drawings, mostly of boats. It might pay teachers to look closely at the musings of their charges ...

Cup'd crusader: John Bertrand, 2004.

Photo: Simon Schluter

INFLUENTIAL PEOPLE

• Paul Elvstrom,
*Danish sailor and
four-time Olympic
gold medallist*

• Buddy Melges,
American sailor

• Ron Barassi

John's competitive instincts and skill in sailing began to emerge when he won national championships in his mid-teens, leading him to compete in the 1972 and '76 Olympics, coming fourth in Munich and winning a bronze in Montreal. "The final race in 1976 was an opportunity of either consolidating and winning a bronze or going for it and potentially winning silver or gold. I carried the burden of the leather medal [fourth place] from '72, and it's worse than coming last because you're so near yet so far – nobody cares for fourth place. I felt that I just needed a medal and that led to me sailing more conservatively.

"Looking back, it became clear to me that, even putting that final race aside, if I had been mentally tough enough it was just as easy for me to have won a gold medal as it was a bronze. I noticed the East German, the eventual gold medallist, had the ability to stay loose and composed throughout the contest no matter the pressure of the international press or the consequences of winning. The East German's attitude became my new benchmark."

There was to be more disappointment and more lessons, including those from an unsatisfying result in the 1980 America's Cup challenge, which ended up like all those before, in defeat. Financially, driving the challenges in 1974, '77, '80 and '83 was Alan Bond. For a convicted criminal, Bond is still respected by many for having a go, paying his dues and doing his time. John acknowledges Bond's frailties, but recognises his talent as both a marketer and big-picture person.

"We were beaten in '74 with a boat called Southern Cross and I said, never again. It was a chaotic program to the point where Bond himself came out sailing in the last race, pumping the handles; he had a lot of raw passion but not a lot of experience and knowledge. I wasn't involved in '77 due to the Olympics and starting my new North Sails business, but Alan had funded all the campaigns – he had tremendous resilience. When we were beaten in 1980, as the boat was sailing in with our tails between our legs, I remember he came on board and said, 'Boys, we now know enough to win the America's Cup.' He could look at anything with the glass half full instead of half empty, and that was one of his great strengths."

John was appointed captain of Australia II for the assault on the cup in 1983. He was in charge of racing the boat, selecting and training crew and pulling them together as a team. At all times these tasks were co-ordinated with syndicate manager Warren Jones. They worked in tandem, overseeing the three links in the chain: administration, technology and people. John was determined that the lessons life had doled out to him, including his missed opportunity for gold in Montreal, would become invaluable in the pursuit of the cup. He wasn't going to miss another opportunity because he was mentally fragile.

Along with the introduction of sports psychologists, John regarded

CAREER STATS

- Olympics 1972 – fourth, Finn class; 1976 – bronze, Finn class
- America's Cup campaigns 1970, 1974, 1980, 1983, 1995
- Winner 1983 as skipper of Australia II
- World champion 1994, America's Cup class
- Chairman, World Wide Entertainment, television production and distribution company exporting to 150 countries globally
- Chairman of the Sport Australia Hall of Fame
- Chairman of the Alannah and Madeline Children's Foundation
- Member of the Order of Australia, 1985

innovation as essential to success and drove a vision with a long-term view. "Our premise was to run a vision-driven model and the vision for us was to become so good that even with the worst luck we'd still be successful."

From John's experience with the Olympics he knew that over any four-year period there was some, usually incremental, improvement in performance. But if you took any 20-year period of the Olympics, across any discipline, then you would almost invariably see quantum leaps in performance.

"We said, purely, all we've got to do is emulate what we think our kids will achieve in 20 years' time and apply those levels of thinking and standards to now. That became a total breakthrough for the organisation because it empowered our young people in particular. That was the start of our thinking

Thumbs up: John at the America's Cup qualifiers, 1988.
Photo: Jim Bourg

__The America's Cup campaign ...__
"We developed the Boxing Kangaroo flag, that was our battle flag. Armies go to war with music and symbols, 2000 years of history tells us that. It's just part of the human endeavour. So we developed the battle flag, which is the pumped-up chest of the pride of the nation, which is the Boxing Kangaroo and red gloves for aggression. That was the flag that we flew with great pride and, after, the music (Men at Work, Down Under) was part of the image of this organisation – to be the best in the world."

behind developments like the winged keel and others."

Enter Ben Lexcen. For a man with just three years of formal education and no formal mathematical or engineering background, he was a brilliantly practical yet creative thinker. Upon arrival at the ship model-testing facility in Holland in 1981, he decided that the weighbridge, for pulling the boats up and down, was not precise enough to give the fine tolerance of lift and drag required to analyse whether a development was fast or slow.

Not content, he actually redesigned the tank system to a point where it is still being used today. "Benny was a creative genius in many ways, and he applied his lateral thinking to many, many areas and, of course, part of that was the winged keel."

The winged keel is one of the most talked-about innovations in Australian sport. As with a lot of creative ideas, it wasn't initially greeted with resounding enthusiasm. "I had great reservations because I'd been through the 1974 campaign, which was extreme in terms of the shape of the boat, and it wasn't tank-tested particularly well, and while we were out in left field the boat was slow, and no matter what we did we couldn't have changed it without building a new boat. All I wanted was an equal boat, and I felt that with the right team, right training, and the right application we could win the America's Cup. I didn't want a roll-the-dice type of environment."

But the tank-test results on the keel were intriguing and led Bertrand to agree they had to build the boat. First tests on the water, sailing against another boat with the same hull and a conventional keel, was a bit disheartening. Heading into the wind for about 12 kilometres you could tie a string between the boats; in the perfect sailing conditions they were exactly the same. However, when they turned, set the spinnakers and went with the wind, the conventional boat just sailed away from them. Was this to be '74 all over again?

"We thought, my God, maybe we've got a dog on our hands. Because the centre of gravity of the winged keel was so much lower, the boat would wobble at a much faster rate and shake the wind out of the sails. With perseverance, we redesigned the sails, the sail shapes of the spinnakers, so Australia II was reasonably competitive with the wind. Interestingly enough, sailing with the wind was never our strong leg, but that was the leg that we won the America's Cup on, the fifth leg when we passed the Americans."

With his engineering and science background (he has two engineering degrees), John was able to give more accurate feedback to the design team. "You take someone like Michael Schumacher. The reason he is so good in Formula One is that he can take a car for one lap and give more accurate feedback to his design engineers than any other driver."

Every time Australia II was lifted out of the water, the keel was covered by a "skirt", causing much consternation among the American team. Their major fear was that they had been out-developed; their greatest frustration was they didn't know.

"In the end, the whole psyche of that winged keel was just as powerful as the technology of the winged keel." John and his team's composure, superior preparation and tough mental attitude saw them turn a 3-1 deficit into what has been regularly nominated as Australia's greatest sporting triumph.

The victory broke 132 years of American domination and, as a result, broke the longest winning streak in modern sports history. The Confederation of Australian Sport voted the team performance as the greatest in 200 years of national sport.

In his reflections after September '83, some 20 years, three Olympics and five America's Cup campaigns after that psychiatrist noted her concerns, her thoughts were laid to rest. "After winning the America's Cup, I became a very content person compared to someone who was driven to the extreme to be successful.

"And it also became clear to me that once you attain contentment, which is a wonderful thing in life, and I can highly recommend it, you don't then become world champion again because the all-consuming drive leaves you and you start to smell the roses and you start to achieve a more, what we call a balanced life, which is a wonderful thing to have."

LAWS OF LEADERSHIP

- Love what you are doing – with passion

- Teach the values of integrity and honesty

- Communicate clearly and concisely to the team

- Develop the ability to succinctly analyse situations, make decisions and communicate them

- Encourage and empower your people

- Take off the blinkers – have no limitations

- Prepare – so no excuses to lose

- Set clear goals that people can understand and believe in

- Never give up

- Zero in on the process

- Have fun

PETER **BROCK**

"We do revere our sporting people in Australia, there's no doubt about it. And with that comes great opportunity. You can either take the money and run, which some do, or you can put something back into the world around you by encouraging others to seek personal excellence."

PETER BROCK *Motor Racing Champion*

POSTSCRIPT: As we went to print, Peter Brock passed away competing in Western Australia. We spent three weeks as Athlete Liaison Officers in Athens in 2004. He was a wonderful person to share time with, so positive in his outlook and so generous with his time and his spirit. Many knew him so much better than I, but he will be missed by all.

It was a sight so familiar. Peter Brock, up on the podium, holding the trophy aloft, speaking into the microphone, accepting the accolades of the crowd and revelling in his latest victory, telling the world how good he felt. A familiar sight, yes, but not a familiar background. Was it Bathurst? Definitely not. How about Sandown? Don't think so – he looks a bit young for that.

In fact, on closer inspection … far too young. He's only 10 years old and the footage is his father's home movie and, yes, Brocky has won another race, but this time not on wheels. It was the under-12, 75-yard running race at the interschool carnival and Peter was the winner, a full year younger than the youngest of his competitors. Watching the video copy years later, he wondered, "Where did that come from? Who taught me? What confidence did I have?"

"I've still got the trophy, it's my most treasured trophy. There is something in that confidence stuff that comes through as a kid in sport. When you feel comfortable in your surroundings and in your peer group, when you actually feel you belong there, that's when the success comes."

As a kid who loved sport, Peter's surroundings were ideal. He was the second born in the family and subsequently spent his formative years chasing and competing against his elder brother on the family farm. His challenge was to run a bit harder, jump a bit higher, and be a bit tougher so that he could fit

"There is something in that confidence stuff that comes through as a kid in sport."
Peter Brock, 2004.
Photo: Eddie Jim

INFLUENTIAL PEOPLE
• Harry Firth, *racing driver*
• Ted Griffiths, *headmaster Hurstbridge Primary School*
• Geoff Brock, *father*
• Ruth Brock, *mother*

in with the older kids – and that he did, on many occasions coming up trumps. From running at the age of seven, he graduated to behind the wheel of the car, or the tractor or whatever machinery he could find. Whether it was ploughing a paddock at three kilometres an hour or driving a truck or a tractor, he loved it. Riding old pre-BMX bicycles around a self-constructed obstacle course, with the stopwatch on, and beating all his mates, was another favourite.

His great uncle, Henry James, was a pioneer of Australian motorsport who together with his father, Geoff, inspired him to tinker with the vehicles on the farm, and later to take an interest in motorsport and a hero by the name of Norm Beechey. "Norm Beechey raced an early-model Holden and he drove the thing crazy – he drove it wild. He drove it with tyre smoke and he'd wave to the crowd at the same time. I used to think, 'That's pretty good.' We were awestruck with this guy. We even made up songs about him and we'd sing them on the way to the track. But I didn't really follow his style, although his flamboyance impressed me. I enjoyed doing it really fast, neat and accurate. That influence came more from the Formula One style of doing it rather than the crash-and-bash touring-car style."

Peter had natural talent, athleticism and enthusiasm, qualities that were harnessed and nurtured by his mentor Harry Firth. People take to mentors for similar reasons and for different reasons. They take to them to learn, but also because they are interesting or quirky people. Harry was the sort of guy who could touch anything and make it work. As a dispatch rider in Tobruk, he once captured a broken-down old German motorcycle and fixed it by making a piston out of a piece of wood. Harry was to Peter what Percy Cerutty was to Herb Elliott. "I've spoken to Herb about his relationship with Percy and mine with Harry, and we both came to the conclusion they were very strange people. They had us doing some really weird things that we resented a bit at the time. But he had a very, very focused mind on what the outcome should be, so he taught me some very important lessons."

Harry, for instance, in the early days, never gave Peter new tyres or any new equipment, rather he got his teammates' cast-offs. At the same time, he expected Peter to beat his teammates – and he didn't disappoint. "I thought that he was lousy, I thought that he'd lost the plot, I thought all these things, but he was very clever about what he did. He made me dig deep; he made me

"I was winning these races and doing all these things successfully, but where was my life going, who was I really? So, strangely enough, success caused me to look within myself, not failure."

see a part of myself, which was about achieving personal excellence and about proving myself, rather than anger. I thought, righto, and I'd really buckle down, and that made an enormous difference to my career."

Peter took a passionate and almost artistic approach to racing. As a result, when Harry described how to round a bend or take a corner his body would move with his description. "When you come to a corner, you know, get it … a bit like this … then straighten up a bit like that …" Peter knew instantly what he meant and he let it happen. Together, he and Harry created some magic.

As time went on and Peter became the focal point and leader of the Holden Dealer Team, he saw his job very simply to "go fast and reward them for their efforts". He knew that results and feedback, both positive and negative, would provide that cohesive element and create a team that was focused and confident. Peter was close to his team and just as happy getting down and dirty with them in the workshop preparing the car as he was being the driver. It was a familiar sight to see him getting the coffees or under the car tinkering

"I enjoyed doing it really fast, neat and accurate." Peter racing in a Holden Monaro, undated.

CAREER STATS

- Bathurst Enduro winner 1972, 1975, 1978, 1979, 1980, 1982, 1983, 1984, 1987
- Bathurst 24hr-race winner 2003
- Sandown Enduro winner 1973, 1975, 1976, 1977, 1978, 1979, 1980, 1981, 1984
- Repco Round Australia Reliability Trial winner 1979
- Australian Touring Car champion 1974, 1978, 1980
- Australian Touring Car runner-up 1973, 1979, 1981, 1984, 1990
- Australian Touring Car championship wins 37
- Australian Touring Car championship poles 57

and suggesting, but being careful not to get in the way. He struck the balance between being one of the boys and being the boss, and had the respect of all around him, a respect that afforded him the right to demand and receive excellence. Open and honest communication was the key.

"You need massive dedication and passion. If something's not right, a good engineer will pull the car apart half a dozen times, maybe more, and work until they get it just right. But guys that are just OK are the ones who go, 'Oh, yeah, I think that's pretty right. Yep, that's fair enough.' They don't have that energy for the team that's going to make you operate at that elite level. You've got to have people who say, 'We will give you everything. We know you'll give us everything out there driving, and together we're going to come up with some magic.' "

Peter's greatest moment in sport didn't come at Bathurst, as you might expect, but in 1979 in the 14-day, 21,000-kilometre Repco Round Australia Reliability Trial. It was the last race held on Australian soil that was so arduous, and one can safely assume there will never be another like it. Peter's entry into the contest was seen more as a publicity gimmick in the eyes of the media. He was up against the best rally drivers in the world.

"It was the single most difficult and challenging motorsport event I've ever done in my life, and I defy anyone to invent anything tougher. They will never run a motorsport event like that ever again on the planet, and never have since. [Occupational health and safety issues have seen to that.] We were driving for up to 48-60 hours with only very small stops for fuel and stuff like that, and then you would get an eight-hour break. I worked it out that from the time I started the event to the time it finished 14 days later I had less than 30 hours sleep, and I drove virtually the whole way myself. It was just adrenalin. People got killed in that event because of the sheer fatigue." For the stretch along Gibb River Road, from Broome to Kununurra, more than 600 kilometres long, the drivers were expected to average more than 100 kilometres an hour. Peter's was the only car that "cleaned" it, leaving all the others in his dusty wake.

Unlike a lot of people who learn more about themselves from their mistakes, a period of unparalleled success taught Peter to look deeper within himself for answers. "At one stage in my life, I won so many races so easily that they lost their appeal. There was no great sense of fulfilment, there was a sense of temporary satisfaction, but there was also this feeling that there's got to be something more to it. I was winning these races and doing all these things successfully, but where was my life going, who was I really? So, strangely enough, success caused me to look within myself, not failure."

For a man called "Peter Perfect" by fans, he was, by his own admission, anything but. His journey was a search for balance, and while at times he lost the odd battle, it was always a work in progress, a work he devoted his life to.

It was this emotional maturity that allowed him to deal with issues and not suppress them, and to be content with being the person that he was.

"I don't feel like I have to please everyone. I have always been cognisant of the fact that you have to be yourself and you have to be transparent. That's it. That's me, and if you don't like it, well, I'm sorry, but I've got to look at myself in the mirror, and if I'm happy with what I see, then I know the rest of the world will fall into place."

Not being preoccupied with those around him enabled Peter to focus on his own performance, and it was this intensity of purpose that drove him to success. "Other drivers will perform to beat other drivers, that's their deal. I drove to beat myself, and there's a big difference. If it wasn't enough to win on that day, it wasn't enough to win on that day. But nine times out of 10 it was because I knew that getting the technique right, getting myself focused on it, getting the whole energy and moment-by-moment focus happening, was going to give me the best result possible."

A pattern emerged with Peter as to what he considered the important ingredients for successful leadership. It was a pattern blending the soft skills with the hard skills, the emotional with the physical, and the heartfelt with the practical. For him it was about being responsible for his own actions, in setting a great example while remaining compassionate and understanding; encouraging others and giving them the freedom to feel good about themselves and their accomplishments; being humble and self-effacing yet confident and proud; tolerant and forgiving yet demanding of excellence; and about giving energy to those around you on a full-time basis.

Through the whole journey and all the success Peter remained true to himself, and that was why he was loved by Australian sports fans.

"I find it very difficult to get interested in what I've done. I'm far more interested in what I am doing more so than what I have done. I've never had a problem with feeling like I was this almighty person, this Peter Brock person. I'm just me, Brocky. I was just a kid from Hurstbridge who made good. That's the way I see it."

LAWS OF LEADERSHIP

- Take responsibility for your own actions

- Set a great example

- Be compassionate and understanding to let others feel good about themselves

- Remain humble

- Develop tolerance and patience

- Have a passion for what you do and a commitment to it

- Focus on the outcome

- Be honest

43

JOHN **BUCHANAN**

"Your strength is often your weakness, and our strength at that time was that we were a very aggressive side in the way we played a game. That's not talking about sledging or anything, but it is just about your body language and how you batted and bowled, field placings and the way you care for yourself. India were a team that stood up to us [in the 2001 Test series defeat], and we hadn't really thought how we would deal with that. I remember saying to myself that if we ever got into that situation again it would be different."

JOHN BUCHANAN *Australian Cricket Coach*

Even the most successful and confident coach needs affirmation, especially when instituting change. Why? Because all change has risk and part of that risk is rejection, rejection of an idea or innovation at best, and rejection of the person themselves at worst.

When John Buchanan started as Queensland Bulls coach in 1994, his goal was to win the Sheffield Shield that had eluded them for 69 years. His quiver had to include not only the conventional armoury of cutters, cut shots and cameos, but also a brave new world of tactics and technology.

Even his application for the Queensland job was unconventional and risky, too. "In the interview, I told them I am not here to win them the Shield, but what I am here to do is to put in place a set of systems and processes so that Queensland will dominate domestic cricket for the next 10 years, and in the process maybe pick up a one-day competition or a Shield along the line."

In this role, John was not going to be caught behind the times. He would be at the leading edge of the new age of cricket. That was the plan, anyway …

"Fundamentally, we looked at the game of cricket as being a game based on numbers, but we didn't necessarily accept that they were the right numbers. Until we could actually record some further stats, though, we couldn't really dispute them, so initially the idea was for the technology to

Hopeful Queensland batsman: John practising for his first appearance at the MCG, 1979.

support us looking at how we wanted to play the game and give us feedback to that effect."

The players knew that something unusual was going on. For a start, there were computers in the change room and people entering data all the time. The general reaction was to leave well enough alone – if they don't disturb us, we won't disturb them. And they didn't … not for about three or four games. Then, one afternoon after training, the players found a couple of sheets of paper on their cricket cases. They were the new stats. "I left some simple feedback for each player and observed exactly how they reacted. Some actually read it and some put it in their case, which was fine. Then I watched Allan Border."

In 1994, there was no bigger name in Australian cricket than A.B. He had retired from Test cricket just months earlier as the most-capped player, with the highest number of Test runs in the history of the game, and was playing on for Queensland to help them finally win that Shield.

For John, Allan's reaction was crucial. "He picked up his sheet and started looking at it … then glanced over to me … and then looked at it again. I thought, 'Well, this could be one of the great springboards to the future, where one of the greats of the game, who had been around for so long and had always done things his way, suddenly embraced this new technology; this could be where technology and sport all just fit.'

"He looked at me again and started walking towards me … All my heavens had come at once … just one question from Allan … I don't care how annoying, it would be sensational … Then I could use that interaction amongst the group to gauge their reaction … Now he was upon me … *This is going to be great* … Then he looked at me, crumpled up his paper, threw it at my feet, and walked back to his seat." John made a hasty retreat … right out of the room.

"I guess I would have liked A.B. to have reacted differently, but it did teach me a couple of things. He was a great player, and he had his way of doing things and, really, what was this piece of paper going to do for him at this stage of his career, anyway. In the end, all these experiences, so long as we don't let our egos get in the road, help us to learn a little bit more."

From such an initial reaction, it is hard to imagine such brilliant success, but that first season John took Queensland to the Shield, and created the foundation for the Bulls to play in eight and win five of the next 11 Shield finals. Subsequently, in 1999, on Steve Waugh's recommendation, John took over as coach of the Australian cricket team one match into their 16-Test match world-record winning streak. Four years later, he was the architect behind the defence of their World Cup one-day crown as well. For a man so publicly questioned, he has come up trumps.

As a player, John dreamed of the baggy green, of striding out to open

the batting for his country to the cheers of his nation. It never happened, but not for lack of effort. "I was a young player wanting to do extremely well, and I would listen to everybody and everything and, while that's an important part of learning, the other important part is knowing what is important to you. I couldn't do that. When I wasn't successful I would take in more information and try harder and harder, and the more that I tried the worse I became and the less confidence I had in myself. It got to the point that eventually I had to give it away."

John's green dream was over, but his experience helped him to understand that it isn't the quantity of information being absorbed but the quality and its relevance for a particular player. He knew he must understand his players and in turn understand how to help them reach their potential, something he wasn't able to do himself.

"To actually get near my potential [as a player], I needed some other support around me, I needed people that properly understood me and helped me to understand myself better than what I did. I guess in those days it was really sink

Support: John in the nets at training in Brisbane before leaving for the Ashes tour, 2005.
Photo: Andy Zakeli

The next big thing ...

"The future of cricket will be about match-ups. Bringing on specific bowlers to bowl to specific weaknesses of batsmen ... If you go back to baseball, once the batter steps up to the plate they decide which pitcher they should actually have on the mound to pitch. They know where his strengths are, and equally the batting side knows the weaknesses of this pitcher and what's the best batting or the best shot to match up against this pitcher. So going back through all our data and all our vision, so that, for instance, with Brett Lee going to the World Cup we have data and vision on him bowling to whoever it might be. It shows where he has been successful and where he hasn't been successful. Now that's how we use that as a team. That is the next step."

or swim – you were picked, and it was up to you to deliver. As a result, I now feel very strongly as a coach that it is about the knowledge of each individual within your team, how they mix in your team, where they are at personally, how they understand themselves, and how they can best deliver their skills."

The return of players from World Series cricket helped make John's decision to call time on his career. He knew he wasn't good enough. Instead he began his journey to one day coach the team in the baggy green.

His new pathway, a series of careers in health, education and sports administration, would take him north to Townsville, back to Brisbane, south to Canberra and overseas to Canada. At one point, he found himself teaching marketing and sports administration to rugby league players Mal Meninga and Gary Belcher. (John modestly asserts he is probably the reason neither of them pursued further interests in that field.)

His combined experience created a coach prepared to turn conventional wisdom on its head, leading to both the Queensland Bulls and the Australian XI setting new benchmarks. It was this creative approach that led to one of the most amazing innings and matches in one-day cricket – Australia vs South Africa at the Wanderers Stadium in Johannesburg on March 12, 2006.

In the 1980s, conventional wisdom pegged 200 as a match-controlling score in one-day cricket. By 2000, 300 was, if not unbeatable, then almost a sure thing. Four hundred, or eight runs an over, was one-day cricket's four-minute mile, considered unobtainable. But, says John, "I always had this notion that there was no reason why this particular team couldn't score 400 runs."

His reasoning was sound. In an innings, where they would score 330 or 340 runs, which was not so unusual for this team, they would only score off 140 to 160 of the available 300 balls.

"We were not using about 50 per cent of the available deliveries so imagine what could be achieved if we actually started using 10 per cent of those. Then the question became how. Maybe it was by shot selection, maybe by introducing a new shot, maybe better running between the wickets or increasing our skill training."

The Australians, off more than 180 deliveries, amassed a total of 434 runs – a world record. At the interval, the Australian dressing room was awash with pride. On the contrary, the South African players were disconsolate as the Australians' world record was also theirs in reverse. Their heads were down, until Herschelle Gibbs came into the rooms and said, "I think they're about 10 runs short." Many a serious word ...

"We had come off the field so excited about what we had done and didn't actually work out that there was a second half to the game. Not that we went to the field saying that we had won, but mentally we weren't practically clear on what decisions we had to make to do so." The Australians grabbed an early wicket, further contributing to what they saw as an inevitable result, but then Graeme Smith and Gibbs produced a partnership which turned the impossible into the unlikely, and finally into the reality.

"I don't think that we were mentally tuned into exactly what was going on, and technically we weren't delivering exactly what we needed to deliver. So, amazingly, the next team to get through the 400 barrier was the South Africans in that next innings.

"The dressing room was just dazed and in total shock, and I remember breaking the silence when I looked at Adam Gilchrist and just laughed. He had a laugh as well – there was nothing else we could do, it was just an amazing match. We had achieved something unbelievable, but then the very next innings we got knocked over. We talked about the Bannister effect, where once a barrier is broken everybody seems to break it."

John has broken many barriers with his style, and it has led to much success. "Everybody's a coach, anyway. As a parent, you're a coach, as a manager you're a coach and, obviously, as a sports coach you are a coach, but generally all of us coach in some shape or form because we try to interact with people and influence or guide or assist in whatever we do."

LAWS OF LEADERSHIP

- Learn from every experience, good and bad

- Believe in the ability of your team

- Have a vision of where you want to take the team

- Use the resources you have around you

- Establish honest and open relationships – trust is very important

NATHAN **BURKE**

"Football is what I do, not who I am."

NATHAN BURKE *Former AFL Player*

Cometh the hour cometh the man … but sometimes he doesn't. With a solitary behind by Barry Breen defining St Kilda's only previous triumph 31 years earlier, all was humming at half-time in the 1997 AFL grand final against the Adelaide Crows. With the Saints looking strong and leading by 13 points, the stage was set for another group of heroes to emerge. They did, but they were South Australian. One in particular was Darren Jarman, who kicked five goals in the final quarter to spearhead a Crows debut flag.

That grand final was a defining moment for Nathan Burke. "I look back now and realise that we had an opportunity, and leadership is all about taking opportunities, no matter how small. After a game is over it is too late. I left it to the coach and his assistant coaches to make the moves to try and stop Jarman; all I could do was really encourage the guy on him to keep going, keep going, keep going. But, at the end of the day, perhaps if I had the gumption I could have dragged another player to stand on him."

It was a tough moment. We all have them, and sometimes we simply make the wrong choice. Even making no choice is making a choice. It is making a choice to let chance play a greater part in your destiny than it necessarily needs to. "It's such an important point about leadership. To be able to grab an opportunity right there and then, especially during a game, because after a

Kick away: Nathan with Carlton's Earl Spalding behind, 1992.

INFLUENTIAL PEOPLE

- Barry Burke, *father*
- Ken Sheldon, *coach*
- Darrel Baldock, *first coach*

CAREER STATS

- St Kilda (1987-2003) 323 games, 123 goals
- Co-captain 1996-98
- Captain 1999-2000
- Club best and fairest 1993, 1996, 1999
- All-Australian 4 times
- Represented Victoria 11 times

game it's often too late. After the grand final I felt miserable, but had to make others feel better so we could overcome the loss and, importantly, learn from it. That's hard to do when I was also gutted by losing."

Nathan's leadership role at St Kilda was activated by one of his coaches, Ken Sheldon, who took him aside during a game of golf and issued him with the challenge. "Look, Nathan, it's about time. You've been playing in the back pocket, been playing peripheral roles for five or six years. Now's the time you really need to step up and become not just a good average player, but something a little bit better than that. I'm going to play you on the ball, give you a chance there, and it's up to you whether you take it. I'm going to have faith in you and stick with you. You may have a couple of poor games, but I'm going to actually stick with you."

His words and his time were not wasted. "It showed that Ken had a personal interest in me, and that was a defining point, learning that being a leader is about having a personal interest in someone rather than just the basic player-coach relationship. It felt like he wanted me to personally succeed, and that made a big difference to my confidence. It made me feel that not only do I have to try and succeed for myself and my family, but this guy wanted me to succeed as well, so I wanted to succeed for my coach because he had faith in me."

And succeed he did, becoming captain of St Kilda and, until recently, the club's most capped player. But it took Nathan time to understand exactly what the responsibilities of a leader were, and to understand that he had to think beyond his regular scope. Like many, when Nathan stepped into a leadership role he had to overcome the obstacle of needing to be liked, rather than respected. "Early on, decisions were put off or changed due to the need to be liked. I was not great at confrontation, and the job of a leader is to sometimes confront. I always felt compelled to lead by example and thought this could compensate for action. It didn't. I had to learn to have those hard conversations to make those hard decisions. Then I realised that I had to take myself out of my comfort zone of being liked, and I realised that the person I was confronting would respect me because I was coming at it from the right angle, coming at it from, 'The team needs to improve, you need to improve and we all need to improve'."

Nathan's motto was: "Football is what I do, it is not who I am." This distinction is not common among young people, and especially young sportspeople, who are typically feted more for kicking a goal than a doctor is for saving a life. But it explains why, as time progressed, he was not afraid to be different. In the macho world of AFL football, where a drinking and good-time culture sometimes prevailed, he was teetotal. "I was in the minority, but to a degree I'm a bit of a control freak and one of the reasons why I didn't drink was because I always wanted to be in control of the situation. Also, to achieve things you've got to make sacrifices and to me that was always one. If you can make some sacrifices in your life, it becomes a habit and that was just a habit for me, and typified the fact that, for this small amount of time in my life when I'm playing football, I had to give it my all."

Nathan didn't want any regrets, a factor reinforced by his first coach, Darrel Baldock, when he said to him about four games into his 323-game career. "Listen, son, no matter how long your career lasts, whether it's one year, five years or 10 years, there's going to come a time when it's finished and you'll be sitting in a chair, and you don't want to spend your whole time thinking, 'Well, I wish I had done this, I wish I hadn't done that, I wish I had not drunk or I wish I had concentrated on my weights a little bit more' because you will have regrets. It's up to you. You can have no regrets or you can have a lot."

Nathan has few regrets, and a lot of lessons to pass on, just as his father Barry passed them to him. "My father was always in leadership positions and was always my role model. Every Saturday was spent at the football where he was coaching and I was always in the room before the games, at half-time and after the game. ... Leadership is about empowering others to share the load of leadership. I always found that if a leader makes themselves too relied upon, then when they are not there it can leave a hole ...

"Being a leader requires you to be both interesting and interested; it's a two-way street. To be interesting means that you are able to, for a variety of reasons, grab the attention of your team and have the opportunity to turn this attention into a positive influence. However, an interested leader seeks to know about the people they lead because if you are really interested in that person that is a much more powerful form of leadership, and you will become a more effective leader."

Nathan has never had to have a schooner and a half of beer to give him a glass and a half of personality. He was always interesting from the start. "I set out to play as long as I possibly could because I thought if I played this game for a long time that's a measurable goal, and to achieve longevity I had to be doing my bit for the team. I needed to be remembered as a person who gave his all no matter what the situation."

LAWS OF LEADERSHIP

- Have faith in yourself and the team
- Leadership is having a personal interest
- Understand the difference between being liked and being respected
- Be prepared to go out of your comfort zone
- Make the most of your opportunities
- Do not make yourself too relied upon, as there will be a time when you're not going to be there
- Only worry about things you can control, not those you can't
- A good leader focuses on his team both in the game and away from it

RIC **CHARLESWORTH**

"One of the big mistakes coaches make is they stop coaching the senior players, and it is critical that you don't do that. Most of the senior players, if they are good, are really good, and they actually want to learn and they are open to it. But what happens, and what happened to me, is that you get to a level where you have a particular status in the group and you don't get coached enough and that's a mistake."

RIC CHARLESWORTH *Former Olympic Hockey Captain and Hockeyroos Coach*

Unconventional: Ric Charlesworth, 2006.
Photo: Greg Totman

How do you make everyone in your team a leader? Isn't it obvious? You make no one in your team *the* leader. It was this cryptic approach to leadership that master coach Ric Charlesworth adopted for the Sydney Olympic campaign of the Hockeyroos – Australia's women's hockey team. Outside of the under-8s footy team, where captaincy is shared like lollipops, it was a unique approach in which Ric used eight different captains in the eight games leading to Olympic gold.

"I don't believe in hierarchies in teams, I don't believe in some person exemplifying all the qualities you need. My experience is that everybody has something to offer, and the thing that we were most concerned about was what I call 'social loafing' – where as soon as you identify somebody as a leader, then the other people take less responsibility, are less involved, less curious, and sit on their hands. I wanted everybody to exemplify leadership, everybody to behave like a captain. While over time we built six or eight people as captains and co-captains in our team, in the end we didn't even have one."

Although unconventional at times, Ric understands success, leading the Hockeyroos through eight consecutive years as the No.1 team in the world. He is a man who has seen sport through the eyes of a player, captain, medico and now coach, so his revelations about captaincy were in no way whimsical.

INFLUENTIAL PEOPLE

- Lester, *father*
- Herb Elliott
- Horst Wein, *hockey coach*
- Ron Barassi
- Ian Chappell
- Merv Adams, *hockey coach*
- Wilfred Thorpe, *primary school hockey coach*

"One thing I did learn from politics is that you better listen to people from the other side because people with a different perspective often have a very good point to make ..."

He has documented some of his insights in his book, *The Coach*, in which one chapter is titled, "Beware of Aspiring Captains".

"You get people manoeuvring for the leadership. Some people want to be captain for the wrong reasons, and that is not necessarily a good thing. I was captain of the national team for six or eight years, and sometimes I didn't operate in the interests of the team as well as I might have. Sometimes when I was captain of the team I distorted the interests of the team for my own purposes. It might sound terrible; I think it is human nature. People do not do it maliciously, but it's because that's how we are, and you don't even realise it at the time. Sometimes I was a bit too self-centred and self-orientated. I recognise that in myself, and I am sure that it occurs in other people as well."

His philosophy recognised that leadership in a team is better done as a collective rather than as a hierarchy. In his days as a state cricketer for Western Australia, he played with decisive captains he respected, such as John Inverarity and Rod Marsh, yet they also allowed debate in decision-making on the field. In Ric's preferred sport of hockey, a fast-tempo game where play rarely stops, he required decision-makers everywhere on the field. People had their set responsibilities and they remained accountable for them, but the captain of the day held slightly more responsibility in that match. This encouraged people to give their best, in their own way, all the time.

"Some people set an example at training which lifts the tone of the training session. Some people do inspirational things on the field. Some people are inclusive in the social environment, and they bring in others who are on the periphery of the team and who don't feel as comfortable. Some will stand up in front of the group and disagree when that is not the orthodox view. Some people will take criticism really well and set an example for the rest of the group. In our team, nobody had all these qualities, but everybody had something to offer, and the best way to actually get them to do so was to say, 'We aren't going to have a captain, we expect you all to lead'."

Ric has learnt a lot of lessons in his time, and many of those have been through his disappointments. As a player, he was selected for five Olympic Games, but only attended four due to the boycott of Moscow in 1980, a political decision he rates as crazy. As a team expected to play in the Olympic

COACHING CAREER

- Australian women's hockey team, 1993-2000
- Champions Trophy: winners 1993, 1995, 1997, 1999
- World Cup winners 1994, 1998
- Olympics 1996, gold; 2000, gold
- Commonwealth Games 1998, gold
- Australian Coaching Council Team Coach of the Year 1994, 1996, 1997, 1998, 1999, 2000
- Appointed Master Coach by the International Hockey Federation in 2001
- Named Western Australia's greatest ever hockey player and coach in 2005

Pursuit: Ric gets the ball past New Zealand's Chan Chhiba on the way to a 5-2 victory at an AIS international.

final, they felt robbed of a genuine opportunity to win gold. Personally, it was both shattering and a turning point. Shattering, because his withdrawal as captain of the West Australian cricket team to concentrate on his pursuit of Olympic gold ended his cricket career. Life-changing because Vietnam and the Moscow boycott were two issues that galvanised his political resolve and led him into politics. He spent 10 years in Federal Parliament, which he describes as "interesting job, terrible lifestyle".

In 1992, he decided to leave politics and go back to medicine, but in the interim was approached by members of the Hockeyroos. They were disappointed with their results in Barcelona and convinced him to apply to be coach of the women's team. At 40, he subsequently sat for his first job interview. His breadth of experience as a player, politician and medical man held him in good stead. It was all useful, even the politics. While he saw politics as generally the antithesis of teamwork, he knew that no experience was a total waste of time, as you could always learn from a bad example.

"One thing I did learn from politics is that you better listen to people from

CAREER STATS

• Hockey
  Australia 1972-
  1988, 227 games

• Olympics
  1972; 1976, silver;
  1984; 1988

• World Cup
  1975; 1978, third;
  1982, third; 1986,
  first, player of
  the tournament
  and leading
  goal scorer.
  (International
  goals scored:
  more than 90)

• Cricket
  WA, 1972-1980;
  captain 1979-80

• WA Sportsman
  of Year 1976, 1979,
  1987

• Sport Australia
  Hall of Fame 1987

• Member of Order
  of Australia, 1987

the other side because people with a different perspective often have a very good point to make – as a coach, exactly the same thing applies – you better listen to your athletes. I learnt more about teamwork in my time in medicine than I ever did in sport. An operating theatre involves a whole range of people with different capabilities under the pressure of time, in a stressful situation, having to co-operate to get the result."

Ric followed the credo that you treat everyone fairly, but not the same, and so prided himself on knowing his people and what made them tick. To seek an understanding of his players, he turned to the words of all manner of successful politicians, sportspeople, historians, philosophers, other athletes and coaches and even writers such as William Shakespeare. He was so impressed by Shakespeare's insights into the human character that he penned *Shakespeare the Coach*.

"There have been lots of messages from the Bard. Shakespeare was the first psychologist in English literature. He was the first person to really put meat on the bones of his characters and actually describe why they failed and succeeded. Shakespeare defined personality in English literature. The messages are age-old and timeless messages about character, about what works and what doesn't, and why people are evil or successful or whatever they may be." When pushed as to which Shakespeare character most represents him, he falters, ruling out just the one. "Shakespeare's characters were pretty terrible, and Falstaff was a drunk, and I'm certainly not that." If only my year 10 teacher had explained that Shakespeare could have helped my sports career.

In taking on the women's team, Ric was forewarned of the potential perils of coaching the opposite sex, but he felt there was little difference between coaching men and women. "Everyone told me that they would be difficult, but I didn't find that at all. The rules are the same for men and women in our game, and the important thing is the coach should treat each person as an individual, and whether they happen to be female or male it doesn't matter much. I found them co-operative, determined and hardworking – all the things I would expect.

"I expected of them exactly what I would expect of the men's team, so I didn't make a big differentiation – I don't think there is a big one. In some ways, though, they actually made it easier to build a team. They were much more honest than men were; they were less egocentric and more willing to play for the team, but they weren't as analytical as men, so we had to work a bit harder on that aspect.

"I'm wary of generalisations, but I think women are socialised to sublimate their personal ambitions sometimes, for the family, for instance, and you see that in sport – in terms of their willingness to be team members and to co-operate. And they are honest about what's going on. They say it. People say that's bitchy, but it actually helps you deal with issues rather than them being subterranean. Those were good things."

Helping the team to reign supreme for eight years required Ric to continually focus on improvement in the team and in the individuals within the team. That required an ability and willingness in the players to acknowledge that they had areas to improve. It was this humility that he rates as the greatest and most important quality of the Hockeyroos, both individually and as a group. "Humility underpins an attitude which says 'we can get better, there's more to do, we can improve, how are we going to do it?' For us, it was a collective humility because we had champion players on our team.

"One of the big mistakes coaches make is they stop coaching the senior players, and it is critical that you don't do that. Most of the senior players, if they are good, are really good, and they actually want to learn and they are open to it. But what happens, and what happened to me, is that you get to a level where you have a particular status in the group and you don't get coached enough, and that's a mistake."

The Hockeyroos were categorised as much by the way they played as by their success. In doing so, they had boundaries and rules within the team that they never compromised on their road to success. "We had a rule in our team that we would never cheat. So, for instance, in a hockey match it can be very difficult for the umpire to tell whether or not you touched the ball before it flew into the net. In our team we would never accept a goal that we didn't score. We would never cut corners; we were not going to kid ourselves about our performance. We set standards which were realistic and we didn't take a freebie or a lucky mistake. As a result, we developed better skills."

And it was those skills and that attitude that drove Ric and the Hockeyroos to glory again and again, and again. "I have never been much of a believer in innate leadership skills. Leadership is the capacity to be candid and honest with people consistently and reliably, and to provide purpose and direction for the program to assist the person."

LAWS OF LEADERSHIP

- Use your experiences to your advantage

- Never underestimate your opponent

- Do what you think is the right thing

- Listen to different opinions

- Set an example

- Be prepared to work hard and take no short cuts

- Be willing to take risks and experiment

- Remain contemporary

- Treating people fairly doesn't mean treating them all the same

- Maintain balance

JOHN **COATES**

"With the Olympic team, we want to win medals, but not at any cost. We must be professional in the way we go about it. It is important that our teams are ethical and they behave well. You have to respect the highest standards of transparency and corporate governance, know your strengths and know those of your competitors."

JOHN COATES *Australian Olympic Committee President*

Revolutionary: John is proof you don't have to be a champion athlete to influence sport, 1998.

Photo: Jessica Hromas

There aren't too many people who can claim they made it in sport because they became overweight, but John Coates can. A combination of weight gain and study commitments fast-tracked him from the coxswain's seat in a rowing boat into an administrative role as manager of the Australian rowing team to the world championships in 1975 and the Montreal Olympics in 1976.

Australia's performance at the Montreal Games, with only four medals, was our Olympic nadir, and it became the catalyst for an administrative-led reform of our sporting system. John has been at the forefront of this revolution, holding a variety of administrative roles at Rowing Australia, the Australian Institute of Sport, Australian Sports Commission and now as the president of the Australian Olympic Committee and member of the International Olympic Committee. Results from Australia's sporting reformation have been outstanding, with Olympic results post-'76, and particularly at recent Games, staggering – at the Sydney and Athens games Australia finished fourth on the medal tally. This is an extraordinary result considering our population and limited budget compared with many Olympic countries.

John proves that you don't have to be a champion athlete to have an enormous influence on sport. He has shown that if you are prepared to

work hard, you love sport and you have a genuine respect and empathy for the athletes you serve, you can make it to the top. For Olympic sport in Australia there is no higher position than that held by John. He has been chef de mission, the head of the Australian team at the Games for the past five summer Olympics, and will again lead our team in Beijing in 2008. He has been president of the Australian Olympic Committee since 1991.

In my role as athlete liaison officer at Athens, a position John instigated at the Seoul Olympics in 1988, I saw first-hand what his responsibilities entailed, and he never stopped. In commanding a team of 482 athletes, the second-biggest of all nations, John led the team Good Shepherd-style – there wasn't an athlete, official or administrator in the team he didn't know, and no one athlete, no matter the profile, was more important than any other.

During an Olympic campaign, John's goal for the team is twofold: to win on the medal tally and to create a unique and special team experience for all. "As chef de mission of the Australian Olympic team, I aim to instil in those under my charge, and that is almost 500 athletes, confidence and pride and the belief that they are not inferior to anyone – in 1976 and in the early '80s there was an inferiority complex amongst our team. It is also very important that with a disparate team, across 28 sports, we are able to bring it together and create a team of teams so that athletes from one sport support the athletes in other sports. That now happens all the time with the Australian team, but rarely with the other countries."

As the leader, then, it is important that John is visible at the venues, mixing with the players and support staff. Protocol is important, but not as important as the people. During an Olympics, each day is tense, with gold up for grabs from the first. A typical day will see John up early and on top of the press clippings before doing the rounds of the venues.

In Athens, one of my days with John begins at the rowing to see the qualification rounds; then we're off to the shooting, where Suzy Balogh wins gold; John then watches our women play basketball just before catching the afternoon beach volleyball session and then heading to the swimming for gold, gold, gold. The night finishes at the diving pool, where our team is seeking qualification to the medal rounds.

Between these events there are the official functions and the detail of office work to stay on top of. It may sound appealing, but the pace is hectic and unrelenting for the 15 days of the Games. John, like any great CEO, stays on top of his athletes and his administration.

John's start in administration was as secretary of the local church cricket side, at the suggestion of family friend and former Test cricketer Alan Davidson. Alan, retired and sitting as president of the NSW Cricket

Eye on the ball: For John, it is about enjoying the success of those he works with, 1992.
Photo: Colin McConnell

Association, guided John constructively in those early years. So well in fact that a few years ago John found himself at odds with his mentor and the NSW Cricket Association, when he added his support for Sydney University to remain in the Sydney grade competition.

"When I put my head up to support my old university, I know Alan was not impressed, particularly given I had achieved nothing in his game." It was no deterrent for John, but a lesson reminding him to be careful when buying into sports that he may not be too familiar with and which are not his responsibility.

Australia's focus on and success in team sports has been a source of particular pride for John. The crowning stat was that Australia qualified for 11 out of 14 of the team sports for the Athens games, topping all nations other than Greece, which had automatic qualification rights due to its host nation status. The US, Russia and Germany each had no more than eight teams qualify.

The Australian Youth Olympic Festival ...
The biennial Australian Youth Olympic Festival is fully funded by the Australian Olympic Committee. The AOC provides $2.7 million for each edition of the festival. After three very successful events in 2001, 2003 and 2005 the AOC has committed to another AYOF in 2007.

The main aim of the AYOF is to develop our Olympic stars of the future, and to provide aspiring Olympians with an idea of what the Games are all about. The AYOF incorporates many aspects that athletes will experience in an Olympic Games – opening and closing ceremonies, medal presentations, athletes' villages and drug testing. AYOF is a multi-sport event for young Olympic aspirants generally between the ages of 14 and 19. It is conducted in co-operation with the national sporting federations and features the best young male and female athletes from Australia, Oceania, East Asia and, in some sports, the world.

Twenty-seven athletes from the 2001 and 2003 festivals won selection for the Athens Olympics, winning a total of eight medals, including three gold.

Our strength and pride in team sports, though, is under threat through lack of funding. It costs a lot more to bankroll a team to win a medal than it does an individual, though it counts just the same on the medal tally.

"To emulate our success is fast becoming a harder task for each successive Australian team, as other countries are seriously increasing their funding to achieve greater sporting results.

"There is some bewilderment as to how Australia have been so successful in both hosting a great Games in 2000, and in our medal tally and team performance at recent Olympics, but we cannot muse for too long because people are trying to knock us off.

"The Chinese are throwing a whole army of athletes at the world and a lot of other countries like Britain, Russia and Germany are upping the ante with the amount of money they are putting into sport. As well, many countries have taken the view that they are in the business of winning medals and, given a disproportionate amount of money is required for one medal in a team sport, taking the view they are better served by directing their funding into multi-medal sports.

"But being a member of a team is character-building and part of Australian society. We have a greater spread of sports in our country, and as kids we can play all sports at school, and I hope that opportunity continues."

While massive commercial and logistical problems pass over John's desk throughout any given day, they are not the worries that keep him up at night. One of his biggest worries actually went up in flames – the flames of the Olympic cauldron.

It is curious that two of the best-kept secrets of the world are both revealed with derivatives of fire. The Vatican signals a new Pope has been elected with a puff of smoke, and the lighting of the Olympic cauldron reveals another secret just as tightly held. It was this latter secret that played on John's mind for months in the lead-up to the lighting of the flame in Sydney.

Speculation about whether it would be Don Bradman or Dawn Fraser, Herb Elliott or Betty Cuthbert ended as Cathy Freeman lit the cauldron at the opening ceremony in September 2000. But for John the biggest question remained unanswered – would this task put too much pressure on Freeman and cost her the chance to win gold?

John was one of two people who made the decision to choose Freeman to light the cauldron. In itself, that was easy – he knew the power of the symbolism and he knew that she had earned the right. What he didn't know was whether it would affect her one chance at gold.

"I personally felt a lot riding on that night of her race because winning that 400 metres was the most important thing for Cathy. She had to trust that she could do both. She carried the weight of the nation that night, and that was a very big effort. When I asked her if she would light the flame, in a restaurant in Los Angeles in March of 2000, and warned of the added pressure, she responded, 'John, I like pressure. That is when I perform at my best.' Her confidence gave me a lot of confidence."

Success for John is about enjoying the success of those he works with and watching young talent reach its potential. Whether he is mentoring a young executive at David Jones (where he is deputy chairman) or leading another Olympic campaign, he knows what counts is not only what you do, but also how you do it.

"With the Olympic team, we want to win medals, but not at any cost. We must be professional in the way we go about it. It is important that our teams are ethical and they behave well. You have to respect the highest standards of transparency and corporate governance, know your strengths and know those of your competitors."

LAWS OF LEADERSHIP

- Have confidence

- Maintain a high standard of governance

- Don't be afraid to delegate responsibility

- Ensure your team has the right people in it

- Remain calm

- Maintain some separation from the team as far as leadership

- Establish respect, not fear

- Develop discipline

- Know your strengths and those of your competitors

BARRY **DANCER**

"For all the talent in the world, you've got to pay the price,
and the price is a lot of hard work and personal sacrifice."

BARRY DANCER *Australian Men's Hockey Coach*

**Insight: Kookaburras
coach Barry Dancer
presents a seminar
at Illawarra Hockey
Centre, 2005.**
Photo: Wayne Venables

Nationally, it didn't have the impact of the America's Cup but, outside of a rugby Test, watching the Kookaburras' gold medal in Athens was one of my favourite sporting moments. And I wasn't alone, as an Athlete Liaison Officer sitting in the stand among hundreds of really fit Australian supporters – swimmers, rowers and athletes of all shapes, sizes and flexibility – supporting our team. We were lucky to have such great seats, though, because most of us almost didn't make it.

The day before the final, team activity co-ordinator, former Wallaby and Australian swim coach Laurie Lawrence, covered every spare wall, door or noticeboard around the Olympic village with invitations to support our boys as they attempted to win Australia's first Olympic gold in men's hockey.

He failed to anticipate the team's enthusiastic response. Armed with 18 tickets, Laurie watched as 180 Australians piled onto the designated buses for the journey to the hockey stadium. If he was concerned, you didn't know it. Maybe his mind went back to a certain man some 2000 years earlier who had multiplied loaves and fishes; more likely he was making it up as he went along.

The buses arrived simultaneously, so Laurie assembled the throng of green and gold. To the closest 18 people he handed tickets and, then, Moses-style, held up his arms to speak. "Those people with tickets and passes go through

INFLUENTIAL PEOPLE
• Merv Kinnane

"There is a poster of Winston Churchill that says 'Deserve Victory', and that is a catchcry for me."

the gate first and then the others follow. If you have any problems or get stopped let me know." Laurie went through first with his access-all-venues pass, then the next 18. When the first person without a ticket or a pass tried to enter, they were stopped. Dutifully, they put their hand up and called to Laurie, "They won't let us in."

Laurie looked at the lone Greek attendant and then at the throng of flag-waving, green-and-gold-draped Aussie supporters, and yelled back, "RUN! JUST RUN!" Like a group of children told they had a three-minute free-for-all in the candy shop, they needed no further encouragement. The green-and-gold army were here to witness their piece of history – and they did so in style, watching the Barry Dancer-coached Kookaburras beat the Netherlands 2-1 in extra time.

But gold medals are not all about celebration. For those on the other side of the fence that evening, the players, the journey had been longer and more challenging. The Kookaburras had known heartache, falling at the final hurdle before. Dancer himself was a player in the men's team that lost the final in 1976 to New Zealand. Even if it wasn't as relevant for the current players, the weight of expectation was significant. Newspapers spoke of the monkey that had grown into an ape, and was now a gorilla.

The team knew they had to concentrate on the job, and nothing that went before mattered now. They clinically prepared for the Athens final with a "can do" in their attitude; this was an achievable task. In their own minds they knew they had earned the right to be there on that day, and they were every bit as good a chance to win as the Dutch. Unlike Barry and the team of '76, they had left no stone unturned and nothing to chance.

"There is a poster of Winston Churchill that says 'Deserve Victory', and that is a catchcry for me," says Barry. "For all the talent in the world, you've got to pay the price, and the price is a lot of hard work and personal sacrifice. It doesn't matter how much talent and potential you have, it is about how much you use it that is going to, in the end, make you satisfied or dissatisfied with what you have achieved out of your sport."

Barry was never satisfied with what he achieved as a player; his efforts had been so in contrast to Churchill's message, and that lesson gave him particular insight as a coach. Even when his team won the silver medal in Montreal, which was the best result of all Australian teams at the Games, he

PLAYING STATS
• Australian national team 1973 -1979
• International caps 48
• World Cup Kuala Lumpur 1975, 5th
• Olympics Montreal 1976, silver
• World Cup Buenos Aires 1978, bronze

knew within himself that he hadn't made a strong contribution so he never considered it a personal milestone.

"In the end, I was disappointed when I looked back on my career because I didn't put as many demands on myself as I should have and didn't feel I reached my potential as a player. The time when I really needed to commit my most and leave other things to the side of my life, I tried to mesh them all together, and that was foolish because I really didn't give my development what it needed.

"I was a bit of the golden-haired boy, I'm afraid, and sometimes when there is that sort of perception people don't want to criticise you. Stronger hands and stronger messages along the way would have been beneficial in guiding me and asking me to be more committed and more focused. Ultimately, though, it was my responsibility as a player, and ultimately I didn't take on that responsibility strongly enough."

The one person who did give Barry feedback was Merv Kinnane. Merv

Strong hands: Barry (left) with Australian women's hockey coach David Bell.

COACHING STATS

- Australian men's hockey team, 2001
- AIS head coach, 2001
- World Cup Kuala Lumpur, silver, 2002
- Commonwealth Games Manchester, gold, 2002
- Champions Trophy Amsterdam, silver, 2003
- Athens Olympics, gold, 2004
- Coach of the Year, Australian Sports Awards, 2004
- Great Britain and England men's hockey teams, 1998-2000
- European Cup, bronze (England), 1998
- Commonwealth Games Kuala Lumpur, bronze (England), 1998

was like the Godfather of Hancock Brothers Hockey Club in Ipswich, just outside Brisbane. Hancocks was a very successful club, at one stage winning 17 premierships in a row, and Merv was the man who knew everything and everyone around the club, and was respected accordingly.

When Barry was coaching the A-grade team there, it was Merv who took him aside for a quiet word to let him know that he had to be more open to other people's ideas – he was too much of a closed shop, just taking the advice of one. When the substance of this conversation crystallised, Barry began to focus more on using the talent and resources he had around him.

Barry understood from Merv that to be a great team you had to know what outcome you wanted to achieve as a group, and most importantly how it was that you wanted to operate as that group. Respecting both what and how ensured you lived by a value system that was important to you.

One of the important values the Kookaburras lived by on the road to gold in Athens was humility, so it was a concern to Barry in their Olympic match against India when he sensed this aspect of the team was slipping. Just after half-time the Kookaburras scored two goals in quick succession, after which both scorers engaged in what has become a ritual of sport these days – the goal celebration. Barry detected a difference in these celebrations, though: they were premeditated and no longer revolved around the team as much as they did the individual.

Within minutes India struck back …bang … bang … 3-3. In a must-win game, the team was in trouble and all because they had lost focus. With just seconds remaining, Australia scored the winner from a brilliantly executed corner. They had their victory, but the taste was soured.

"I was frustrated, and I think it was a very good learning experience for myself and the team. It's one of the biggest things I learned out of Athens – how to manage a situation like that better.

"I made a mistake at that time in a press conference, being mildly critical of our goal celebrations and our distractions as a group from the task at hand. I didn't recognise the repercussions that that sort of public comment could make in an Olympic environment with a team that isn't exposed to the day-to-day, week-to-week, microscopic media analysis that our other professional teams are in Australia."

The news was back on the team immediately, prompting Barry to apologise

India struck back … bang … bang … the team was in trouble and all because they had lost focus.

to the group. He didn't regret his thoughts but he vowed never to publicly criticise his players again.

"Overall, our team is better for it. Now we don't get individual egocentric goal celebrations; we get team-orientated goal celebrations and people in our team recognise the broader team contributions rather than just the goal-scorer. Our team has always had a very strong team bond and a mateship that's been very strong, and our goal celebrations were at odds with that. Now our goal celebrations are very much in sync with that teamship and that mateship bond that's within the group.

"Humility is a very important part of this team and an important part of ongoing success of any group, so I'm pleased that there's not a great deal of individual ego in the team. There's a real pride in the team about what the team can achieve and has achieved."

Success is a tightrope, and so it was in the final as they went to extra time level at 1-1. The Kookaburras had stayed composed all night after being 1-0 down at half-time. They went back on the field each time confident they didn't have to do anything differently and knowing that they must stay patient. They did so right to the golden goal that signalled time.

"The move involved Jamie Dwyer finishing with the ball and he was to flick the ball at the net from where he was, but he chose to hit it and he did so through the narrowest of gaps in the middle of the goal," Barry says.

"The play was a variation on a move that we had developed over the last 12 months. It originated from one of our National Training Centre coaches on a pitch in Belgium where he just put something a little bit different into a variation that then led to something else that led to something else.

"It was another example of how from the fringe of the group somebody can add that something extra that makes such a big difference. It was one of those Merv Kinnane moments – just to be wary of what other people can offer."

LAWS OF LEADERSHIP

- Be open and prepared to listen to ideas

- Surround yourself with the right people

- Take responsibility for yourself

- Have confidence in yourself

- Never publicly criticise

- Know what you want to achieve

ROB **DE CASTELLA**

"The greatest leaders are those that are able to inspire people when things aren't going well, to be able to turn around games and matches, and to perform under pressure."

ROB DE CASTELLA *Marathon Runner and Former CEO Australian Institute of Sport*

Mental ability: Deek on his way to a record in the 3000m at the APS Sports, 1974.

T he hardest moments of the marathon are over the final five kilometres. You have run out of petrol, the glycogen stores in your muscles are gone, it feels like you are drawing your energy from the marrow within your bones, your body has started to tighten up, your ligaments and joints are starting to lock so you can no longer run as smoothly and as efficiently as you were in the early stages, you have blisters, you have lost toe nails, and you have chafing.

"But the overwhelming limitation in the marathon is this huge burden of fatigue that you build and you carry. It is over those last five kilometres, or the last 10 to 15 minutes of a 2 hour 10 minute race, that that burden of fatigue weighs you down."

Bruce McAvaney describes calling the marathon as like reading a novel – you tell the story unfolding before your eyes. He makes it sound romantic. He doesn't run marathons. Rob de Castella makes it sound gruesome – more *Silence of the Lambs* than Shakespeare. Rob runs marathons.

There has always been much ado about the marathon, beginning with the inaugural Olympic race of 24.8 miles (40 kilometres) in 1896 in Athens. Legends have been created and stars born; people respect the race because they understand just how difficult it is.

Among the 17 runners in 1896, 13 were Greek and, because the Greek

> "You have to be aware of what is around the corner. The realisation that you are going to get to that point of exhaustion and mentally preparing yourself to confront it, or confront yourself, as that is who you are really battling with."

athletes had not been successful in their home games, there was much anticipation of glory for this final event. Australia was represented by our first Olympian, the gold medallist in the 800 and 1500 metres events, Edwin Flack.

Soon after the halfway point of the race, the four foreigners were leading, but the exacting conditions began to take effect. Three of them retired, but Flack, in his first race over this distance, continued. In the final five miles, those that Rob de Castella describes above, Flack, a victim of fatigue and exhaustion, collapsed on the track and was carried off.

The race was won by Greek shepherd, Spiridon Louis, who had qualified just days before the opening ceremony. In second place, some seven minutes later, came Charilaos Vasilakos, and third was Spiridon Belokas. The story, though, was not complete, as it was discovered that Belokas hitched a ride in a carriage for part of the journey and he was subsequently disqualified. Belokas may well have been the first cheat in Olympic history; he was certainly not the last and certainly not the first marathon runner to have the urge to call a cab.

That urge to hitch a ride or to just give up is the essence of the marathon – a discipline where mental toughness is as important as any physical requisite. Deek had both. Well, sort of. His stature wasn't exactly that of a traditional marathon runner – running weight for him was between 68 and 70 kilograms and for his opponents about 55 kilograms, so he was giving them 10 to 15 kilograms and, over 42.2 kilometres, that adds up.

Still, he had surprisingly few serious injuries and was able to consistently do large amounts of training. At the same time, he seemed to have better results than many of his training partners – so his body adapted to his workload and showed the anticipated improvement quite quickly.

The battle for mental toughness is waged through little victories. For Deek, they began as a 10 year old, when his father would wake him at 6am to go for a run around the streets of Kew in Melbourne. He hated it with a passion, but the era and his respect for his father ensured he ran. It built in him a discipline, a base fitness and, by the age of 15, a love of running.

Deek loved running with his mates – for him it was vital that he enjoy the

company as much as the challenge, and it was the company that pushed him to train harder and break through the inevitable barriers he faced.

"You have to be aware of what is around the corner. The realisation that you are going to get to that point of exhaustion and mentally preparing yourself to confront it, or confront yourself, as that is who you are really battling with. It is a matter of awareness and accepting that it is going to happen. The training is not about preparing yourself for the first 30 kilometres, which are relatively easy, it is about preparing yourself for the last five kilometres. That is what the mileage, and the conditioning, and all the other background training and preparation are for."

A key to confronting his inevitable agony was Pat Clohessy, Deek's coach throughout his career. Pat reinforced the benefit of winning the mental battle at training, because if you did it gave you an opportunity to do something extra when the big competition was upon you. But winning the

CAREER STATS

- Won his first marathon in 1979
- The only Australian to have placed in the top 10 at three consecutive Olympic marathons
- Completed more than 20 marathons, winning nine and finishing in the top 10 in all but two
- Fastest time: 2.07.51, in Boston in 1986
- Held the world marathon record from 1981 to 1984

mental battle at training required long-term application and dedication, not just short-term focus.

For Deek, each session was like tearing a page out of a phone book; you won't notice a difference if one or two pages are gone, you will hardly notice a difference when 10 or 20 are gone, but you will notice a marked effect when 100 and 200 disappear. "That is one of the limitations of a lot of very good athletes: in a pressure-cooker situation they are not able to rise above what they anticipated they could do, and rise above other people's expectations and do something truly spectacular.

"It's that extra mental ability, and I don't know whether it is taught and trained or whether it is something you are born with. It enables you to rise above and take that quantum leap and do something that you never thought you were capable of doing. It will take optimism, confidence and a little mongrel and toughness to get that out.

"I thrived on the thrill of competition and I used that to actually motivate myself and strive over those closing stages of the marathon when I was physically and mentally pretty tired."

Deek is unique in his perspective on elite sport because, while still competing internationally, he became head of the Australian Institute of Sport. His challenge was not unlike that many business people face as they move into leadership positions. Or that many parents face as their child assumes independence. It was a challenge of losing control.

"All through my athletic career I was the one who had the final say. If I wanted to compete in the New York marathon, I would bounce the idea off my coach and others, but I would be the one who made the final decision.

"At the institute, decisions were made by consensus, and it was a matter of trying to convince people of the justification for the decisions that you wanted to make. That was difficult to grapple with as I had always understood that you don't win medals by consensus."

One of Deek's frustrations was the ingrained belief that "sport owned sport" – meaning that in spite of the AIS having some of the best coaches, sports scientists and facilities in the world, if a sport wanted to do things its way, then the bureaucracy allowed that to happen, even if it was to the

"It is not about being good, it is about being the best. You don't get to be the best without experimenting and without being prepared to occasionally make a couple of mistakes."

obvious detriment of the sport. This has largely changed in recent times, with the AIS exerting much more control over sporting organisations, particularly with their administrations and high-performance programs.

It was a demanding role for Deek. As well as 10- to 12-hour days in the office, he was training early mornings and late evenings in preparation for the Barcelona Olympics. Again, his exceptional discipline and ability to juggle competing priorities enabled him to do both. In doing so, he relentlessly challenged those he led in the workplace.

"I tried to cultivate in the coaches a preparedness to make mistakes. The institute is about sporting excellence. It is not about being good, it is about being the best. You don't get to be the best without experimenting and without being prepared to occasionally make a couple of mistakes.

"This is a little bit foreign to how bureaucracy works. In a bureaucracy, you get into a lot of strife if you start making too many mistakes. I was constantly at the coaches to get out there and try new things, to do something that no one else was doing.

"That was what was going to be required to take the performance of the athletes from being good to being great. I gave them the confidence to know they weren't going to be crucified if they made a few mistakes or they lost a few events."

Deek made his share of mistakes and had his share of disappointments, but he was never disheartened. For him it was all part of the learning journey of life, a journey that is a marathon – good and bad, blood and guts – not a sprint.

"At the end of the day, my approach throughout my career was that I needed to be able to look myself in the mirror and be proud of who I am and what I did. I never wanted to look back with regret and say, 'I wish I had done that.' I always went out to give my best performance, and if it was enough to win, spectacular; if it wasn't, then that's all I could be expected to do.

"Regardless of whether I came first, second or last, I had to be proud of the performance I gave."

LAWS OF LEADERSHIP

- Enjoy your performances

- Satisfy yourself, not others

- Step outside the comfort zone

- Rise above expectations

- Doing your best is always good enough, win or lose

- Be prepared to make mistakes

- Know your stuff

- Inspire confidence in the people you are leading

- Work hard

- Do things for the right reasons

ANDREW **DEMETRIOU**

"Being in a sporting team is a great teacher. You make great friendships, you get to interact with people … You start to learn about time management and disciplines."

ANDREW DEMETRIOU *AFL CEO*

Don't dabble. That was the advice up-and-coming all-round talented sportsman and student Andrew Demetriou received at a school football clinic, and the words hit their mark. "One of the Carlton players came to the school for a footy clinic – it was a big thing for a VFL player to come to your school – and this particular player knew that I was not bad at football and not bad at cricket, and he just said, 'Don't dabble. Concentrate on what you're good at because you can't be good at all these things'.

"It was the best advice I ever got when I was young and terrific advice at the time because I was tossing up whether to do cricket and footy or to do all these things, and he just said, 'Don't dabble, focus on what you're good at and just get better at what you're doing'."

The youngest of four sons, Andrew grew up in the northern suburbs of Melbourne in a competitive yet fun environment. The arena was the Woolworths car park, the asphalt doubling as the footy oval in winter and the cricket pitch in summer. Competition was fierce both among his family and against the other boys of the neighbourhood. The unforgiving surface took its toll, just as it did all around the country, where a knee without skin or a cut under the eye were not so much disfigurements as badges of honour.

Andrew found he was better than most at sport, being selected in state and

**No dabbling:
Andrew at a press
conference after an
AFL AGM, 2005.**

Photo: Erin Jonasson

INFLUENTIAL PEOPLE

- Malcolm Blight
- Bjorn Borg
- Jack Nicklaus

national junior cricket teams, but he was still dabbling. "I was one of those guys that liked sport and would try to adapt to each sport and then persevere until I thought, 'That's OK', and I'd move on to another sport. But football was more luck than anything because I always thought I was probably better at the other sports than football. I always thought that I would be more on the academic side than sporting side as I had never actually thought I would do as well playing sport as I did."

Don't dabble. Andrew concentrated his efforts on Australian Rules football and enjoyed an unspectacular career of 103 games as a winger for North Melbourne from 1981 until 1987. He followed this with a brief stint at Hawthorn, where he played just three matches in 1988. History will not document Andrew's on-field contribution to the game as even a patch on his off-field performance, but he did learn many lessons from playing sport. "Sport is a great teacher. From being involved in a sporting team and sporting competitions you make great friendships, you get to interact with people that you don't think you will, you're meeting board members and sponsors, you're doing media, and you are starting to learn things about time management and disciplines in team-oriented activities." And so Andrew crafted his future opportunities; opportunities far beyond those he may otherwise have had.

Don't dabble. Andrew instead focused on business where, after combining his playing career with working at the Royal Melbourne Institute of Technology, opportunity led him to become CEO of the Ruthinium Group, a business importing and distributing acrylic teeth. "It was probably a very boring commodity, but we grew that business to become a national business which ended up buying our parent company in Italy. It was a great experience, learning, negotiating and raising funds for acquisition."

It was also a difficult time for Andrew, as he had to combine a demanding travel schedule with the tragedy of having a very sick wife. Simultaneously, back in the world of football, a few AFL players such as Brendon Gale, John Longmire and Peter Mann decided it was time the players became organised. As part of a process of discovery, they conducted some research attempting to uncover what was needed to put the Players' Association on the map. "Out of that report came a recommendation to find a chief executive officer, and I was asked whether I would be interested. I actually said yes because it afforded me an opportunity to stay at home with my wife [she passed away in 1999. Andrew has since remarried and has twin girls, Francesca and Alexandra] at the time I honestly didn't even know what the Players' Association did."

Don't dabble. The Players' Association wanted a CEO who, possibly through a playing career, had empathy with football but at the same time had a business background and experience in negotiating. Andrew had just

Ahead of the pack: Andrew spears a handball as teammate John Law and St Kilda ruckman Warren Jones look on at the MCG, 1987.

negotiated an enterprise bargaining agreement on behalf of his company, so he found himself well positioned. "I said to the players that I was happy to take on the role on the condition and the understanding that we go to the AFL and work with them and become a partner with them to help grow the game. I didn't want to go in there and be adversarial, and I didn't want to be militant. We could achieve our outcomes if we worked with the AFL."

The first thing Andrew did was to have lunch with Wayne Jackson, the CEO of the AFL, whom he hadn't met, and Ian Collins, the general manager of football operations, whom he had. "That is how we broke the ice. I introduced myself and we had an enjoyable lunch, and I told them of our aspirations, and I committed to them that we wouldn't be an adversarial organisation. We wanted to get some outcomes, and I'd come back to them with what they were. We'd work with the AFL because if the game grew, if we developed the game collectively, if we generated revenues collectively, then the beneficiaries would be the players, the clubs and everyone else."

The Players' Association surveyed their players to uncover the critical issues and they came back with three key areas: retirement, welfare, and education and training. "As a result, we set up a retirement fund which is second to none, and it means that for every year of a player's career they get $12,000 or $13,000 put aside for them. A welfare program was available to aid them with things like grieving, marital issues, financial and career counselling. And we insisted on a day off a week and an educational and training grant for the players to give them an opportunity to do some on-job training or some educational training. I have no doubt that our players today are coming out of the system far better than they ever did before."

Don't dabble. After about 20 months as head of the Players' Association, Andrew replaced Ian Collins running the AFL's football operations. In his new role, he developed a new-found respect for the AFL as it became apparent how much of the nitty-gritty work they did to get things right. Before long Wayne Jackson was leaving and Andrew was installed as the new CEO of the AFL. "I've always regarded the role as a great privilege and a great honour to serve the game. My chairman once said to me, 'You're a custodian, you get to borrow the game for a while, you can't have equity in the game, you can't get shares or options, you get to borrow it, and then you give it on to the next person, and you have to ensure that you leave it in better shape than when you took it over.' And that's how I've always thought."

Andrew was taking over a healthy game, but he wasn't going to sit on his hands. He rearranged the management team, bringing in new blood and a new focus in certain areas.

Don't dabble. One of Andrew's first tasks in light of the impending renegotiation of the broadcasting rights was to move Ben Buckley out of commercial operations into a new area he called broadcasting strategy and major projects. "We spent the 12 months prior to negotiation preparing for those rights, and that was the best preparation and the most well-executed planning that I've been involved in. Ben Buckley, with our broadcasting subcommittee, had done so much work on the value of the rights and what the networks were making we knew what their rights were worth, and I think I was consistent from day one when we started negotiations. We knew what our rights were worth and we wouldn't sell them for less."

The result was another record figure for broadcasting rights in Australian sport – $780 million, which goes a long way to solidifying the future of the sport. But the AFL considers itself and its players first and foremost to be leaders of people and of society. With this is mind, they have taken leadership roles on issues such as racial and religious vilification and the attitudes towards women in the community. "We've got a great vehicle, our sport, which can influence so many things in the community. I think that type of leadership is far more important to us than being the leaders in sport."

Don't dabble. Andrew wants to focus very strongly on broadening his sport's national reach before concerning himself with international expansion, although he concedes that the first international opportunity could come from Africa and, more specifically, South Africa. But national expansion is the priority. One criticism of the AFL is that it is not an international sport and, although true, Andrew does not consider this a problem. "One of the strengths of our sport is what people consider our weakness – that we are just a national game. We are not the game played in heaven, and we are not the world game, we are the indigenous game and it's no coincidence that 10 per cent of our player population are indigenous."

Don't dabble. "Often in business you are very tempted to diversify, you're very tempted to go outside of your core business, very tempted. I've done it at times, and sometimes I haven't, but often if you stick to your core business, stick to what you're good at and keep getting better at what you're good at, it pays dividends. I hope my legacy is that we will secure the future of our 16 clubs, our players will be looked after, we will invest significantly in the growth of the game through grassroots, and we will invest heavily in NSW and Queensland going forward. We will have a huge push into South-East Queensland and the western suburbs of Sydney.

"The AFL has achieved what it has achieved over a long period of time because it's an organisation that is never satisfied; it's always wanting to do things better. Even today, as an organisation we are in a position where people could say things are going pretty well. But we're not satisfied, we're not happy, we're not standing still; we want to do what we're doing better and better; you want to put the game on better, you want to generate more revenues better, you want to work out ways you can deliver value to your supporters better. We're always wanting to do things better."

In the final analysis, the AFL and Andrew Demetriou have done things better because they didn't dabble.

LAWS OF LEADERSHIP

- Be professional at all times

- Leave a legacy

- Be consistent in all your actions

- Find your own balance in making decisions

- Always learn from those around you

- Understand your priorities

MARK **ELLA**

"Sport was a passion but it wasn't my life."

MARK ELLA *Former Australian Rugby Union Captain*

Imagine if your first experience as captain of your country involved key players standing down and refusing to do what you told them. Imagine those key players are your brothers. The year was 1982 and Mark Ella, the first Aborigine to captain Australia in any sport, was chosen to lead the Wallabies on their three-Test tour to New Zealand. To add to the degree of difficulty for the 23-year-old, nine Queenslanders and one New South Welshman made themselves unavailable for the tour, causing the squad to be christened the "unknowns".

"Glen and Gary just revolted. They didn't want me captain at all. They hated me as captain at Randwick, Sydney and NSW and the very first training session in New Plymouth, we were playing against Taranaki in the opening game of the tour, they refused to train. Bob Dwyer took the forwards and I took the backs, and when I called a move they just held their positions."

The session stopped, with everybody looking to see what Mark was going to do. It was the first test of his leadership. From his brothers' perspective, the root of the problem was inequality. Due to Mark's playing position as the five-eighth he only had to run three or four metres in playing each move. Gary in the centres was covering about 15 and Glen from fullback about 30. When multiplied many times over, it just wasn't fair. "It was like an enterprise bargaining agreement I had to negotiate. I was calling all the moves out wide

INFLUENTIAL PEOPLE

- Geoff Mould,
  rugby union coach
- Cyril Towers,
  rugby union coach
- Sir Nicholas
  Shehadie,
  *former ARU
  chairman*
- Bob Dwyer,
  *former Wallabies
  coach*

"If you lack a bit of confidence in revving up the players, or you fear that you are not going to say the right thing at the right time, then you can certainly lead by example."

and as the five eighth I would basically just catch, pass and stop. They just said, 'We're not running, we hate you, you're a bastard.' I guess I convinced them that after every second or third play I would take the ball off the winger, and they were happy with that. As long as I exerted myself they were happy."

In reality, Mark probably held the same authority over his brothers that any sibling has over another: none. In his case, it was compounded because he was one of five girls and seven boys who shared three bedrooms in their La Perouse house. Competition in his house, and in the Aboriginal community, was tough but it shaped his future. Because there were so many children and such a small house, they tended to spend a lot of time outside. "It was competitive in our own household let alone competing with the guys next door and down the street. We always had a football, a cricket ball, a tennis ball or we'd be diving for coins off the bridge. It was a very competitive environment, so sport and outdoor activity was always a part of my growing up."

Mark and his brothers were educated at Matraville High and coached by Geoff Mould, who recognised their talents and secured their services after school for the Randwick Rugby Club. At Randwick, they were further tutored by Cyril Towers, a master of running rugby. "Geoff Mould used to bring Cyril Towers to training and Cyril basically went through the flat alignment that my brothers and I became so famous for: the catch, pass, support regime. We were indoctrinated into the basics of the game, and we probably did it better than most people." The catch, pass, support game under flat alignment is extraordinarily difficult, requiring the backline to execute perfectly under extreme pressure, so it is rarely adopted by modern sides in an environment that encourages percentage play ... but not every team has a Mark Ella in control of the backline.

Mark's skills earned him selection for the Wallabies on their 1979 tour of Argentina, but the news was too much for his mother, who fainted immediately upon the announcement. She did the same again when he was first chosen in the starting XV to take on the All Blacks a year later. Leadership positions were a responsibility that came early for Mark when, at the age of 20, Bob Dwyer chose him to captain the Randwick first-grade side. Captaincy, however, wasn't a responsibility Mark coveted, and he would be the first to admit that it didn't come naturally for him either. "Bob Dwyer

Family (from left): Glen, Gary and Mark at Matraville High, 1974.

Photo: Kevin Berry

CAREER STATS

- Wallabies (1980-1984) 25 Tests, 10 as captain
- International debut June 21, 1980, v New Zealand (Sydney), won 13-9 (Age 21)
- Final appearance December 8, 1984, v Scotland (Murrayfield), won 37-12
- During 1984 Wallabies Grand Slam tour of UK and Ireland scored a try in every Test
- First indigenous Australian to captain a national sporting team
- Young Australian of the Year 1982
- Member of the Order of Australia 1984
- Sport Australia Hall of Fame 1987
- International Rugby Hall of Fame Inaugural XV 1997

handed it to me and I didn't want the position. He just said, 'Obviously you need other people to sometimes tell you what you're good at.' He had confidence in the way I played and as a coach had a particularly good relationship with me, thought I had the capability to be captain, and that I had the innate ability to lead players on the rugby field." When Mark was chosen to captain the Wallabies he declined. "I told them I didn't want the position, 'Thanks very much, it's a big honour but … I'm not interested.' They said to me, "Bad luck, you've got no choice. We've picked you as captain."

Throughout his time as captain, and particularly when he was first chosen to lead his country, Mark found he had to adjust his pre-match preparation. Traditionally, he was the type to be almost so relaxed in the rooms before a match that some might think he was sleeping. He at times retreated to his own world. This had to change. "I had to keep the guys focused on their jobs without affecting my own game. That's a role that you become accustomed to, but in the first three or four Test matches I was probably feeling the pressure of being both one of the key players in the team and continuing to play well, but also leading the other 14 players. It did have an effect early, but once I settled in it wasn't too bad."

When in doubt, Mark just threw himself into the action. "If you lack a bit of confidence in revving up the players, or you fear that you are not going to say the right thing at the right time, then you can certainly lead by example. You do that by playing the best you can. So when I was a little bit nervous about what exactly to say at the time and about revving up the big ugly forwards in the heat of battle, well, sometimes you just go in there and do it yourself."

Being the first Aborigine to captain his country in sport brought different attention on Mark, but didn't interfere with his focus and how he prepared as a player, person and captain. "Towards the end of my career, I felt more pressure about my heritage than when I was playing in my younger days because we tended to be in numbers, there were always a dozen of us around, and if anybody said anything, we'd just belt them up," he says with a smile. "Everything you do in life you primarily do for yourself and for those you care about, so my focus was on Mark Ella playing rugby … I just wanted to be the best five-eighth that I could at the time. So the focus is on your own ability, your own career, and then when you have time to reflect after a match you can look at what influence you can have on a broader scale."

Mark and his brothers have more recently been influential on that broader scale through the Lloyd McDermott program. Lloyd was the first indigenous rugby player to represent Australia. He played on the wing for the Wallabies in the 1960s and went on to become a successful Sydney barrister. In 1991, to assist indigenous rugby players, he set up a foundation which runs tournaments around the country regions, focusing mainly on development of 16-year-old rugby players. "In Australia, we haven't fully utilised the talents of indigenous Australians. The AFL do it particularly well, and through the Lloyd McDermott program we are developing indigenous talent in rugby. As a company [Horton Ella – Mark's marketing company], we do a lot of their fund-raising, and Glen and Gary have both been presidents of the Lloyd McDermott Rugby Development Foundation.

"The state of Aboriginal issues across the board hasn't really improved greatly over the last 15 to 20 years, and both sides of government need to do more. But at the same time it's not a simple issue of throwing $20 or $30 million at indigenous communities. There are lots of problems out there, and it's going to take years for those issues to be resolved. There's violence, substance abuse, poor health … where do you start? Essentially, you have to get these guys to feel like they are contributing to their own future, that they're working for their families and their communities, but it's difficult."

Today Mark coaches a Central Coast under-17s side and, while it is something he enjoys, coaching is not something he wants to pursue. He did once, coaching Milan in Italy for four years with his mate David Campese as the star player, but those fires burn no longer. However, working with his under-17s, his modern-day mantra is not far removed from those of his mentors Geoff Mould and Cyril Towers. "A lot of kids want to go from school to professional sport, and our advice to them is to: 'Refine your talents; don't neglect the basics of the sport; don't get a big head; you don't get anywhere without hard work; be patient; work on your game; and don't be somebody you're not.'

Mark believed firmly that a good player had to be driven from within. "I just wanted to win. I am a passionate person, but when it came to winning or losing, I'd rather win than lose. Part of my ethos was to enjoy myself, and with my brothers we certainly enjoyed ourselves, but you enjoy yourself so much more if you win."

If ever there were an example of someone who retired at their peak, then it is Mark Ella. At the age of 25, just after he had covered himself in glory on the 1984 Grand Slam winning tour to Britain, scoring a try in every Test, he called a premature end to his career.

Six years later, I played an invitational match with him and his twin brother Glen in Cairns against the touring English club side Bath. The Bath team were the current English champions, and included British Lions and England internationals. We were young and inexperienced by comparison. The game was close and no result was apparent until the dying minutes when Mark, in cahoots with his brother and through his genius, crafted a win out of nothing. I could only imagine what wonders he had left undone on the international stage; it was a notion that bothered everyone ... everyone except Mark.

"Sport was a passion, but it wasn't my life. I did it because I wanted to play rugby. In some sense, I used rugby to get to where I did, and rugby also used me, so it was an amicable deal. I wanted to get out of the game while I was young enough to build a career. I didn't want to finish at 29 or 30 and then all of a sudden think about what I was going to do for the rest of my life, so I was basically thinking ahead. I always planned to retire at 25. I played the game because I enjoyed it and not because I was obligated to play it, and at the end of the day it was an easy decision and one that I've never regretted."

I cannot echo those sentiments ... Mark Ella may not have regretted his own retirement at such a young age, but everyone else has.

LAWS OF LEADERSHIP

- Know the basics and know them well

- With everything you do, do it because you are passionate about it

- Allow yourself to grow into a leadership role

- Take on responsibility, both on and off the field

- Always lead by example

- Value the importance of a good education and use it to your advantage

- Be patient and work hard

- Don't be somebody you're not

HERB **ELLIOTT**

"Human beings only grow if they're outside their comfort zone. If a human being is comfortable, they're not growing. In fact, if they're not careful, they might actually be going backwards."

HERB ELLIOTT *Olympic Runner and Businessman*

Herb Elliott has a theory, albeit slightly tongue-in-cheek. First, you try cricket, because that's the easiest game to play. If you are no good at that, you try footy and, if you are not good at that you take up running. If you take up running, you try sprinting, because that is the easiest, and then you keep going until you find your mark. People who run marathons never found their mark anywhere else. Herb got to the 1500 metres and the mile and discovered that was what he did best. The rest is history.

Growing up in Scarborough, Western Australia, after school Herb passed time in the sand dunes chasing his mates. For hours, he would run, and that was after having already run to the bus or to school and back home again. "I liked winning, and probably the first time I realised that I was about 10 or 11. I was at a YMCA camp at Rottnest Island and they had a race. I don't remember how far it was, but we headed off somewhere down the road, and we ended up back on the beach. Belting along the beach, some guy had just come in with this big catch of fish which he had in a great heap on the beach. I just ran straight through the bloody pile of fish. There was no way I was going to divert around this fellow. It was the first time I realised that I had the fever in me to win."

Herb, now almost 70, lives in Byron Bay, and competitiveness seems the

Winning streak: Herb on his way to victory in the mile at the Empire Games, 1958.

furthest thing from his nature. Byron can do that to people with its rural/seaside calming effect. In his yard sits a grand Moreton Bay fig, probably about 200 years old. The appropriateness is neat. Herb, considerably younger, has left a legacy in Australian sport that endures like the fig tree. His success is a product of passion, competitiveness, intelligence, the importance of a good mentor, and a robust self-awareness.

Herb's natural ability may have been nurtured through his love of running, but it was enhanced by his singular determination never to compromise his standards. This winning attitude was ingrained in him by his coach and great mentor Percy Cerutty. It is a coach-athlete relationship as famous and as enduring as any in Australian sport. "I was very lucky that very early in my life I met Percy Cerutty, because the first time I actually sat down and had a conversation with him, he made some comments that stayed with me right through the rest of my life, in sport and in business."

Percy was an athletics coach of some note. Herb, who was still at school, had caught his attention. They met at Herb's house. "I was expecting a big sales pitch to get me to join his training group because he had made some very nice statements about the fact I was going to be a great runner one of these days. It didn't turn out that way at all. Basically, he challenged me to explain why I wanted to waste my time being an athlete. I remember him saying, 'Why would you want to do that? All you're going to do is run around in circles and end up back where you started from.' "

Herb was forced to analyse why he wanted to run, but it also made him realise that by taking his talent as far as he could he would grow into a better person with greater self-respect. "Percy explained that human beings only grow if they are outside their comfort zone. If a human being is comfortable, they are not growing. In fact, if they are not careful, they might actually be going backwards. So if you want to grow, be outside your comfort zone. Now that is a message I have taken with me right throughout my life, and it is something that enables you to stand out from the pack because most people don't want to be uncomfortable, they don't want to go outside their comfort zone. Moving outside your comfort zone means a change of behaviour, and a change of behaviour means lots of practice and lots of practice means lots of boredom and most people get defeated by boredom and tediousness."

Percy's training regime was relentless, which was at odds with the amateurism and "don't burn yourself out" mentality that pervaded his era. But Herb and his coach admired the training regime of people like Emil Zátopek, the legendary Czech distance runner who trained in military boots so that his running shoes would feel light. Sometimes he used to see how far he could run without breathing. Once he did so until he fainted.

CAREER STATS

- World records in 1500 metres and mile, 1958
- 1958 Empire Games: 880 yards, gold; mile, gold
- 1960 Rome Olympics: 1500m, gold
- Retired in 1961, unbeaten over the mile and 1500m
- Awarded MBE in 1964

"You determine how you are going to compete in the race by the way that you train. I don't think you can expect to train with one frame of mind and then to race with another, and win. Our goal was to combine stamina, speed and intelligence. It's not just ability, grit and determination – some people are going to have all of those things yet choose the unintelligent path. You have to think about how you do things. There are many ways to the top, but there are some ways that are never going to take you there."

To simulate the conditions of an event, with competitors determined to run past him, Herb trained imagining a competitor running right on his shoulder. To tighten the screws, he imagined that competitor had the ability to see into his inner being. "I had this person sitting on my shoulder looking into my heart and my mind and my soul and being aware of the weakness that was flowing around inside me at that particular point. He was ready to pounce on me so I could never slow down. I practised that millions and millions of times in training so in a race if someone came up along side me to pass me I knew how to react to the point where it became instinctive."

That competitor never passed Herb – not once – not through all those sessions, and not through any one of his races. He never relented and never lost. "There was no moment where I was so zoned out that I didn't feel the pain. Apparently, Roger Bannister used to get to this point where all of a sudden the pain would go and he'd fall across the line and collapse. Well I never got there. The closer I got to the line, the harder it hurt."

The fever to win gave Herb uncontrollable nerves that hit their crescendo in the couple of hours before the race and, the bigger the race, the bigger the nerves. He would feel lethargic and often yawn. Percy had some timely advice, "That's just your body resting itself before you really go with it, Herb." It allowed him to remain cool enough not to get distracted by the external noise while allowing his emotions to drive him towards a great performance.

Rome 1960 was the culmination of Herb's athletic ambition. Olympic gold was his crowning glory, proof he could perform under extreme pressure. He was favourite but not at his best. "I was struggling before I got to Rome. I had a great year in 1958; I broke world records and won Commonwealth Games gold medals. Then, in 1959, I got married – which was a great distraction – and started to prepare myself to go to Cambridge University. I really lost interest in running. It was so hard to get myself fired up again that when I did it was a bit late. So I didn't have an ideal preparation for Rome. I had competitors who were running 3.54 or 3.55 miles, and I was running 4.10 in Sydney and vomiting afterwards only six weeks out from the Games."

Herb was vulnerable in this environment and had every reason to feel so. Nonetheless, he went to Rome behaving like the favourite, even though he

"My greatest moment was a nondescript moment. At the Empire Games in 1958 in Cardiff I won the 880 yards (the half mile) against a much better English runner, Brian Hewson. A week or so before, he had beaten me over that same distance at White City in front of a crowd of 70,000 people. I was invited to run against Hewson again to decide who was the real man out of the two of us. I ran in this race and the Pommies had lined three or four of them to box me in. At one stage, I had to run five wide to get past them. I did get past them and I broke the Empire record, beat Hewson. It was the fastest that I'd ever run over that distance, even faster than at the Empire Games. I said to Percy [Cerutty], 'Let's go back to the pub and have a beer or something.' And he said, 'No, you've got another race.' What!' And he said, 'I've lined up a race for you at Watford.' I said, 'You've got to be joking.' He said, 'No, you've got to do this for me, I've made a commitment.' I figured he must have been getting some money for it. We got straight in the car and headed off to Watford. When we got there I looked around at the field and there was nobody there of any note. I thought, 'When the gun goes off I'll amble out a little bit and I'll put a bit of effort in at the last lap, and knock them off.' Unbeknownst to me, Percy had got other competitors all together in a group around behind the grandstand and said, 'Is there anybody here who can run a 50 second quarter?' One of the kids said, 'Yeah I can do it', so he said, 'Here's five quid, go and do it.' So the gun goes off and I sort of ambled out, then all of a sudden I look up and here's this kid off at a million miles around the track. So I had to bloody well go for it, and I just caught him with about 100 metres to go and did another time that was faster than the previous Empire record before I set it that afternoon."

didn't feel that way. He had his doubts, but he was not going to give in. He had dedicated a lot of his life to win this race, and now there was some chance it wouldn't happen. But for that to happen someone would have to pass him ...

"I would rather die than have someone go past me. I would actually try and focus before the race and think about squeezing every last drop of energy – emotional, physical and spiritual – and pour it out on to the track where I would be near death but wouldn't die ... It wouldn't have been very intelligent to actually die as a concept – no race is worth that – but at the time I'd rather die than let these bastards get past me. That's how I used to think." When in Rome, he ran and ran and broke the world record with a time of 3.35.6. That would have won seven of the next nine Olympic 1500 metres finals. His athletics career was complete.

The corporate world was different for Herb. No longer was it just about him. "The first time I was a manager I had six guys working for me, and they all hated me. I thought that it was my job to be the font of all wisdom and I had to tell these blokes what to do. Since those early years. though, whenever I have been in executive positions I have been totally confident within myself to have the people who work for me know their job far better than I know it. My job is to encourage them and to learn from them how I, as the chief executive, can help them do their job better."

It was typical of Herb's approach as the greatest mile runner of his time, and as the budding and then successful businessman, setting standards and rigorously adhering to them as they drove him towards outstanding performance, performance that will forever have him admired in Australia as an exemplar for all.

I'm glad Herb chose the 1500 because, while cricketers and footballers are a dime a dozen, there has only ever been one Herb Elliott. Like the sprawling fig tree in his yard, he commands attention and remains at ease with his surrounds. And while, as Percy suggested, he ended each of his laps where he started, each has taught him lessons that have made his extraordinary journey so worthwhile.

"It's not the gold medal that's the key contribution to your life. Although it may appear to be so, and it has huge advantages in a way that people respect you and look up to you, but the most important respect of all is self-respect – knowing that you can rely on yourself and that you can respect yourself.

"And that doesn't come out of winning, it comes out of setting your mind to a task and then carrying out that task, day after day, week after week, month after month, through boredom, through all the challenges, and each time that you're challenged to compromise, not compromising.

"The end result is that eventually you start winning a few things, but that learning experience as a person and the self-respect and self-reliance that you get out of it doesn't come from the victory, it comes from working your way up to the victory.

"The winning is a sign that you used some intelligent training and that you've got some natural ability, but the real benefit is putting yourself through an experience of getting the best out of yourself over a period of time."

LAWS OF LEADERSHIP

- Remain calm

- Use your emotions to benefit your performance

- Keep your life balanced

- Maintain the focus

- Develop mental toughness

- Don't compromise on anything

- Recognise your weaknesses

- Maintain and preserve your integrity

LIZ **ELLIS**

"You've got to have a huge amount of belief in yourself to stand up when something goes wrong and make it right the next time you get the opportunity."

LIZ ELLIS *Australian Netball Captain*

I f Australia's most-capped netballer, Liz Ellis, figures in a team that reclaims the world championship crown in Fiji in 2007, then all of us can thank Guus Hiddink and the Socceroos. For it was the moment when John Aloisi kicked the decisive goal to send us to Germany that her nationalistic passion was reignited. "I was three weeks post-op from my knee surgery and I thought to myself, 'I have to get back to play for Australia again. I want to be like that. I want to be part of a team that achieves something unique, something special. I'd like to have 80,000 people screaming my name.' "

Well, two out of three ain't bad!

Liz's experience is a familiar one for Australian sportspeople that highlights the uniqueness of our sporting culture. It is to our advantage that the many and disparate sporting teams that Australia produces feed off each other for a greater collective result.

1999 was a stellar year for Australian sport, with a variety of our teams involved in world championships. In June, our cricketers overcame the much-vaunted South African challenge in the semi-finals and triumphed against Pakistan in the final of the World Cup. In October, our netballers (Liz included) beat New Zealand with a goal in the final second to clinch their title. The Wallabies also beat South Africa's Springboks in an extra-

Own goal: Liz at home in North Curl Curl, 2004.
Photo: Jenny Evans

On role models ...

"My biggest hero when I was growing up was a player called Keeley Devery, who was a defender in the Australian team. When I first made the Australian team, it was at the expense of her. When they named the team it was, like, "I'm in" and the girl who was my idol, she wasn't. And that was a terrible feeling. But as it turned out she was a great person to have as an idol because she walked up and congratulated me and told me she was going to do her best to make sure she was in there next time. She fought her way back in to the team the very next time, and thankfully it wasn't at my expense. She's someone who I looked up to, not only for her physical skill, but also for her sportsmanship. She was always someone who really respected the rules of the game, and everything that she did was for the benefit of the team, and that was a nice thing to know."

time semi-final before eclipsing the French on November 6 in the final. And among the inspired from that afternoon were the Australian Davis Cup tennis team, who proceeded to Nice to claim the final 3-2 against the French.

Each gained momentum from the other; inspiration morphed into responsibility and then into achievement. Australian sport was in a purple patch at the top of the world in one of our greatest years.

So Liz clearly is not just the inspired; through her various guises as world champion netballer, team captain, lawyer and businesswoman, she has indeed been the inspiration. This time, though, the challenge is different and a lot harder, having suffered a serious knee injury along the way. In a one-off match against New Zealand in October 2005, she blew out her knee which required a full reconstruction. At 32, it could have been the end of a career.

However, life delivers messages in strange and sometimes painful packages, and learning often comes through agitation rather than ease, so it is no surprise that in her time of darkness Liz has been enlightened. Whereas patience and sympathy have never been among her greatest strengths, they are now genuine strings to her bow.

"My injury has made me more human as a leader. I have always had a tendency to have huge expectations of myself, and I would pass those expectations on to every other member of my team, and would not have been

"I have to get back to play for Australia again ... I want to be part of a team that achieves something unique, something special. I'd like to have 80,000 people screaming my name."

sympathetic when they've been injured or when they've been struggling with different things."

As with most people, bad times remind you of just how good things have been in the past – "I have had a very sharp reminder of what I'm not going to have when I finish netball" – and she is determined that her body suit has not yet soaked up her last beads of sweat.

Through her rehabilitation, Liz was spurred on by her self-belief and, importantly, her self-motivation. This had always been the way as, while always supportive, her parents never had to push her: as long as she was enjoying herself they were happy. Unobtrusive as they may have been in the leadership of their daughter, though, the acorn never falls too far from the tree, and what did rub off was her father's aggression.

"Dad was a stock-car racer whose nickname was 'Wrecker'. A stock-car racer is someone who drives quite aggressively and many people have said that I play netball like he drove cars."

On the road: a 19-year-old Liz, in her NSW kit, prepares to head to the nationals in Launceston, 1992.
Photo: Amanda Watkins

Best person for the team, not in the team ...
"You can't teach someone the game plan just before you run out. You've got to be working on it all week. You can't control the people who either don't get it or don't stick to it. Generally, those sorts of people often get weeded out, because if you're the only one not executing the game plan then you're not truly in to the team. I guess what I try to do just before we run out is keep my message really simple, just go over the simple points. If you give people too much information, no matter how well they understand the game plan, their head's going to be spinning. So I always remind them to focus on the process. Focus on doing the little things well. If something goes wrong or some part of the game plan falls down, go back to doing what you know. Pick out the key things that I'm going to remind them of in a game plan and go back to concentrating on those things, and then generally the game plan rebuilds itself. It's just keeping the message simple."

Aggression hasn't been a quality traditionally coveted by sporting women, and equally hasn't been used as a common descriptor by the media that follow female sport. Says Liz: "Women are often discussed in terms of how they look rather than in terms of what they're achieving. Women are rarely described as powerful and aggressive, and strong and fast. They're often described in terms like 'they look graceful', for example."

It is part of the battle for women in sport as they compete for identity and coverage in the sports pages, although it is a battle for any sport in Australia that is not football, swimming, cricket or tennis. Somehow, they must compete for the hearts and minds of a public whose time is diminishing.

"For me, I'm trying to change the perception of netball. Netball used to be seen as a bit girly and run by old ladies around a kitchen table, whereas the sport is a modern professional sport and the athletes are aggressive, fast, powerful and strong, and it has become more so in the last 10 years. So if we can just look after our little patch of turf it might make things better in general for women's sport."

While the perception of men's and women's sport may be quite different, the reality of what it takes to succeed in both realms is the same. Both require mental as well as physical control. "Mentally, I'm particularly tough as a competitor, and I think dad was a mentally tough driver, so perhaps I've subconsciously inherited that quality from him."

Mental toughness requires concentration on the task at hand in spite of the distractions on offer. "You learn to focus on the process just by being in those pressure situations. I've always been very good at being really task-oriented. You can't focus on the end goal if you're not prepared to take all the little steps between where you are now and where you want to get to."

And it is that focus and mental toughness that has allowed Liz to return from what could have been a career-ending injury and to eradicate those demons that may have otherwise overcome her confidence.

"I put all of my confidence down to the fact that I had done everything physically that I could, and that gives me a huge amount of mental confidence."

Just participating, then, isn't an option – the competitive juices are flowing. "How you're viewed by your opposition and your teammates is probably a greater indication of where you sit. At the moment, I want to be the best goal-keeper in the national competition, and I want to go back to being the best goal-keeper in the world."

And all moves well in that direction – in July 2006 the Australian netball team beat New Zealand for the first time since 2004. The story was the main feature on the back page of *The Sydney Morning Herald* and co-captain Liz Ellis was the focal point of the picture.

Guus and the Socceroos, netball supporters and Australians all round thank you for lighting the competitive fire within Liz again. We're confident that, with her qualities, she can do the rest herself. "The greatest thing that you can do is set the example … you don't call time unless you're broken or you're bleeding."

Only a brave soul would stand in her way.

"You can't focus on the end goal if you're not prepared to take all the little steps between where you are now and where you want to get to."

LAWS OF LEADERSHIP

- Passion – find something that you love

- Mental toughness

- Empathy for your teammates

- Take personal responsibility for your actions

- Have confidence in your ability

- Be humble

- Respect your opposition

- Find a leadership mentor

- Focus on the process, not the end result

- Take the initiative

NICK **FARR-JONES**

"My early mistakes revolved around me thinking that I had to change and be someone different from who I was."

NICK FARR-JONES *Former Australian Rugby Union Captain*

Presence: Nick in flight at Twickenham during the Rugby World Cup, 1991.

There I was, just 21 and on rugby's biggest stage. It was moments before kick-off in the World Cup final between Australia and England at Twickenham. England had just sung *God Save the Queen* and we had sung *Advance Australia Fair* and, while indeed young, I felt anything but free – not of anxiety, anyway.

My position just before kick-off had me hugging the left-hand touchline, metres from the crowd, with the competing chants of support and abuse heightening the tension. Searching for relief, I turned to my right and caught the eyes of my captain, Nick Farr-Jones. No words were spoken; they wouldn't have been heard above the din even if they had been. They weren't required.

All Nick gave me that afternoon was a smile. It was confident and it was reassuring. The shrill of the referees whistle was like a penny dropping in my mind. If Nick was so composed then why shouldn't I be? Game on!

Great leaders have a certain presence about them. It is often hard to pinpoint what defines that presence, but by its nature it implants confidence in those they lead. Nick Farr-Jones imparted a confidence in me that Saturday afternoon that was calming and enabled me to focus at a crucial moment. At that moment, looking across the field at Nick, it seemed so natural that he be there, so natural that he feel so calm and then so natural that I should, too.

INFLUENTIAL PEOPLE

- Andrew Slack
- Bobby Charlton
- Jack Nicklaus
- Bjorn Borg

What I didn't consider was that not much more than 12 months earlier Nick may have played his last Test.

Sportsmen tread a fine line, sporting leaders an even finer one. And so it was in the third Test against the All Blacks in July 1990, just over 12 months before the World Cup. The Wallabies were down 2-0 in the series. Another loss and the growing voices calling for the heads of Bob Dwyer and Nick Farr-Jones may have had their wish. Nick's place was under question and as a tour selector he sat out of the selection meeting when it came time to pass judgement on the scrum-half. The selectors stuck with Nick and he in turn promised them a "captain's knock".

A few nights before the Test, New Zealander Sir Bob Jones, a good friend of Nick's, organised a meal with Nick, Michael Lynagh and another Knight of the British Empire, New Zealand cricketer Sir Richard Hadlee. It was a sombre occasion, with the odd joke about the Last Supper passing around the imminent gloom of the room until Hadlee, familiar with the situation the Australians found themselves in, offered Nick some advice.

"Hadlee just said, 'Look, Nick, I can recall times when our New Zealand team was down and we had a simple catchcry. Any time when someone felt the need we would simply call out 'WIN'. It was a simple mechanism to change our negative mindset into a positive mental attitude. Just 'WIN', that was it.'"

Recalls Nick: "It was so simple and I spoke to the guys beforehand and we decided to carry it through and it created a really positive attitude right from the kick-off. The conditions on the day were not great for rugby, but Hadlee's input about our commitment to ourselves and to each other and our positive determination to get on the front foot meant that nothing was going to stop us. During any lull in play the call went up, and with any big hit the call went up again. It was not a trite three-letter word but a call to arms. There was never a thought that we wouldn't win. When we did win it gave us a belief that we could beat those bastards and that took us through to the 1991 World Cup."

Much to Nick's satisfaction, that win against the All Blacks in 1990 was where the Wallabies started to fulfill their promise of becoming a consistent rugby team. From when he became captain in 1988, and for the first two years he was in charge, the Wallabies were an inconsistent team that performed superbly in some Tests and poorly in others. In 1989 they beat the British and Irish Lions convincingly in the first Test only to lose the next two, then they beat the French at Strasbourg only to lose in Lille. Coming home from that trip to France, Nick had had enough.

"I remember organising a weekend with our coach Bob Dwyer, assistant coach Bob Templeton, and vice-captain Michael Lynagh to discuss our inconsistency and look at how we could fix it just under two years from the

CAREER STATS

- 63 Tests, 36 as captain
- Played in inaugural World Cup
- Captained Wallabies in 1991 World Cup victory
- Member of the Order of Australia

Team spirit: Michael Lynagh and Nick during a parade to welcome home the world champions, 1991.

Photo: Wayne Venables

World Cup. Great teams are consistent teams and we were not that. Essentially, that weekend we planned to change the culture of the team. We were too scoreboard focused. We thought that every time we had the ball we had to score a try to become the first team to win a series in France. To be more consistent, we had to become a team that was process driven. We demanded people understand their role in the 80 minutes on the field, but also beyond that. During the game people had to focus on their role and trust the other 14 guys to do the same; at the end of the 80 minutes we would then look up and see what the scoreboard had to tell us. It didn't change overnight, it probably took about six to nine months, but in the last 25 Tests I played we would have won about 21 of them." And that included the World Cup final.

Another factor in Nick's serenity as a leader was his faith. He didn't grow up with a church upbringing but the Lord works in mysterious ways and, at 17, following a couple of girls to church, Nick discovered the Gospel. "My Christianity has been a rollercoaster ride, but I know that my best years

In defence of Campese (a letter to the editor)
Sir, not only as captain of the national team, but as an Australian, it disturbs me to hear and read the constant and at times vilifying attacks by rugby followers and the press on one of our greatest sportsmen, David Campese.

Campo's blunder last Saturday was careless and costly. But few of the Australian players would be satisfied with their performances, including myself. Campo will hopefully learn by the mistake and the whole team, I am sure, will not only show the tremendous spirit in Australian rugby but will improve on individual performances when matched against the might of New Zealand in August.

To Campo I say: Yes, one bad mistake on Saturday which I know you will learn from, but, mate, if I was a selector you would always be one of the first picked, with no handcuffs or chains to inhibit you.

Nick Farr-Jones.

Take note: Nick's letter on July 19, 1989, to *The Sydney Morning Herald*.

have been those when I have been a Christian. To be able to connect with God has given me the calm and the peace to know that I could recover in the tough times and it gave me a great sense of self-belief and the confidence to continue with strong leadership."

He required faith when he was elected captain in 1987. Nick was a guy who liked to be liked. He enjoyed people and they him, but when he was first chosen by Paul Dalton to captain the Waratahs there was almost a revolt from a group of players that supported Simon Poidevin, the incumbent Wallabies captain, for the job. Even the Wallabies coach at the time, Alan Jones, called Dalton and suggested that Nick would not have been his choice. Dalton, though, backed himself because he saw leadership qualities in Nick that he really needed. These leadership qualities, though, took time to come out from underneath the covers – the covers that many leaders use to protect themselves. "My early mistakes revolved around me thinking that I had to change and be someone different from who I was," says Nick. "All of a sudden I started to think, 'What would Andrew Slack (Nick's first Wallabies captain) do in this situation?' It took me approximately a year to realise that Dalton and Dwyer had seen in me natural leadership qualities and so I should use them."

Nick made mistakes, but in learning from them he built confidence in himself as a leader. As well, his Christianity had subdued his stubbornness and impatience, allowing him a greater willingness to try things, and an acceptance of his mistakes in doing so.

"Towards the end of his life Le Tourneau [an innovator at the turn of the 20th entury] was asked: 'Where did you get your great judgement from?' He responded, 'From my experience'. The follow-up question was, 'Where did you get your experience from?'. He replied 'From my bad judgement'.

One of Nick's qualities was that he always backed his teammates. In doing so he built an environment where people were comfortable chancing their arm. To him, that was an important part of being Australian. Famously, after David Campese had thrown a poor pass behind his own goal line, effectively losing the British and Irish Lions series for his team, Nick remained loyal. Amid calls for Campese's sacking, Nick was moved to write a letter to *The Sydney Morning Herald* in Campese's defence. It is history now that Campese, who was so distraught and on the verge of quitting because of the vitriol, kept playing and went on to win the Player of the Tournament honours at the 1991 World Cup.

As a captain, Nick was able to lead in such a way because of his self-belief. "When I was riding high, when I was confident individually, and confident with the way the team was going, I was a good leader. When I was sapped of my confidence, for whatever reason, even if I was having a disagreement with someone in the team, I would wake up at three in the morning with the cracks in the ceiling getting wider and it could affect my captaincy."

Throughout the World Cup campaign in 1991, Nick had been confident and composed. Training may have been edgy at times, sometimes it had to be, but he knew exactly when to tighten the screws and when to relax.

"Andrew Slack was someone I admired greatly for his personal qualities, his leadership qualities and his understated way. The balance he brought to the team was crucial. He called it the on/off button. There were times when you had to be deadly serious when preparing for victory and yet there were times when it was important to be laid-back, to realise that, yeah, this is important, but there are a lot of other things in life that are important as well."

That was also Nick's way and the team loved it. He had the perfect judgement as to when to turn it on and when to turn it off, and to a young forward that November afternoon he got it just right.

LAWS OF LEADERSHIP

- Have the ability to change a culture through young people

- Don't change your leadership style once you become a leader – that's why you got there in the first place

- To be great, a team must be consistent

- Be self-aware enough to step back from the team and see its problems

- Talk is not always the best form of communication – if there's nothing to say, there's no need to talk

- Focus on the process, not the expected outcome

- Create an environment in which people are prepared to make mistakes

- Have a firm sense of self

- Right place, right time – make the most of your opportunities

- Don't be afraid to delegate

- Acknowledge your weaknesses

- Be passionate

- Lead by example – the way you behave and what you stand for is very important

- Know when to turn off and when to turn on

- Know when to finish

BRAD **FITTLER**

"A lot of being a good player, a good sportsman, a good anything, is about how you react to good and bad stuff. If you're open to the good stuff with humility then when things are bad you find you react to them better."

BRAD FITTLER *Former Rugby League Player*

Most celebrated: Brad in action for the Kangaroos during an Anzac Test match, 2000.
Photo: Steve Christo

R ugby league is perhaps the toughest of Australia's four football codes. There is no other code where one individual, running at pace, is lined up by two or three opponents possessed with the sole intention of stopping him – almost dead – in his tracks. There is little pretty about it and a lot to fear. Brad Fittler was a great rugby league player – one of the greatest.

Upon his retirement, he had played the second-highest number of first-grade club games in history, earned state and national honours at a younger age than anyone and – with premierships, State of Origin and Test victories – finished with one of the most celebrated records. "I played rugby league because I was good at it and I found it stimulating. My philosophy as a young kid was that I've got to do something so I may as well get good at this. So that's what I did."

Brad's talent was not latent. He oozed it, so much so that he was chosen to make his second-grade debut at the Penrith Panthers in 1989 as a 17-year-old, a boy among men. Or so they thought, and so did he. It was to be a short-lived career in second grade, one week, in fact, as he scored two tries against the team that ended up winning the competition. His next match was in first grade, where he again excelled. "I set up a couple of tries, and from that moment on I just wasn't scared. The big thing about stepping up and starting to play men was the fear, and after the game I no longer had that fear.

INFLUENTIAL PEOPLE

- Royce Simmons, *rugby league player and coach*
- Phil Gould
- Christine Fittler, *mother*
- Marie, *partner* and Demi and Zac, *children*

That was a big step; it wasn't as though I had made it, but now I felt that I belonged. I really felt that this was where I could be happy'."

At one point in his debut first-grade match, Brad chip-kicked over the fullback and teammate Greg Alexander scooped up the ball to score. It was an audacious move for a man so young, and one that incurred the wrath of his most experienced and respected teammate, captain Royce Simmons, who told him, perhaps somewhat more colourfully, "If you ever do that again you'll never play another game of first grade in your life." The message to Brad was clear. He was not the best player in this team – not yet, anyway – and he was answerable to other people, his teammates.

A ticket to play rugby league, let alone to be a leader in league, requires that you are tough. Brad may have lost his fear of men early, but he was in a good side, a tough side, and that was a great help. "For the first couple of years at Penrith I wasn't scared of anyone because I had these big mountain men behind me who really looked after me. But you still grew up the hard way, you were very rarely cuddled and you were treated like a man a lot quicker than they do these days. I worked out from a young age that rugby league was pretty tough, and you were going to have to play injured and you were going to have to take knocks."

It was the little disciplines in the game that were ingrained in him. Rule No.1 was that the ball was precious, and no matter what else you did you never did anything that risked giving it to the other team. "You could be copping punches in the head and want to retaliate, but you would never jeopardise losing the ball. A lot of people these days are a bit looser in their standards; they are more talented, but they don't have that starch and grit. They were naturally more mentally tough back then. You were really taught to be what was considered a man."

Brad's biggest influence, though, was his mum, who brought him up as an only child without a father (he didn't meet him until much later) in a flat in Ashcroft. She was all he had, and he loved her dearly. "Mum was just a really good person. She never really did much in sport apart from a bit of swimming, and she was not a renowned leader. We just grew up doing the hard yards, and she was just a really nice person. She had really good morals and standards so, if anything, I hope that I took those qualities from her." Brad's on-field standards were exemplary, both as a player and as a sportsman; not an easy balance in such a fierce arena. At times, he even compromised winning opportunities in the name of sportsmanship.

One of those was in the decisive moment of the 1994 State of Origin series against Queensland. "I see it on video replays all the time, when Mark Coyne scores that famous try; they call it 'The Try'. About five metres from

the line he steps inside me and scores a try and they end up winning the game. Because I knew he had this incredibly sharp right-foot step I believed my only option was to head-high him. I can remember in the instance saying to myself, 'I should head-high him. I know I'm going to get sent off but there's only 30 seconds to go. I should head-high him; just smash him across the face.' But I didn't do it. Maybe there in itself lies one of my deficiencies, I lacked the win-at-all-costs mentality, and that may be why I am not a great, great player." No Brad, we think that's actually one of your strengths, one of the reasons that you are a great, great player. Thank *you* Brad's mum.

Brad's first foray into captaincy was with the Panthers at 23. For him and for everyone else it seemed like a natural progression. After all, he was one of the most experienced players in the team. But it wasn't until he transferred to the Roosters in 1996 that he began to understand what leading and being a captain was all about. "I did the job from a playing point of view pretty quickly, but it wasn't until late in my career that I understood about consequences of behaviour and what was right and what was wrong, that it actually dawned on me as to

No fear: An 18-year-old Brad when he was playing for Penrith, 1990.

CAREER STATS

- Played 1989-2004
- 336 first-grade games
- Clubs:
  Penrith, 1989-95;
  Sydney Roosters,
  1996-2004
- First-grade debut:
  Penrith v Wests
  at Orana Park,
  August 20, 1989
- Points:
  526; 122 tries;
  14 goals; 10 field
  goals
- Premierships:
  Penrith 1991,
  Sydney Roosters
  2002
- Representative
  career:
  NSW: 1990-2001,
  2004, 31 games;
  Australia: 1991-
  2001, 34 Tests;
- World Cups:
  1992, 1995, 2000
- Kangaroo Tours:
  1990, 1994, 2001

"One of the things that improved me as a leader was getting myself in order. I really had to work on myself. My footy was never a problem, but I had plenty of problems being undisciplined."

what leadership was all about. One of the things that improved me as a leader was getting myself in order. I really had to work on myself. My footy was never a problem, but I had plenty of problems being undisciplined at times. As I started to get that in order, and realised that it was very important, the more respect I got and the more I enjoyed being a leader. I got rid of a lot of things out of my life which weren't that great even though I thought they were at the time."

Alcohol was one such demon for Brad. He had a lot of good times growing up, but found that as he got older it was something over which he had to exert more control. No longer could he have a big night and then train the next day. "Alcohol made me really loose and took a couple of days out of my life. Towards the end of my career it wasn't ideal for me. Some people can do it, but I felt that I wasn't a great influence on other people. It's very hard to be telling people to do certain stuff when you're not doing it yourself.

"Everyone's responsible for themselves, but I was lucky to always have good support groups around me. Alcohol isn't illegal so you can't stop people doing it, and in the right environment it can serve a great purpose by bringing down barriers, but it's just a matter of trying to use it responsibly."

Brad understood the role of sacrifice in leadership, and whether it was his partying, diet or extra summer training, the little things he went without made him stronger each time. Once it was bread. He loved bread for breakfast, lunch or dinner, but decided to cut that out of the diet for three months. Then it might have been milk. With each sacrifice, his belief in his worth as a player and as a leader grew.

He also saw it as "compartmentalising" his life – breaking it up into the different areas of interest, so that when he was playing football it had his total focus, when he was with his family they were everything, and when he was relaxing he got the most out of that as well. It was all part of the learning journey; learning to know himself and gaining in confidence to be himself. "I masked a lot of anxieties and inefficiencies when I was younger, but as I got older I tried not to mask anything. I was just myself. Some people don't like that, some people don't agree with you, but that's just life. In sport, they're pretty hard to fox, they're pretty hard to lie to, they can tell when people are ditching them, and so you have to be yourself."

Brad was true to himself, and his teammates loved and respected him for it, and it showed in his ultimate moment in sport, captaining the 2002 grand final victory over the Warriors. It was a satisfying victory with a group of mates who had set goals together, stuck to standards and achieved them. They would do anything for each other and particularly for their captain, as Brad was so important to the team. So when one of the Warriors props hammered Brad with a semi-illegal knock, they took action.

"The next two times that bloke ran the ball up, he just got smashed by our two props. He took it up twice, he got smashed by Adrian Morley and dropped the ball, then smashed by Peter Cusack and dropped the ball. That was the standout moment for me, the respect those blokes showed me that I had earned."

Brad played on for two more years, but essentially his career ended as it began, with him the star player, never shirking responsibility no matter how tough, but always with his mates looking out for him and protecting him. "I worked really hard towards the end. I ticked off a lot of boxes, but when I finished I was tired of most of it. I felt like I had been running my whole life."

Brad Fittler is a unique character in rugby league and in Australian sport. He was a boy who before our eyes quickly became a man. Disarmingly honest, he has confronted his challenges and triumphed. He is a man who, physically, as a person and as a leader, has earned respect from both within and outside his code of football. "I had no idea what Steve Waugh was doing at training to make him a better captain, but I admired and respected him from afar. But I tried to take a lot more from people that I knew, that I trusted, and people that I liked because I could see their strong points being laid out in true life. A lot of it comes down to things like trust and basically just being a good person.

"You know, when I look back on my career, I think that maybe I could have matured a bit earlier, but then I've had a great life, I've smiled the whole way. I've been under pressure at different times and pretty much come through, so I wouldn't change a thing."

LAWS OF LEADERSHIP

- Be prepared to make the necessary sacrifices

- As a coach, player or captain, be yourself

- Have standards and stick by them

- Earn respect by your actions, not your position

- Leadership is all about influencing others

LINDSAY **GAZE**

"I learnt a long time ago that many athletes don't want to be coached. They accept coaching, but ultimately they want to make their own decisions."

LINDSAY GAZE *Melbourne Tigers Basketball Coach and Former Australian Coach*

Twelve months to the hour that my father passed away I am sitting opposite Lindsay Gaze interviewing him for this book. The moment is surreal. If I close my eyes I could swear that I am sitting with my dad. Lindsay is the same age as my dad. He is a tallish man like my dad. And through the wisdom of the same grey hair he is teaching the same lessons that my father taught me. It's like that with father figures, even when they are absent they have a profound influence on your life.

Lindsay is popularly considered the father of Australian basketball – not his words, but those of just about everyone from within as well as outside the sport. It's understandable, too, when you consider the role he has played in developing basketball in Australia.

When Lindsay started playing basketball there were just 1500 registered players in Victoria and no basketball-specific stadium. Times have changed. Now there are 120,000 registered players and more than 60 basketball stadiums in that state alone. He has been very busy. So busy that Australian basketball at both the elite and community levels would not be what it is without his leadership.

The good old Gaze: Young Lindsay, 1968.

Lindsay identifies with three styles of leadership: "Firstly, there are those who consult with their members, find out where they want to go and take them there.

INFLUENTIAL PEOPLE

- Ken Watson,
  basketball coach
- Bill Bradley,
  US basketballer
- John Wooden,
  US basketball coach

> "You give people choices, let them know what the consequences of those choices might be and educate them and guide them along the pathway that leads to their success."

Then there are those who take their members to where the leader wants to go, whether the members like it or not. And then there are those who take their members to where they want to go, even though they didn't know it at the time.

"In my case, I am pretty much in that third category. I like to teach by guided discovery. You give people choices, let them know what the consequences of those choices might be and educate them and guide them along the pathway that leads to their success."

This is the approach he has taken with basketball in Australia. Like a good father, he had a vision for his children, whom he has guided towards their goals – allowing them to learn from their own mistakes along the way, he takes greatest joy out of watching his people succeed, and he does so with altruistic intent.

Lindsay never had a father figure of his own. His parents separated when he was very young so his greatest inspiration was his mother. Perhaps her most significant influence was instilling in her children a strong sense of responsibility for their own destiny.

"When I was about six or seven, mum told me that George Bernard Shaw once told a young autograph collector to 'Go out and make a name for yourself.' I am not sure what his intentions were at the time, but I took it as him saying that he was not that important himself, but what was important was each person making their own pathway in life. That stays with me today and has really had a strong influence."

He certainly took Shaw on his word because the Gaze name is one of the biggest in Australian basketball. Not that it has been a one-man show.

Lindsay is quick to recognise that, as with most endeavours, the development of basketball in Australia has profited from the contribution of many. One Lindsay rates highest is Ken Watson, a former mathematics teacher at Swinburne University and Australia's first Olympic coach.

"Ken was a great thinker and a lot of the good things in our sport were introduced by him. Sometimes I get credit for things which he introduced. I might have run them, but he was the man that had the inspiration, and he was the one that kept basketball alive during the war years of 1939-1945."

And son: Lindsay and Andrew Gaze at the NBL grand final, game 3, at Melbourne Park, 1997.

Photo: Ken Irwin

This is typical of Lindsay's modesty, a quality, along with longevity, that he admires most in people who have succeeded in sport. Modesty, however, should never be confused with lack of ambition, for Lindsay's goals for the sport have been lofty.

"I had a very firm determination that we wanted to win. Australian basketball was relatively unknown and not very well respected. Our goal was to win gold medals in international competition, but no one believed that was a realistic option. We have already done this with the youth and junior levels now, and the women have won silver, while the men have finished as high as fourth. We have come a long way, but still have a long way to go."

Gold ambition had to start with baby steps and, while many consider the birth of basketball in Australia to be the inauguration of the national league in 1979, Lindsay suggests it all began with the construction of Melbourne's Albert Park in 1958, the first basketball-specific stadium in Victoria. That's a 21-year gestation period.

Gaze on Mal Speed, CEO, International Cricket Council …

"All coaches take great pride in their prodigies even if they take a different path. He was one of our juniors, started him off at under 12, came through basketball, and I was influential in recruiting him to the executive of Basketball Victoria. He went on to be president of Basketball Victoria, president of Basketball Australia, chairman of the National Basketball League. Now he is the boss of cricket. He is somebody who has come through our system.

We only had a small part of the development in his formative years. And there are others; we have professors of mathematics, professors of chemical engineering in the US and all over the world, who have been part of our system growing up.

Getting letters from these people, reflecting on their youth and how it was important to them, I feel good about that."

"Basketball is a major sport throughout most of the world, and at the time I could not understand why it should be any different in Australia. But to develop it we needed facilities, coaching, teams and experience. Albert Park was constructed in 1958, and I was appointed to manage it. It was our first facility. That was the starting point of administrative progress and a planning board for the development of our sport."

Lindsay and his team grew the sport, targeting a community/club-based structure to act as its foundation. They also saw it as vital that the game be recognised and represented in the education system.

"I spent 10 years teaching the phys-ed students at Melbourne University how to teach basketball, and they in turn introduced it into their curriculum in schools. And then, quite by accident, the government introduced a recruitment system of American teachers to cover a teaching shortage. Many of these were very good basketball players and teachers so it was an injection that helped the education of our sport."

As well as being a visionary administrator, Lindsay was an influential coach, borne of his love of the game and the players he led. Also, with a father's generosity, he has never been paid as a coach. The simple reason: he could always see better uses for the money. As a coach, he strived for his players to become not only better basketballers, but also better people, and in doing so preached the virtues of balance.

"As a sportsperson, there are three aspects in your life that you manage: there is your sport; there are your studies or career; and there is your social life. Combine any two of those three and you can do well at them, but it is very difficult to get the three of them in there. If you are thinking about being great in sport then you have to put your social activities on the backburner for a while, although obviously not to the extent that I have done – I have been accused of being a social cripple."

While he has influenced so many, Lindsay understands the paradox of coaching. "I learnt a long time ago that many athletes don't want to be coached. They accept coaching, but ultimately they want to make their own decisions. They want to have their own future in their own hands rather than be limited by what the coach says.

"My mentor and teacher, Ken Watson, had a theory: in the classroom, the students will try desperately to break the teacher with their behaviour, but in turn be grateful for losing that battle, because then the teacher will be able to elevate the kids' knowledge. The same applies in team sports. The players want to do their own thing, and they test the coach, but ultimately they are grateful they lose and improve."

If there is one area in which Lindsay Gaze could be accused of being derelict of his duty it is in not fathering more children. As the unofficial father of Australian basketball, it is appropriate that he fathered its greatest player, Andrew Gaze. That said, he believes a parent's role in their child's sport is to provide a lot of love, care and support, to act as a taxi driver, and to watch from as far up the back of the stands as you can.

To practise what he preached, he didn't coach his son until Andrew was 15 and the boy's talent, nature and ambition were obvious. When Andrew was selected in the 1984 Olympic team, there were some accusations of nepotism because Lindsay was the coach, but with his talents so obvious that was the last complaint anyone heard.

So now, approaching 70, having played for Australia, coached Australia, administered at all levels, inspired generations of basketballers, sportsmen and Australians in general, where to from here?

Well, a father's duty is never done, and while Lindsay is retired he and his legacy continue. A year after my father's death, he still teaches me daily. When someone close to you and significant in your life moves on, their profound influence continues. Lindsay's voice will echo for many generations to come, and when those gold medals arrive we will know who to thank.

LAWS OF LEADERSHIP

- Build the right base

- Have lofty goals

- Inspire others

- Parenting skills – allow your kids to make mistakes and sit at the back of the stands

- Balance your life and the choices you make

- Love of the game

- Communication, organisation and planning are vital

- Everything happens for a reason – "Everything is for the best in this best of possible worlds." *Candide*, Voltaire

- Desire – you cannot coach it, but it is the most important ingredient

- Understand your style of leadership

DREW **GINN**

"When I watch sports teams now, and various things with business, I look for the person who actually has the ability to demystify things and hand control and ownership to others around them. Also, the exceptional coaches that I have had have said, 'You are who you are and I am going to let you be that way and just give you some guidance along the way.'"

DREW GINN *Australian Olympic Rower*

Drew Ginn's debut in an Australian rowing team was poor. The 11th place by the men's eight at the world championships in Finland in 1995 was one of the worst by an Australian crew. For Drew, a high achiever all his life, it was to get worse: the coach blamed him for the result. "I just stood there and thought, 'Wow, this hasn't happened before'. Previously in my sporting career, through my enthusiasm alone, I always had coaches on my side. For the first time, enthusiasm wasn't enough; the coach wanted me to challenge myself further. I decided then and there I didn't want to be in that position again. I didn't want to be seen to be one of the younger members of the team who had less experience and have people question whether or not I should have been there."

At the post-race wake, Drew sidled up to the "Oarsome Foursome" – Australia's most renowned crew. They, too, were mourning a poor result, fifth. With two parts the courage of youth and 10 parts lager he announced that by the end of the following year – the Olympic year – he would be in their crew. "The coach sort of looked at me, and probably thought that for a young guy I was a bit cheeky. I was feeling pretty shattered about what I had just gone through, and I could see they weren't happy, but I thought, 'If I can make it work, if I can improve, then there is no reason why I can't make the Four'."

Days turned into weeks and weeks into months, and before the sun set on

1995 Andrew Cooper's retirement created a vacancy for a bow-side rower. Drew, a bow-side rower, hoped he might be a chance, a fact confirmed by coach Noel Donaldson, who told him that he was third in line … but he would get his chance.

Drew made the Foursome, enjoying every minute learning from each of the three disparate characters – Mike McKay, Nick Green and James Tomkins – all the way to the 1996 Atlanta Olympics. One of the most powerful lessons came after a poor performance in the semi-final at Atlanta. They did enough to qualify, but not to build confidence. Tempers flared. Fingers were pointed. Donaldson sent everyone off to cool down. When they reconvened, McKay admitted he could have raced harder in the semi-final. His frankness set the tone for a session where harmony was restored within the group through brutal honesty. It became known as the "honesty" meeting.

"It was so valuable to have a person slightly removed in the coach, to say, 'Hold on, let's just settle down.' That little time and space was critical," says Drew. "It was that meeting the following morning that things went from Maybe It's Not Going to Happen to This Is Going to Happen."

Although they continued selling fruit on television, the Oarsome Foursome disbanded after Atlanta, and the lead-up to Sydney saw Drew partner James Tomkins for the pairs. All was going to plan until Drew broke down in their qualification regatta eight weeks before the Games. He was shattered; he had let down a mate and, with his rowing future in doubt, thought he would never be able to repay James for all he had done.

He was desperate to purge himself of the guilt. "For the race in Sydney, I was on the concourse at about the 1500-metre mark and when James and Matthew Long passed me they were in fourth place. I hadn't been able to do any exercise for six weeks and so was pretty unfit. When they passed me, myself and the guy standing next to me took off running and cheering.

"The security guard tried to stop us going over the fence for the last 250 metres by putting his hand up, but that wasn't going to stop us. We just jumped the fence and kept running. He was shouting and we were shouting, and as we were doing that the guys were surging into third position. When they crossed the finish line I felt that I had helped in some way."

The big lesson for Drew from Sydney was to play within his limits and not let his ego or bravado interfere with acting rationally. His back injury originated from a preventable event in the gymnasium at the start of the 2000 season. "I had only just come back from four weeks off and found myself getting competitive with two guys I was good friends with in the gym. As the weights were going up, I thought, 'I am starting to struggle here', but I ignored that warning. There were so many times when I could have opted out and said, 'That's enough for me today', and that would have been fine.

"Something inside me was driving to say, 'No, I want to keep up with you guys as the weight goes up.' When finally I felt the slightest of pinches in my lower back, I put the weight on the rack and lay on the floor thinking about what I had just done." James never doubted Drew's ability to come back successfully, so Athens became a loyalty race for Drew. James had stuck by him. Drew, in return, was just as determined to come back. The relationship is a true partnership of equals, with neither dominating and both working together around each of their strengths.

Drew, for example, took on the responsibility of analysing their competitors. James, much less into the finer details of analysis, encouraged this initiative and, together, as they planned their race strategy, they used the information to move from fourth in the world to first.

"When I watch sports teams now, and various things with business, I look for the person who actually has the ability to demystify things and hand control and ownership to others around them. Also, the exceptional coaches that I have had have said, 'You are who you are and I am going to let you be that way and just give you some guidance along the way.'"

Ironically, given the lesson doled out by his coach in 1995, life rotated full circle and Drew found that after the 2002 world championships he actually had to communicate similarly to James. "James, being as good as he is, at times does things almost like he is only in fourth gear, and he gets away with it. After that regatta (2002 world championships where they came fourth) we had a discussion that from here on we had to start pushing ourselves further. The international competition was actually advancing, and if we didn't start to get a move on, and if we didn't start to challenge ourselves with our capacity, then we were not going to stay in front. He was fantastic in actually taking that on."

Some teams are just meant to be together, and Drew and James are one of those. Their status was sealed with gold in Athens and could well be added to with more in Beijing in 2008. "At times I have actually preferred to do the following role, which is leadership in itself. I am only now starting to find that I am doing some of the things I have seen Michael, James and Nick do. "It's taken for them to almost finish up their time in sport to realise that I am now one of the top people at the top end of the sport, with people looking up to me."

And as they look up to him now they'll be liking what they see.

LAWS OF LEADERSHIP

- Make the most of any opportunities

- Respect the different qualities of your team members

- Know your competitors

- Set an example

- Share your ideas

- Communication is essential

- Respect yourself and your teammates

- Make the decision

BRIAN **GOORJIAN**

"When I played I felt I didn't come to the game or I didn't come to the practice feeling responsibility. As a coach, every single day, every single training session, every single game you have a responsibility."

BRIAN GOORJIAN *Australian Men's Basketball Coach and Sydney Kings Coach*

Brian coaching Eastside Melbourne, 1988.

Picture: Len Lamb

To say that Brian Goorjian has become more Australian than American in the way he coaches basketball may not seem too complimentary. For if there is one sport at which Australians continue to learn more from Americans than from any other nation it is basketball. After all, they invented the game.

This was reflected in Brian's attitude when he arrived in Australia knowing only the American way, a way indoctrinated from a very young age and so different from the Australian way. "America caters to the top 3-4 per cent of children. If you have 400 kids in the playground at elementary school, 10 are in the team, whereas in Australia everybody gets a go. Then when you finish school in Australia everybody still gets to play; State Bank plays ANZ Bank every night at six o'clock. At that age in the US, if you are not in the NBA then you are watching it on TV."

A basic comparison shows that while in Australia the salary cap for an NBL team is about $800,000, in the US LeBron James's seven-year shoe contract is reportedly worth more than $US90 million ($119.6 million). For the struggling individual in the States, sport becomes a first-class exit from the slums, rewarding and reinforcing some non-team – and very selfish – behaviour along the way.

INFLUENTIAL PEOPLE

- Ed Goorjian, *father*
- Johnny Wooden
- Jerry West
- Elgin Baylor
- Magic Johnson
- Paul Kelly
- David Parkin

The downside to this system is obvious, as it builds individuals preoccupied with self-interests as opposed to the interests of their teams. If a competitor is paid $2 million a year to do his job, that is what he will do, but that is all he will do. It is an environment more about Me than We, and this grates on Australians.

"If you spoke to Chris Anstey or Andrew Bogut, they would miss the Australian teamship – the sense of being part of a team. It's not the same in the United States. I love the system in Australia. When I came out here as an import, and I was playing ahead of someone, those people would still invite me to their house at Christmas time because I'm the American – and they would even have Christmas presents for me! In the United States, if he was playing ahead of me, I'd be sitting on the bench hoping he'd break his leg. I know that sounds harsh, but that is the reality."

The upside of the US system is that, it caters exceptionally for the brilliant individual. "If I had a really talented kid who's 16 years old and has a chance to play in the NBA or the NBL, then their [the US] system is phenomenal. However, if I've got a kid who likes basketball but wants balance, then Australia's system is the best. So when I go back to the United States and we talk offence and we talk defence, I take a lot of notes. When they talk about how to blend a star player into a team, that's an area where Australia's great."

Brian's initial on-court influence was his father Ed, a man with a military background who ran his team and his son with an iron fist. His father's philosophy was built on an untiring work ethic and respect. He led by example, running everything himself and making all decisions. As a young boy, Brian watched his father coach the Crescenta Valley Falcons, imagining himself as the star of the team, winning and playing for his father.

He eventually played, won and captained for his dad – all important steps along his basketball journey, which eventually brought him to Australia as one of the first imports in the NBL. While his first impressions of Australian teamship couldn't have been better, he was less than impressed with some of the coaching.

"When I first came to Australia, I noticed a lot of practices where the coach would be sitting on the bench with a coffee. I would think, 'God, the coach is sitting down. He's sitting down on the job.' He'd just sit there talking to his assistant. I was amazed because I'd never seen this in the States."

"The worst times are the hard decisions. And the hard decisions are always about people."

Brian was frustrated in this environment, and vowed that when he coached he would be different – that he would excel with the attention he paid to the people he worked with. Coaching had to be about the players and about giving them the best opportunity to improve.

"I have made a conscious decision such that, if it is a choice between sitting in front of a computer and watching video or spending 10 minutes talking with a player, I'll spend the 10 minutes with the player every time. The guy may have a problem at home or he may be sleeping in the car – a lot of coaches would not find that out. I want to be on top of their problem so I need to invest my time with my players."

He quickly realised that coaching was a significantly more difficult gig than playing or captaining. His job as a captain revolved around leading a team on the court during a game, which is different from the leadership required from the all-consuming perspective of the coach, where you have a whole system

On top of any problem: Brian pushes the Kings to victory over Brisbane, 2006.

Photo: Tim Clayton

127

CAREER STATS

- Coached the Sydney Kings to become first NBL team ever to win three consecutive championships
- Coached more than 600 games in the NBL with a 68 per cent winning percentage
- Won five NBL championships – a feat achieved by no other NBL coach
- Coached teams to 11 grand finals
- Coached teams to be minor premiers nine times
- For the past 17 seasons his teams have reached the NBL semi finals or better
- Voted Coach of the Year four times
- In 2003, was named the NBL's greatest coach in the league's 25-year history
- In 2005, reached yet another milestone by winning 400 games

to orchestrate. On top of this, he tried to do too much himself. "In my early coaching days, everything was run through me, and that clearly was a fault of mine. When I left Melbourne, I had six weeks where I didn't have a job, and I really looked into myself and got some help. The result was that, with the Kings, I put together a very strong management team and leadership group within the team and empowered them to make decisions. I have stepped back more. While that has been very hard for me to do, that decision has had a lot to do with our success."

The spoils of empowerment are leadership, and Brian has revelled in the leadership shown by the players in the Kings squad, although he acknowledges that the environment could never have been created without his letting go. Which doesn't mean he has eased his focus or decreased the demands on his players. "You must be 100 per cent committed, which I am. When you see me walk up and down the sideline in a game it is the same as I am at training. Whether it is a game or whether it is practice, the players know that the pressure is on. They know to be ready. If they are not ready, then I am all over them."

The other side of focus is the "off" switch, and a trawl through Brian's past is not only entertaining but proof enough that he is yet to master that skill. Once, heading to a game, he searched for his keys for an hour before finding them in the freezer. Then there was the time he left his then 12-year-old daughter Gemma at the stadium, only realising she wasn't with him one block from home.

My favourite story, though, is when he had just endured a spate of forgetting things in the overhead lockers of planes. Rather ingeniously, he thought, he took off his left shoe, placed a document that he could not forget in it, and put it in the overhead locker. When the flight landed, he was up and walking away from his seat before the penny dropped. It is always hard to turn off if you care.

Brian will never lose focus when it comes to selection. In the late '90s, during the under-23 world championships, he met Jerry Krause of the Chicago Bulls and learnt a valuable lesson.

Over three days of the championships, Brian developed a liking for a particular player, and he mentioned as much to Jerry. Jerry rebuked him. "What would you know? I've been watching you for three days and you have no plan and no idea what you are looking at."

It inspired a more civil conversation and a system of selection that Brian ranks as the most important ingredient of his success. It has three parts: physical (the speed of their hands and feet); competitive spirit and skill.

"The most important one is competitive spirit, because I don't think you can teach that. The second one would be hands and feet, which is difficult to teach. The third one is skill, because I can teach a kid how to shoot and dribble and pass.

"When I go to a game I look for a guy diving on balls, a guy slapping his teammates on the butt after a play and pointing to them when they make a pass and he scores. And if he drives into the lane and knocks somebody down, because he's too aggressive, which is a bad play, that is somebody that I have a lot of time for, because I feel that I can put a rope around his neck and pull him back. I think I can fix that. But if I see a guy who's really talented, but looks disinterested, that guy is a tease and, in my job, that guy is going to get you fired."

Brian is good at making the hard decisions and making them early. He doesn't enjoy them, but he knows those same tough decisions and the hard conversations lead to some of the most satisfying moments.

At his high school basketball team's 20-year reunion, he was taken aside by a former teammate, Mark Deluna, now a lawyer with four children. In college, Mark was the 12th man on the team Brian captained, and he recounted a story of how scared he was on the first day of practice after he had just been ripped into by Brian's dad. Afterwards, he didn't know which way to turn. Before he had time to dwell in the negative, Brian grabbed him and said, "Hey, man, if he's not yelling at you he doesn't care".

"He told me that, from that time on, dad could get all over him and it had no effect. It changed his outlook; it had an effect on his life."

For a leader who is passionate about his men, these are the moments that drip with gold. "When over time it is confirmed that, as a coach or a captain, you have had an effect on the development of the kids that you have worked with, those pearls, now that I'm in my 50s, have given me the best feelings that I have had."

LAWS OF LEADERSHIP

- Empower your team and those around you

- Leadership can be taught

- Maintain your focus

- Give 100 per cent commitment

- Be flexible

- Ensure clear communication

- KISS – Keep It Simple, Stupid

- Practice makes perfect

- Remain composed

GEORGE **GREGAN**

"Confidence is a funny thing, as soon as you lose it, you know it and then that starts to have a really adverse affect on a lot of the good things which make the team successful."

GEORGE GREGAN *Australian Rugby Union Captain*

They're called "death eyes", and if you've ever experienced their stone-cold glare you will know exactly why. Through my final years in the Wallabies, George Gregan was a great support as vice-captain, but he curried no favour with anyone – if you were out of line, he was ruthless. Even the captain wasn't immune.

You didn't get the look for any old mistake, but for a mistake out of laziness, a mistake out of not being your best. In my time, I was the recipient and lived to tell the tale, better for the experience. George's gaze demanded the best of you, and it worked because he himself was so well respected within the team for his exemplary standards of performance and preparation.

"I won't yell at blokes, but I can be really direct and precise in terms of my talk. Guys know I am pretty serious about it and that they should not make that error again. I use the 'eyes' on players if I feel that it was a particularly lazy mistake or if within the team's framework, or within their own game, they know that they should be doing better than that. I don't like to yell at someone. I don't think you gain much from it. It's more like, let's focus on correcting that mistake because it just wasn't good enough."

The risk with George's approach is that people stop trying new things, but for him that would be a disaster because he rates innovation as the

The eyes have it: George during the Wallabies v Springboks at Subiaco Oval, 2005.
Photo: Mal Fairclough

130

INFLUENTIAL PEOPLE

- Viv Richards
- Allan Border
- Mark Ella
- Ricky Stuart
- Miles Davis
- Tiger Woods

cornerstone to all success. To make sure they don't lose confidence, at the next piece of good play from the "victim", George will be the first on the scene to encourage him and endorse his efforts. I was on the receiving end of a few of those as well; our team wouldn't have been the same without them.

George's crusade for innovation led to the almost immediate success of the Brumbies in provincial rugby and to much of the Wallabies' success of the past decade. His inside pass from the base of a ruck to a player coming from an obscured position became known as the "Gregan ball" and changed the focus of defenders on the edge of the ruck forever.

His implacable pursuit of the perfect (training) recovery regime has contributed to his durability, missing very few Tests over his long tenure.

And his love of coffee has inspired the Brumbies' and Wallabies' cappuccino sets, not to mention a burgeoning chain of coffee shops run by his wife, Erica, under the name GG's.

His penchant for innovation also explains his respect for jazz musician Miles Davis. "I like people who change the way a game is played," says George. "Miles Davis is someone that has done that with jazz. He was bebop and he went to cool jazz. People said, 'What the hell is this?' But everyone still talks about it. It's one of the most revered jazz albums of all and it's called *Kind of Blue*. He just kept changing until the time he died. He was never happy where he was."

George is similar, content in his discontent, always searching to improve and always searching to be different. He has had to be. You don't play more than 127 rugby Tests over 13 seasons without unnatural resilience and an ability to set standards beyond those of most who have gone before you.

With remarkably few injuries over his record number of Test matches, George's physical resilience has been impressive. But it is his mental resilience that has been just as relevant.

It is hard to imagine a player in any sport in Australia who has experienced more concerted vitriol over his place as a member and as captain of a team than George.

When his career began, it was the opposite. In 1994, in just his fourth Test match, he made the tackle of the century, knocking the ball out of All Blacks winger Jeff Wilson's arms as he dived over the line to score a try that would have won the match and the Bledisloe Cup. The ensuing outpouring

"I won't yell at blokes, but I can be really direct and precise in terms of my talk. Guys know I am pretty serious about it ..."

of publicity lionised the moment and the man alike and set the bar of
expectation exceptionally high. He was cushioned by good people, such as his
parents and friends, who ensured he maintained perspective and didn't get as
carried away as everyone else. These early experiences sustained him in times
when things weren't so favourable.

"When you are under a lot of pressure, sporting people have that ability to
focus on the things they can control – things which you know help with your
performance and your preparation.

"You tick all the boxes which hopefully lead to your best possible
performance and you do everything you can to control those things. This gives
me clarity which I am then able to provide for the players around me. When
the heat is on you in the press, you can't go away from the fact that the other
players are reading it, and it does have an affect on the group. You have to
make sure they are not distracted by it."

While there has been every reason for George to lose his own confidence,

**Control: The
Wallabies halfback in
action against New
Zealand, 1994.**
Photo: Craig Golding

133

CAREER STATS

- Club: Randwick (NSW)
- Super 14 team: Brumbies 1996-
- Super 12/14 points: 117 (19t, 4dg)
- Super 12/14 caps: 123
- Test points: 99 (18t, 3dg)
- Test caps: 127

"When I first took over as captain, I assumed that if I said something the players would do it straightaway, but that wasn't the case."

he hasn't, trusting himself through the toughest of times. At the same time, in the absence of enough senior leaders in the team, he has had to build the confidence of his teammates. When the pressure is on, without confidence and experience the heads drop and the shoulders droop.

It happened in the Rugby World Cup in 2003 against Ireland. In the second half, the Irish scored to come within a point of us; the Australian bodies spoke the language of losers. If it weren't for a few of the senior players in the team who remained calm, we wouldn't have won the match.

George used it as the exemplar heading into the semi-final against the All Blacks two weeks later. The lesson got through, but that isn't always the case.

"If a confident person is down on themselves or even irritated at themselves for a short moment, they will lock out of that moment and move onto the next piece of play. That is a confident player. Someone who is lacking a bit of confidence will probably stay in that negative moment for a long time. That long time could be a couple of minutes. In sport that is a long, long time.

"All of a sudden that error compounds to two or three or four and then there is a massive hole. It can be really hard to dig them out, especially in the sport that we play as it all happens very quickly. You don't want to be digging two or three players out of these holes all at the one time. So it's important that they learn that skill to move on to the next thing that they can control because that moment is lost – it's in the past."

While the learning journey can be frustrating, the rewards are satisfying, especially when people get it: throughout one particular off-season George and Mark Chisholm at the Brumbies had been working on a set running line for Mark, but he just couldn't get it right.

"Mark and I had been working on a running line to expose the defence in a certain way, but it relied on him staying hidden," says George. "My job was to engage a defender and the space would theoretically just appear. We had been working on it all through the trials and we almost got it right against the Bulls in Pretoria the week before.

"I had to ask Mark to slow down and hold back and convince him that he would get there and I would leave the ball for him in space. Against the Sharks in Canberra the ball was there for him and he scored the try – pretty much untouched. Instantly, he turned around and smiled. It was one of those moments where he got it. We had been working really hard at it, but finally it registered in him to just hold back and that hole would appear – he was pretty happy about it. He calls the move every time now but sometimes Stephen Larkham overcalls him – I always hit Stevie if I hear his voice."

George's biggest mistake since becoming captain has been in making assumptions too readily.

"When I first took over as captain, I assumed that if I said something the players would do it straightaway, but that wasn't the case. There was a learning process for those new people to come through, which I probably fast-tracked a little bit. There was that stage where we needed them to walk and talk and to experience it before it was learnt. As soon as you assume someone knows something, their deficiency may be exposed, especially under pressure in a big game. That's when you realise it was probably a shortcut you shouldn't have taken."

George has had more than his share of critics, but history will judge his record-breaking career kindly, regardless of whether he achieves his current ambition for World Cup glory in France in 2007.

The greatest praise is often that from within the team, and George's respect among the team is as strong as his stare is cold.

"I would like to be remembered as respectful. I feel as though I am respectful for the game, definitely competitive, but at the same time a good sport. I play the game hard, I play it competitively but I respect the game, too.

"If I am remembered in that way, I'll be pretty happy."

"I play the game hard, I play it competitively but I respect the game, too."

LAWS OF LEADERSHIP

- Ensure motivation for yourself and the team

- Focus on the things you can control

- Ensure honesty and trust within the team

- Understand the importance of communication

- Don't assume anything

- Know your role in the game

- Believe in yourself

- Encourage others

- Maintain balance and perspective in your life

- Earn the respect of your teammates

GRANT **HACKETT**

"For me, one of the reasons that I was selected as captain of the team was because of the experience I have had … great disappointments to great victories."

GRANT HACKETT *Olympic Swimmer and Australian Swim Team Captain*

Golden moments:
Grant celebrates
after winning the
1500m final at
Athens, 2004.
Photo: Vince Caligiuri

Grant Hackett is representative of a body of athletes who have led Australia in our most successful Olympic sport, swimming. Whether due to our weather, our talent, our facilities, our attitude or perhaps all of the above, Australia has been one of the most consistent and successful of all nations in the pool. What's more, the representatives of this sport, many of whom skip school to compete, lead our nation with standards of sportsmanship and behaviour that upstage many older and more experienced athletes.

The standards are amazing: no other Australian sportsmen or women are under such intense scrutiny from so young an age, no other sport produces such a continual stream of fresh and presentable talent and no other sport has such an unblemished public image. With an honour roll that includes the likes of Andrew "Boy" Charlton, Murray Rose, Shane Gould, Tracey Wickham, Steve Holland, Kieren Perkins, Michael Klim, Susie O'Neill and Ian Thorpe you begin to understand why this reputation exists.

The images of any one of those champions are lasting: gold draped around their neck, voices hoarse from belting out the national anthem … again; waxing lyrical about their performances on TV, saying hi to mum, dad and grandma at home and thanking their teammates. It couldn't be more impressive if it were rehearsed – maybe that's what they do as they track that black line up and

INFLUENTIAL PEOPLE

- Mum and Dad
  – *they are your ultimate leaders*
- Pat Rafter
- Michael Jordan
- Tiger Woods
- John Eales
- Steve Waugh
- Roger Federer

"With swimming there is no easy way. Like anything that is worth achieving, there is one way to be successful, and that is to work hard."

down the pool for hours a day. It would certainly help explain it … stroke … stroke … I'd like to thank my mum … stroke … stroke …

Amazingly, Australia has not had a formal captain of its swimming team since the Moscow Games in 1980, although in all our years of swimming, right back to when Frederick Lane won two gold medals at the 1900 Paris Olympics, there have always been leaders.

Enter Grant Hackett, the first official captain of the Australian swim team, and he takes the job very seriously: "The Australian swim team has a very high profile, has been very successful and has a very good image in our country. Every other successful sporting team has its captain, but this was something that was missing from swimming.

"To be captain of this team carries a huge responsibility to lead them correctly. I have to ensure that I give my best to the team in terms of leadership and bringing everyone together, but at the same time I must still focus on my own performance."

Focusing on his own performance should prove no problem for Grant, for there can be few athletes in Australia who are more fastidious about their preparation. At 14, as his ability began to emerge, he set his sights on comparing himself to the biggest and best in the water for his event – "superfish" Kieren Perkins.

With the precision of a NASA scientist, he charted Kieren's times as a 14, 15, 16, 17, 18 year old and in the open category, for the 200, 400, 800 and 1500 metres. Every year he set the marks in his sights, and 80 to 90 per cent of them he gunned down. Kieren was great; he would be greater. Grant had an acute appreciation of his sport, the records and the people, and he was going to etch his name upon it.

While minutes and seconds are the ever present measure in swimming, Grant's focus in preparation and when racing is on process and hard work. "As you become more involved, things become more complicated," he says. "At that point, it is important to be able to undo them and make them simple again. The best way to perform is to focus on the very simple aspects of the race and put yourself in that frame of mind so that you do not worry about your competitors and do not worry about your time. If you can do that, you can execute the perfect race."

For success in swimming, there is no substitute for work ethic and clocking the kilometres in the pool. Unlike some sports, where perfect technique can compensate for hard work, no swimmer has been able to shirk the "money in the bank" of a consistent and heavy training regime.

"My parents' discipline and commitment to their family and their jobs has ingrained in me that if you are going to do something, you do it properly – you commit to it, stick to it and don't give up. I have to take this same discipline and commitment to my office in the pool, where I have to produce 15 kilometres each and every day."

An image of machine-like production comes to mind: precision mechanics, rigid discipline and certain outcomes. It is a relentless pursuit for the edge, and over a 1500-metre race that edge might come in your rhythm, in your stroke, or in one of your 29 turns. Minute inefficiencies in technique multiplied by strokes, laps and turns become extra seconds on the clock and define success and failure over an olympiad.

Teen believer: 17-year-old Grant swims to victory in the 1500m at the Australian Short Course Championships, 1997.

Photo: Vince Caligiuri

Hackett on mind games ...

"I don't (psych out his competitors) because I just like to do it in the performance, because I think that as soon as you sit in a marshalling area or leading into a race or newspaper articles or anything like that where you try to out-psych your competitor, you have given them the edge because you are willing to take a little of your time, a little of your energy to show them that they are actually worthy of playing mind games with. [That] They are actually good enough or competitive enough against you. You are complimenting them indirectly by saying something about them, saying you can beat them. You are taking a moment of your time and energy to show them that you want to intimidate them because they are worthy of it. I have absolute respect for my competitors, but none of them are worthy of that."

For it is that 1461st day, that one day at the end of four years of effort, that will determine whether your dreams culminate in delight or devastation.

One of Grant's unique challenges as captain of the Australian swimming team has been to blend his team of champions. Swimming is an individual sport, yet the Australian team is the envy of all with their conspicuous team mentality. This is trickier than it may seem, especially when you consider that your words and actions as a leader must resonate as meaningfully with a 14-year-old girl as they do with a 30-year-old man.

At the same time, Grant must be available and willing to help a teammate who could be his greatest competitor for gold. In Australia, it is quite likely that your No. 1 competitor actually comes from your own backyard. This requires a type of sportsmanship that human nature rarely supplies, yet the men and women of the Australian swimming team seem to have it in abundance. It requires the delicate balance of selfishness and selflessness.

"You are a good leader if you can treat everyone as an equal, but when you compete you must quickly shift your focus from being in front of the team and selfless, to being selfish behind the block. You have to focus on beating the competition, regardless of where they are from, who they are, or what they are trained to achieve. Once you have touched the wall, as the team captain, you have to congratulate the person beside you and support them whether they finished in front of you or behind, and you must back yourself with a smile."

The longest and the loneliest race in the Olympic swimming schedule, the 1500 metres, requires a singular dedication, so the additional responsibility of leadership has helped balance Grant as a human being. For a young man who was at times considered aloof, he now enjoys the reputation as one of Australia's most-loved and respected people – and not just sportspeople.

It has been a journey of watching and learning from those before him, such as Kieren Perkins, from those in other sports, such as Pat Rafter, and those close to him who have challenged him with some of life's harsh realities. At all times, Grant has recognised where he has come from and how lucky he is.

At his house on the Gold Coast one day, Grant's father, Nev, was hitting golf balls into the canal with his 10 iron. Hackett jumped in to have a turn and, as he swung, his grip slipped and Nev's favourite club ended up in a watery grave.

Without a word, Grant went inside the house, togged up, put on his goggles and headed down to the waterline, his father's words reverberating through his swimming cap. "Just because you can bloody well swim you think that you can do anything." Outside 10 irons there are no favourites in the Hackett house.

"Most people have a leader within, and it is a matter of having the right influences to extract it out of them. I have brought some of my strengths to this role, and in other cases learnt as I went along.

"Of most importance was my performance. It is important for a leader to perform in the big moments – like when Ricky Ponting hits a century. I also must be approachable and relevant to everyone in our squad from the 15-year-old girl to the 30-year-old man.

"To be respected, I must be conscious of doing the right thing and making the right decisions. I have had to be selfless in my approach and, finally, I must never disrespect either a teammate or a competitor."

Grant's leadership will continue to grow and flourish, and there is little doubt that the reputation swimming and its athletes have earned in the public's heart has only been enhanced by him, through his leadership and his team.

"When you compete you must quickly shift your focus from being in front of the team and selfless, to being selfish behind the block."

LAWS OF LEADERSHIP

- Understand and appreciate your sport

- Work hard

- Maintain balance

- Be disciplined and committed

- Be respected and approachable

- Do the right thing, talk to the right people, make the right decision

- Don't be selfish

- Have desire

- Take responsibility

- Enjoyment

MICHAEL **HAWKER**

"When you get to the stage where you think you should be the leader, no matter what, that's probably the time that you shouldn't be, because you're probably no longer interested in the people you're leading. You're probably more interested in yourself."

MICHAEL HAWKER *Former Australian Rugby Union Player and Insurance Australia Group* CEO

Long-term thinking: Michael Hawker, 2002.

Photo: Phil Carrick

As you enter the IAG offices in Sydney, a sign warns, "No Hawkers or Canvassers". I'm sure they don't really mean it. Since taking the chief executive's chair at IAG in December 2001, Michael Hawker has grown the company from 6400 to 12,000 staff and was named the industry's Best Insurance Executive in 2003 and 2004.

But while he has made his mark more in corporate than in sport, as if scripted for this book, ask him where he learnt most of his lessons for life and business and the answer is direct. "From the sporting field."

Michael has always been driven. Legend has it that on morning bus rides to training on Wallabies tours, while others were digesting the goings on from the night before – a legacy largely of the amateur days – "The Lord" Hawker (named because of his regal presence) would be scouring the business pages of whichever newspaper he hadn't finished reading over breakfast. Banking and business were on his mind. He always took the long-term perspective, and his amateur sporting days weren't going to last forever. "I was in a school classroom years and years ago and the teacher said, 'What would you like to have happen if you died?' One guy said, 'I'd like to come back to my funeral and people say that there was value in me being on the planet.' That's how I look at myself. I am driven by this fear that when you die, that's it."

INFLUENTIAL PEOPLE
• Parents
• Nelson Mandela
• Tiger Woods

RUGBY MENTORS
• Barry John,
Welsh rugby player
• Mike Gibson,
Irish rugby player

When Michael played in Australian rugby's most successful and most celebrated schoolboy team, the 1977 side that included the likes of the Ella brothers, Michael O'Connor and Wally Lewis, tour success was never going to be enough. His ambition was so much greater, both personally and for the team. "Once I got in the Australian Schoolboys, then I was really keen to see how far I could take my rugby career because it was the first time I'd been benchmarked within the sport itself. The team was a really talented group of people, and once we'd played together we realised what we could do with the sport. We wanted to see if we could take our pattern of play – very much a running style of rugby – to the national level, and we became passionate about how we could make that happen, and we were lucky enough to get the opportunity."

It was long-term thinking that paid off. From that schoolboys team, 10 players became Wallabies, a very high graduation rate, and three of them, including Michael, played on the Grand Slam tour of Britain in 1984. The Wallabies beat England, Scotland, Ireland and Wales in the one tour, a highlight in Australian rugby history and the only time this has been achieved by a Wallabies team. "It's easy to do something short-term; it's harder to do things in the longer term, and that's my personal challenge."

It is no surprise, then, that when you scan the list of people Michael most admires, this theme of long-term and sustainable success is very prominent.

Lee Kuan Yew: "How you can create an island (Singapore) in the middle of Asia and make it the economic powerhouse it is, is fascinating."

Nelson Mandela: "How you can be locked up for 25 years and come out with the ability to forgive … It's amazing personal strength and discipline."

John Howard: "He's been Prime Minister for 10 years in a time where stakeholder groups like the media attack you so ferociously, so quickly – he's now Australia's second longest-serving prime minister."

Mike Gibson (Irish rugby centre): "… was the most capped player of all time …"

Jack Nicklaus and Don Bradman: "They were just so far apart from everyone else in the sport that they played."

Michael's relentless pursuit of sustainable success is a complex task in a society that rewards good short-term performance, sometimes too well, but

"Understanding how to become more constructive, and how to encourage constructive conversation, is something which, as the decisions get tougher, it is harder to do."

equally penalises poor short-term performance too harshly if expectations are not met. "Short-term profit at the expense of stakeholder groups is unsustainable. I get a little bit frustrated with the media when at times they say all profit is at the expense of stakeholders, which is a nonsense in my view. The only way to make sustainable profit is if you are providing value to your stakeholders – your customers, your community, the people that you work with, and your shareholders.

"If you're not meeting all stakeholder needs, then at some stage those stakeholders will rile against you, which will detract from profit. Business behaviour that is not appropriate is when someone is pursuing short-term profit at the expense of investment in one of those stakeholder groups."

There is inevitably short-term pain in the pursuit of long-term goals and, while sport understands that sometimes you lose games in pursuit of long-

A community of 10 ...

"If a community only consisted of 10 people, then everyone relies on each other to do something. Everyone needs to do some work, and those who have more capability need to help those who don't. They have a responsibility to undertake a leadership position, as they have been blessed with greater capabilities. I think that any individual who performs well in any aspect of community life, whether arts, sporting, academic or practical, has a responsibility to undertake a leadership role. I don't like people retiring early. I think if you're a community of 10 people and you make a lot of money and then retire and go and sit on the beach, I think that's just as disastrous as someone who's refusing to work and wants to sit on the dole. I think both ends of the spectrum equally don't fit within a well-structured society. And I think that anyone who's got a leadership position, whether it's a sporting leadership position, an arts leadership position, a community leadership position, business, politics, whatever it is, they need to take on responsibility."

term success, the sharemarket doesn't and can mark any "lossess" harshly. "I would like to win every game – but you will lose. There will be disappointments."

For those with a glass half-full mentality, these disappointments are taken as an opportunity to learn, no matter how painful. One such "losing game" for Michael occurred in his time at Citibank, where his boss charged him with closing down a particular business unit. It had to be done that day or the next.

With no time to prepare, by his own admission, Michael did an appalling job, making a lot of people very angry in the process. But the experience taught him a lesson. "It taught me how to manage difficult messages and how not to get a business in a position where you need to close it down like that to start with.

"I had also learnt that by taking tough decisions like these you are more likely to save the jobs of other people in the company, as you are making the business more efficient and competitive."

One of his bosses cited an example of a chief executive in the 1970s who, in letting go 40 per cent of the people in his business, had rationalised that he saved 60 per cent of the jobs. This Michael could understand, and it enabled him to tolerate the soul-destroying task of putting people off, as well as focusing on how he could help them move on.

The amalgam of Michael's life experiences has contributed to his view that there are two types of leadership. One falls under the banner of encouragement. These leaders are typically inspiring and they care for their people more than they do for themselves – their style is motivational, and people make the choice to follow them.

The other leadership style is driven by fear, typified by any of the despots around the world whom people follow, almost blindly, but also because they find they have no other choice. The former is sustainable, but not the latter. Your ability to lead in either way is a product of both learning and your innate value set.

"The innate piece is a value system, which essentially says 'You care more for those you are leading than you care for yourself.' This requires qualities like courage, strength of character, discipline, and a willingness to do some of the tough things in the interests of the collective. These are either values you are born with or learn from a very early age.

"And then there's learning about communication. Learning to understand the other person's perspective; learning about how to become more behaviourally consistent through personal discipline; and learning how to influence others more effectively."

Either way, leadership is tough, and something you are constantly learning. "Some leadership roles have terrified me, and some of the things you have to do in leadership I've put off for a while because they take a bit of courage to do. There have been times where I haven't had the courage to really say what I've felt, which would have been valuable to the person I was saying it to, but I really didn't want to upset them. Understanding how to become more constructive, and how to encourage constructive conversation, is something which, as the decisions get tougher, it is harder to do, but you've got to keep doing it."

It's the transparency in sport and the inherent values of courage, teamwork, discipline, hard work and sense of fun and camaraderie that Michael, along with many Australians, relate to. Egalitarian by nature, sport is transparent because the measurement of your team's performance is on the scoreboard for all to see, and there is nothing complicated about that.

Michael, throughout his business and sporting career, has identified the importance of short-term performance and used it as a guide and as a learning vehicle towards long-term sustainability, and he just keeps driving on.

The long-term verdict will judge Michael Hawker an outstanding success.

LAWS OF LEADERSHIP

- Build discipline within the team

- It takes courage to be a leader

- Be inspirational to those you are leading

- Be motivated by what is best for the team

- Accept the best decision for the team, not yourself

- Understand that everyone needs recognition and encouragement to keep going

- Provide constructive criticism

TREVOR **HOHNS**

"I always kept in the back of my mind that our sport progressed and developed even without Sir Donald Bradman, so no matter who is currently playing the sport will always go ahead and progress. There is no doubt about that."

TREVOR HOHNS *Former Chairman of the Australian Cricket Selection Committee*

P osition vacant: Chairman of Selectors, Cricket Australia.
Job description: Knowledgeable cricket person required to travel the world, watch cricket matches and pick the occasional team.

Experience: Previous experience as a selector not necessary, but it helps to have played Test cricket. You will liaise with Cricket Australia, the coach and captain of the team, the media and everyone with an opinion on cricket. Experience in counselling and breaking bad news an advantage.

Salary: This is a paid position, but you will not be compensated commensurate with the time you put in. It is a part-time role, but you will be expected to put in full-time hours.

Note: If you take on this role, in the course of your employment be prepared to lose friends and anger people. At the same time, you will receive no credit for your good decisions and full blame for your mistakes.

All top sportspeople have taken the selectors' medicine. Traditionally, they hunt in packs of three, forever hiding behind that most unpalatable of lines, "It wasn't me, it was the other two bastards." Whatever, they are dropping you from the team, sayonara …

In business, they call it "succession planning" or "performance management". In sport it's simply "getting picked" or "getting dropped". Whatever you call it,

Trevor in action: Queensland versus Victoria, MCG, 1979.

CAREER RECORD

Player

• Sheffield Shield, 1972-1991 105 matches, 188 wickets (average 38.99); 3965 runs (ave. 28.32), highest score 103

• Test debut Australia v West Indies, Sydney, January 26-30, 1989

• Played seven Tests 17 wickets (ave. 34.12); 136 runs (ave. 22.67) highest score 40

Selector

• 1993-2006, Australia played 46 Test series, won 35, drew 5 and lost 6

• Tests played 149, won 94, lost 28, drew 27, success rate 63.09 per cent

• ODIs played 333, won 223, lost 99, drew 6, tied 5, success rate 66.97 per cent

"If you think what you've done is right, stick with it, despite everything."

gathering the right mix of capability and personality in your team is a crucial determinant of success. Selection is no simple procedure, as sometimes the greatest capability available is not the greatest fit, and vice versa. As a process, it remains one of the most important in leadership, yet it is also one of the most difficult and poorly executed of leaders' responsibilities. It can be a terrible job, but somebody has to do it, and Trevor Hohns did so exceptionally well for 13 years through the most successful period of Australian cricket, only hanging up his pen, pad and binoculars in April 2006.

Trevor's earliest memories are of playing cricket, and his crowning glory was being selected to play for Australia as a 34-year-old leg spinner in 1989. "Representing your country is something that everyone strives for and you keep playing your sport and training with that in mind, but to ultimately be chosen at the age when I was first chosen was very sweet. What felt best for me, though, was actually walking out on to the field for the first time representing Australia and playing against the West Indies and people like Viv Richards and Gordon Greenidge – that was very special."

He never aspired to the role of selector – not many do – it just sort of came along. When he finished playing Shield cricket for Queensland he had a year off and concentrated on his sports distribution business. Then Queensland nominated him for the vacant Australian selector's position and he was successful.

"I was playing the game for my state and used to think, 'Who'd want to be a selector?' Then when I first took the role people were saying, 'Why would you want to be a selector?' But the role keeps people who have played the game involved, and if the game is in your blood why fight it? I thought it would be a good opportunity to stay involved in the game and, also, if I didn't take the job then I may never get another chance. Then after about 12 months in the role, the chairman Lawrie Sawle, who had done a wonderful job and was one of the nicest men that I have ever met, retired and I was asked if I wanted to fill the chairman's role."

As chairman of selectors, the buck stops with you. Lawrie Sawle was a quiet man, but had been very efficient, organised and fair, so Trevor tried to follow suit, at all times aware of the magnitude of his responsibility.

"You're not just picking teams for the present, you are dealing with careers and dealing with the future of the game as well. You do the job the best way

you possibly can; that's what I stuck to. Sure you might hurt people; the players in particular may not agree with you at various times, but you're doing the best you can for the Australian cricket team. Unfortunately, that isn't always the best for the individual.

"Even though it's a combined opinion with the other selectors, the ultimate responsibility is yours, and it's important to be firm but fair. I always kept in the back of my mind that our sport progressed and developed even without Sir Donald Bradman, so no matter who is currently playing the sport will always go ahead and progress. There is no doubt about that."

Trevor and his selectors changed the landscape of cricket forever. They chose a unique team for each of the one-day and Test arenas. Conventional wisdom had it that the best XI for any one day were going to be the best XI for any five days, but in the lead-up to the 1999 World Cup Australia began to run with a different team and a different captain in both forms of the game. It was a move that Trevor rates among the biggest contributions his selection team made to cricket.

Talking tactics: Steve Waugh and Trevor during a test match between Australia and the West Indies at the Gabba, 2000.
Photo: Jack Atley

151

"While the same players were playing both forms of the game, we thought there were players in the state competition that were better suited to one-day cricket than some of our Test players were. It was difficult to educate the players and the public, but with the support of the Cricket Australia Board it enabled us to split the teams.

"It didn't suit some of the players at the time, but it has proven to be a correct decision. The selectors involved at that time got a lot of satisfaction out of Australia winning the World Cup in England in 1999. Sure, we were probably lucky with the odd dropped catch and a fabulous Stephen Waugh innings to get to the final, but it was very satisfying to win, and also to see other countries then follow suit [with split teams]."

The selectors also determine the rankings of players, which in turn determines the amount of money they receive through their contracts with Cricket Australia. This requires independence and is one of the reasons the coach of the team was relieved of his responsibilities as a selector.

"I felt that the coach was better off not being a selector because he needed to get close to the players to help them with their game. Because of this, if they had a problem which they wanted to work on in their game in earlier years some of the players were reluctant to go to the coach."

The essence of selection is making the tough decisions, but those decisions are not always obvious. Even in a game like cricket, where supporters assume the stats, facts and figures are the be-all and end-all, you have to rely on more than just that raw data.

"If you pick the team just on statistics you might as well have a robot doing the job. Sometimes you just have to run with your gut feel, as the statistics don't tell the whole story. A batsman, for instance, might have failed a couple of times, but those couple of times he might have been run out or asked by the captain to go in and throw the bat around a bit. So that's why it's important to have selectors at the game watching and taking those considerations into account."

The toughest calls are always on the more established legends of the game, knowing that your decision may call time on their career. "The charter for the national selectors is to not just pick teams for now, but to pick them for now and the future and find the right blend at the right time for the team. Timing is very important as to when you bring a new player in and let an older player go.

"Over the last 10 years, Australia have been very, very lucky and have gone through a golden period in cricket and had some of the all-time great players in that period. You can't just lead a player out because of his age if their form is fine ... so it is a fine line as to when you bring a younger player through."

If a player is selected in the team, Cricket Australia informs them, but if a player is dropped then it's the chairman of selectors' job. Only once did Trevor delegate that particular responsibility. "I'd just taken over as chairman of selectors, and we made a call on an Australian player, and another selector was on duty at the ground where this player was. For convenience sake, I asked if this selector could tell him the news.

Unfortunately, the player was a fairly volatile character in those days and all hell broke loose. I then vowed never to allow another selector to do that again. In future, I would do it myself."

And he did, many times, the hardest being his conversation with Steve Waugh after he had been dropped from the one-day side.

It occurred the afternoon before the Allan Border Medal presentation in 2002, and Cricket Australia wanted to announce the one-day team for the South Africa tour the next day. It was a bombshell that Steve had not anticipated, and while he accepted it he was not happy. In hindsight, Trevor, while sure it was the correct decision, acknowledges he could have handled things differently.

"I'm not sure that the right thing to do is to go and tell somebody their job is on the line, as it could increase the pressure on that individual too much. Possibly, however, we could have said, 'Look we're not satisfied with what's going on. If things don't turn around we are going to have to move on.'

"Maybe that could have happened, although in this instance there wasn't any time to turn things around as the one-day series in Australia was over and we did consider it was the right time to move on."

Despite Australia's successful defence of their one-day world championship crown, for many the decision on Waugh remains a moot point. But in the final wash-up, for Trevor, the most important ingredient in selection, in life and in sport is respect. "Respecting others will always hold you in good stead. Regardless of whether they respect you, always respect them."

LAWS OF LEADERSHIP

- Do the best you can

- Understand the importance of timing

- Communication – be able to talk to your team

- Develop relationships with those you lead

- Know your facts before making a decision

- Keep a positive attitude

- Acknowledge the value of statistics and when to use them

- Respect other people

ROD MACQUEEN

"I suspect I was always someone that wanted to improve on things that happened, I always thought there were other ways to do things."

ROD MACQUEEN *Former Australian Rugby Union Coach*

It is ironic that at the very moment Rod Macqueen was confirmed as a great coach some players within the team were questioning his contribution. It was the 2000 Wallabies tour of England, three Bledisloe Cups, three Cook Cups, one Tri-Nations and one World Cup after Rod took over as coach when an Australian journalist pulled him aside after the final training session:

"Do you realise that some of the players are saying you do very little as coach, and that they actually come up with a lot of the ideas and the moves, and your coaching staff are running a lot of the show? In fact, you are doing very little?"

Initially, Rod was stung by the disloyalty of some of the team … his team – the team he had helped develop from woeful to world champions – but as the heat left the moment, and the space created clarity, he felt vindicated, as this perception was no accident. It was actually the culmination of many months of long hours and planning.

"At the time, I was a little bit concerned about some of the criticism, but I also realised that was probably when I was at my best as a coach. If I had a business where my employees in that business were coming up with a lot of the ideas and fixing the problems as they came along, that the staff and the management were, day to day, running a lot of the business, and I was in a

This way up:
Rod when he was
NSW coach, 1992.
Photo: Tim Clayton

" ... while they might be a reasonable leader, they're never going to be a great leader until they realise that everyone thinks differently."

situation where I could look ahead, see what was going on and look at the bigger picture, well it would be the ultimate compliment."

Six months, but just three Tests later, Rod retired with the Tom Richards Cup in hand, the prize for a 2-1 series victory over the British and Irish Lions, a first for the Wallabies. He had always said he wasn't a career coach, he had signed on to do a job, and he did it and did it well. And that was his way. It was a job well done. Rod brought a unique perspective to the teams he coached, a blend of his experience from the worlds of sport, business, and life in general.

Most of Rod's early sporting experiences came from the team environments of surfboat rowing and rugby. He loved them both because they reflected his upbringing – outdoors and rugged. In rugby, he was more aggro than artisan, but nothing if not a relentless trainer, which compensated for what he happily describes as his "lack of natural ability". "I played nearly all my football in first grade, but only stayed there because I tried so hard. It would have been nice to have someone take me aside and teach me some skills and get my focus on being able to go a step further along the track."

It was through surfboat rowing, however, that Rod attained his highest honours as an athlete and learnt some valuable lessons. "Surfboat rowing is a very interesting sport, as it's a sport where you can make a lot of excuses because of the conditions of the surf and the unevenness that sometimes can occur. But the thing that I learnt is that the best crew still won, and the reason they won is they set their standards so much higher than everyone else."

One of the most valuable lessons from the sea arose from a national title when he and his crew came away with the silver medal after being outright favourites for the gold. "We'd won everything, we won the state titles, we'd won every race up to the finals, and as we were preparing for the next day's final, my sweep came up to me and gave me a look at the gold medal he had won previously in an Australian title and said, 'Rod, you're gonna have one of these tomorrow'.

"That night all I thought about was this gold medal and standing up on the dais. He might have thought it was a great tactic, but it was the worst thing he could have done because the reality was that I was just thinking of the outcome. I was just thinking about this gold medal the whole time." When the day came, Rod and his crew missed out, only just, in a line-ball decision. It hurt, particularly because he knew that he had not prepared well enough, particularly in those last 12 hours, not so much as in the last 12 months.

"I was the stroke for the crew. If I had been thinking about how I was rowing, making sure that as we got out through the break that I levelled the boat, and making sure that on the way back I had enough energy to pick the rating up when we needed to get on the waves, then I'm sure it could have been different. I'm sure that if I had thought that way, and thought about the processes, it probably would have made the difference of the six inches we lost the Australian title by. That taught me it's about being smart, it's not about necessarily just being hyped up. It's about sitting back, thinking it through and giving yourself the best opportunity."

They were salient lessons for Rod and lessons, which many years later, ensured that I, as captain of the Wallabies with Rod as coach, maintained my focus in the lead-up to the 1999 Rugby World Cup final.

Before each match, our team would meet for the final time before boarding the bus to the stadium. The reasons for the meeting were threefold: it was the penultimate check-in on team tactics for the day – the last being at the stadium itself; it was the time for the jersey presentation by the Classic Wallaby to the team – an innovation of Rod's where a Wallaby of the past would speak and present the jerseys for the Test; and an opportunity for the captain and coach to say a few words to the team in a controlled environment.

Before this meeting, Rod and I would meet in his room to download what each of us was going to say to the team and generally chat about how we felt about the upcoming match. It was a moment we gained confidence from each other and aligned our thinking before leading the team from each of our perspectives. That day in Cardiff, just hours before we ran out to play the final, I told Rod that I wanted the team to picture the opportunity we had that day, and to think for a moment what it would be like to win the World Cup, and then direct their focus on what we had to do to achieve it.

I never realised I was playing Freud, uncovering the mental scarring and pain of all those years prior, but I knew it didn't strike a chord with Rod, as he quickly tempered my approach. "Look," he said, "I'm trying hard not to do that myself, and it's really important that we don't." He didn't go into detail, but I trusted his judgement and we concurred, deciding that the day was all about focusing on the process, not the outcome. And that we did, winning 35-12.

In the late 1980s, Rod's life took a profound twist when what he thought was a bad case of pneumonia laid him out in intensive care at Mona Vale Hospital. The pneumonia itself wasn't the main problem, it was merely a symptom of the far more sinister pituitary tumour in his head. The fit and

COACHING STATS

- Wallabies 1997-2001, won 34, lost 7, drew 1
- World Cup, 1999
- Bledisloe Cup, 1998, 1999, 2000
- Tri Nations Cup, 2000
- Mandela Challenge Plate, 2000
- Cook Cup, 1997, 1998, 1999
- Lansdowne Cup, 1999
- Hopetoun Cup, 1998, 2000
- Bicentennial Trophy, 2000
- Puma Trophy, 2000
- Tom Richards Cup, 2000

motivated coach found himself bed-ridden, overlooking the golf course where he'd run so many times. "I didn't realise how sick I was until the doctor said, 'Look, you are very, very sick, and you'll be lucky to come through this'. There I was in bed looking out over the golf course, thinking how often I'd actually run up those fairways, sometimes piggy-backing someone, maybe with weights in my arms. My realisation, though, was that not once had I sat back and looked at how beautiful this course was, with the sea and all the scenery around it. It was a great lesson for me because it made me realise that there is more to life, and while I think a lot of people talk about near-death experiences being good for them, in my case it definitely was very good for me. It was an eye-opener to what life was all about."

Upon full recovery, Rod, with his wife Liz, always took the time to smell the roses. "Liz and I have been through highs and lows like all couples, but we've been together for a long time and are a great team. I really respect Liz's attributes. At that point, we could have settled back and enjoyed a really easy life, but it is the challenges in life that are very important. We started a new business and I got involved in coaching again at the same time, which was a bit of an outlet for me more than anything. All those things were a lot more enjoyable, and in some ways I was a lot more successful because I had a fairly good balance." Rod's balance involved drawing ideas from many different perspectives to focus on being successful. He had three favourite inspirations – Edward de Bono, the great lateral thinker; Phil Jackson, the great Chicago Bulls basketball coach; and Sun Tzu, the ancient Chinese warlord. It was also Rod's custom to use a lot of inspirational quotes, but at times he would get confused, so when he quoted Kostya Tszyu, the great Australian boxer, and his wartime wisdom, or Michael Jackson and his basketball theory we knew what, and who, he was actually talking about.

For Rod, the legacy he leaves and the manner in which he leaves it are as important as the success he achieves. While Rod's field of endeavour may have changed from surfboat rowing to rugby, and to business, his principles of leadership have remained constant. "High standards are vitally important for leadership. Someone who strives to do their best all the time is generally someone that makes a good leader. It is also important to delegate well and understand people. Very often you can see someone who you might think is a good leader, and they lead from the front, but they expect everyone to be like them and to think like them. So while they might be a reasonable leader, they're never going to be a great leader until they realise that everyone thinks differently, and it is really important for them to bring out those different skills, different strengths and combine them together to make a great team."

The culmination of Rod's career as Wallabies coach was the victory over the British and Irish Lions in Sydney. It was a marvellous comeback, with Australia winning the series after getting badly beaten in the first test in Brisbane. Until that point, it was both mine and Rod's intention to retire two months later, after the final match of the Tri-Nations series against New Zealand and South Africa. On the morning of the second Lions Test in Melbourne, Rod called me to his room. It was too early for our regular catch-up so I knew that something was on his mind. Without dithering, he told me that, win, lose or draw, he was going to announce his retirement after the game, effective the next week after the third Lions Test. He knew his time had come.

"The thing that made us a successful side in the first place was the willingness to change and innovate, and I was now finding some reluctance within the team to look at new ideas and challenges. Sometimes success can be the enemy of innovation. They knew Eddie Jones was coming in shortly, and perhaps felt they really didn't need to listen to the outgoing coach any longer. It was at that stage that I made the decision to go. It had always been my vision when I first got the job to put together a business plan that would make myself redundant, and with Eddie now in place to take over I didn't think the side would be disadvantaged by my departure. In fact, I thought they would be advantaged by my making that decision."

The team won in Melbourne and Rod announced his retirement to the dressing room after the match. The players were stunned. The media likewise. Rod was content. "I was really happy to have that last win against the Lions as a final outcome. I hadn't really thought too much about outcomes until that point, but that was a very special moment walking around the oval and seeing the reaction of the crowd to the Wallabies.

"Sport is great because it takes your mind off other things, it gives you something to do, it gives you things to aspire to, it gives you role models, it gives you health and fitness, it makes you think, and it's a bit like life; the ingredients that make you a good sportsman are generally what makes you a good person or a good businessman."

And Rod Macqueen has been all three.

LAWS OF LEADERSHIP

- Enjoy your sport and give it everything you have

- Set high standards for yourself

- Be prepared to share ideas with others

- Be open to different concepts and their benefits

- Look for solutions internally and externally

- A great team is about combining the different skills of different people

- Accept that everyone has flaws

- Do smell the roses along the way

- Make sure you always have a succession plan

- Set your skills and structure for the future

KIRSTIE **MARSHALL**

"As a member of a team, my job is not to just blindly go where I want to go with completely no regard to everyone else's opinion."

KIRSTIE MARSHALL *Former Olympic Aerial Skier and Victorian MP for Forest Hill*

Focus: Kirstie at home after victory as the Labor candidate for Forest Hill in the Victorian state election, 2002.

Photo: Sandy Scheltema

It must have been some sight to see: a petite, fit, blonde Aussie girl navigating her way through the streets of Shibuya, the busiest intersection in Tokyo and possibly the world. There she was just a walking down the street, hardly singing, skis on her shoulder, backpack on her back. Life was tough for an up-and-coming athlete in the marginal sport of skiing, on the other side of the world, searching for her hotel on a bread-and-butter budget. But it was interesting and kinda fun, too … and it gave her perspective. "I find it easy to put myself into somebody else's shoes. So when I am meeting constituents I now understand very clearly what it's like to feel like everything is against you, the odds are against you, and people are against you."

Leadership is best served if you come from a position of understanding of the circumstances of those you lead, the ability to see the world through the eyes of another. Kirstie Marshall has an interesting perspective. She was a gymnast from a working/middle-class background who struggled at school, took her learning and became a world champion skier, and upon retirement transferred her skills to become a Member of the Victorian Parliament for the seat of Forest Hill. It's quite the CV, and by no means complete.

Sport was important for Kirstie because it instilled in her a self-confidence and a focus that did not previously exist. School certainly had not been such a

INFLUENTIAL PEOPLE

- Martina Navratilova, *tennis player*
- Michael Jordan, *basketballer*

CAREER STATS

- Freestyle skiing 1988-1998 World Cup aerials titles, 16
- World aerials champion 1997
- Joint world record-holder for career wins, 17
- Winter Olympics 1992 (demonstration event), 1994, 1998
- Elected member of Victorian State Parliament, 2002

"Leadership is also about showing unity. People think of leadership as being completely individualistic, but being a leader is actually about showing you can obey rules as well."

joy. As an example, for one year at school she had to sit French classes for six months followed by German classes for the next six months, after which she chose to continue with the French. Her teacher responded in a manner which had become oh-so familiar, "You know, you are not very good at languages so why don't you choose something else." So she did, and it wasn't academia.

"That is how I thought of myself when I was at school. I wasn't a complete disaster as a student, but I wasn't good at anything. I didn't have any desire to be a leader, I just had a desire not to be disregarded, and I felt quite marginalised at school. I knew I was relatively good at sport, a jack of all trades sort of thing, but not great at any one thing. My school was very academic-based and there wasn't any sense of accomplishment of doing well in any sport. So when I got out of that I really wanted to stand out from the crowd. Skiing was the first thing I felt really good at, and I did it for the pure love of it. My first jump was when I was 17, my first international competition was when I was 18, by the time I was 19 I remember having a sense of pride about skiing."

Kirstie loved her time on the slopes, and after one particular training week at Mount Buller she returned to Melbourne to do a ski show in Bourke Street. Finally, people were starting to recognise her and know about her results. It made her feel good and it made her proud. By 1998, she was Australia's first world freestyle skiing champion and the equal record-holder for most victories in her sport. Success on skis was determined by two key factors: personal determination and personal responsibility.

"There are three other people who have had significant results in our sport. Jacqui Cooper, Alisa Camplin and Lydia Ierodiaconou. When I look at all four of us as athletes we are all incredibly different, but I do see things that link us, like personal determination to a level which is quite uncommon. Jacqui would train harder than anyone I have ever seen. Alisa would train to a standard that was higher and Lydia was very similar. For me, I knew that I was often quite injured. I had 13 operations over my skiing career, so I had to train smarter.

"For me, it was also important to take personal responsibility for my program. I wouldn't just do what my coach was telling me. Innately, you must believe that you know what is best for you. In my fourth year, which was the year I became

No.1, I didn't have a coach. Probably because of that instability in terms of coaching, I took that responsibility and said, 'Right, I will make these decisions and I will guide myself.' Whereas some athletes get so focused on being treated a certain way by a coach that they become quite superstitious and everything must be in place for their competition to work, I had to be really flexible."

Leaving sport was difficult for Kirstie. "When I stopped skiing I had to be really honest with what I was good at, with what I was I qualified for. My confidence plummeted at first. But once I started to get away from skiing I realised what I had gained, and then I slowly built my confidence back up by actually understanding what it was I had learnt out of skiing."

In the final analysis, much of Kirstie's lessons from skiing came off the slopes and in administration. Without a team manager or coach in her first year on the world cup circuit, she had to represent herself at team leaders' meetings and safety briefings, and fight hard for her particular needs. Before long, her leadership qualities became obvious and smaller nations approached her to represent them.

Air tight: Australia's aerials world skiing champion practising at Mt Buller, 1997.
Photo: Joe Armao

Kirstie, in turn, was happy to put her hand up and stand up for them against the dominant skiing forces of France, Canada and the US. It was an early taste of leadership and she loved it; she loved the challenge and she loved the journey into the unknown.

"My argument was always that the largest three nations were disadvantaging the athletes that could least afford to be disadvantaged. So that is very much a part of the philosophy of my politics now and this is where it all stemmed from. Fighting for better accommodation, fighting for better facilities, fighting for

Ladies' day ...

"If more women, when they bought a newspaper, went to the back page first, more of the sport that they want to read supposedly would be on the back pages. But the media's job is to sell newspapers or to capture audiences with radio, TV or whatever it is. It's about consumers, and they're fulfilling the consumer demand. So it's all well and good for females in sport or associated with women in sport to say we want more coverage, but until there is a greater demand for it at the end of the day that's not going to happen. We have proven, and even my success and my profile, has proven that it can be done without stripping naked or being wrapped in plastic or wearing tiny little pieces of Lycra."

better prizemoney, fighting for better competition site conditions, for better regulations and for better support. In a very strange way, I was really acting like a union, which is quite ironic."

With the end of her sporting career, she packed her skis and assumed the the rage in politics. "While I think of my skiing as quite extraordinary, I think of my job now as quite ordinary. I go so far as to say I am an example of what anybody can do because a lot of people think you have to go to university and get a law degree to become a politician, and I'm like, 'Oh no, you can muck around for 15 years skiing and still represent.' And that's the great thing about politics, it's a job anyone can do."

When musician Peter Garrett entered federal politics he said, "I'll be really straight about it: politics is an imperfect game … and yet it is the best game we have for making the country work better."

Kirstie, however, is quite positive about the political system and the opportunities it gives her to make a difference. "Skiing was an imperfect system. When I was at school, education was an imperfect system. It is very easy to focus on the negative and the negative alone. People see politics as negative, but I know the positive. If every day was just about the negative, it would be an incredibly difficult job to do, but the good still far outweighs the bad tenfold. I do think the system works."

Kirstie is determined to lend her constituents an ear to make sure they believe their voice can make a difference, citing the Government's recent reversal of its decision on the Snowy Hydro sale as an instance where people power can enact change. She always searches for the hot issues. "We have 45,000 people in our electorate with about 5000 home businesses. I have the eighth-highest median age in terms of electorates in the state, and about 72 per cent of the people that live here weren't born here; they come from overseas, so it is a very interesting and diverse area."

Kirstie understands that being a member of a political party requires her to at times accede to the party's wishes. If she doesn't always win she accepts it's because the team is bigger than the individual. "As a member of a team, my job is not to just blindly go where I want to go, with complete disregard to everyone else's opinion. Leadership is also about showing unity. People think of leadership as being completely individualistic, but being a leader is actually about showing you can obey rules as well."

Through her varied experiences, Kirstie sees leadership quite simply. "Leadership is about making decisions and having the conviction to follow them through, being well organised, self-sufficient, and able to minimise as much stress and drama in your life as possible.

"When things go wrong, that's OK, find another solution. I know that every time I fell, every time I failed, I learnt more than when I succeeded. I evolved through those failures, not through the successes. When I won I tended to copy everything that I did. When I didn't succeed I had to look back and analyse what happened, what didn't work, and what did I need to change to make it better next time. That is when I grew."

It's a good thing that Kirstie Marshall is able to put herself in others' shoes because there are few of us capable of putting ourselves in hers, certainly not at 10 metres in the air and turning somersaults, anyway. Hers has been an interesting and valuable life from both a sporting and a political perspective.

"Sports is fantastically selfish. As the athlete, I could choose what to do, when I wanted, how I wanted. Nobody could make me do anything. I didn't have any real responsibilities to anybody but myself. Politics, on the other hand, is almost not about me at all. I am a medium which other people use to get their results. And so I have no doubts in terms of legacy; politics has the capacity to have the greatest impact, and I also think it's where I would like to have my greatest impact. If it comes to my eulogy and somebody says, 'She was fantastic in sports, yeah, she did politics for a few years' I would be disappointed. I would like my achievements to be listed in terms of priority – from politics down."

LAWS OF LEADERSHIP

- Learn from other people's mistakes

- Consider your words carefully and how others may interpret them

- When you make a decision, follow it through

- Eliminate as much stress and drama from your life as possible

- Fight a good, worthwhile fight that you have a chance of winning

LEIGH **MATTHEWS**

"You are given the title [of leader] because that is what you do, rather than we give you the title, now we expect you to do all these things."

LEIGH MATTHEWS *Brisbane Lions Football Club Coach*

When I ask Leigh Matthews what he wouldn't do in the name of victory, he laughs a little – almost bashfully – and looks up to the left as he ponders. Then, with a straight face and an even pulse, comes his response. "Well, you wouldn't go and kill someone ..."

I like a man who knows his limits.

With four premierships as a player and four as a coach, it is hard to find a better record in the history of Australian football than that of "Lethal" Leigh Matthews. He had very few limitations in his career and, as his nickname suggests, his reputation was built on ruthlessness and an uncompromising pursuit of success, something he acknowledges in hindsight.

"It is probably in some way a failing as a human being, that on the spur of the moment, when I played, I would often have done things that my morality said I shouldn't do."

Competitiveness is at the heart of Leigh's success, driving him to arguably his greatest achievement of three consecutive premierships with the Brisbane Lions. It is even more remarkable when you consider the now formidable Lions were once known as the "Bad News Bears".

To win premierships in sport is difficult, but to win three in succession and strongly challenge for a fourth is exceptional.

Lion heart: "Lethal" Leigh checks the scoreboard during a NAB cup match against Melbourne, 2006.

Photo: John French

INFLUENTIAL PEOPLE

- Parents
- School teachers
- Sports coaches
- John Kennedy
- David Parkin
- Allan Jeans

COACHING STATS

- Collingwood, 1986-1995
- 224 matches, won 125, lost 94, drew 5
- Finalists 1988, 1989, 1990, 1992, 1994
- Premiers 1990
- Brisbane Lions, 1996-
- 194 matches, won 123, lost 71
- Finalists 1999, 2000, 2001, 2002, 2003, 2004
- Premiers 2001, 2002, 2003, second team in AFL history to win three consecutive flags
- Runners-up 2004
- In 2002, became first man in AFL history to play and coach 300 games
- Sport Australia Hall of Fame 1994

"As a coach, 99 per cent of the time you are developing an elite team, because you may never become an elite team. The Brisbane Lions became an elite team and maintained that for three or four years, and that is very rare. It is very rare that you become elite enough to say, 'Now, we will try to maintain it'. Maintaining is very much about short-term decisions, whereas developing is about trying to pick the medium- to long-term as well."

In a sporting system that aims to have 16 different premiers in 16 years, a "three-peat" is difficult, and it requires sacrificing long-term results for the short-term gain. Players and staff of the Lions knew they had an opportunity to create their own niche in Australian sporting history, to become only the second team to win four premierships in a row, after Collingwood (1927-30). To do so, they would have to make sacrifices.

"In our particular group, that meant trying to keep our players together. We had to play within the salary cap, but use whatever mechanism available to us. We had an agreement with the players that if they were on a four-year contract, we would push a lot of the money to the third and fourth year of the contract. We all knew what we were doing, but we are now in the situation where those moneys that were pushed forward are upon us. We always knew that eventually we had to pay the piper."

These sacrifices were only possible because of the team ethic that had been engendered within their squad. Leigh learnt about the importance of selflessness from John Kennedy, his first senior coach at Hawthorn. Kennedy was a school principal by profession who reinforced his words in the way he carried out his life. For Kennedy, sport was about the team coming before the individual, which was a lot more easily said than done. Leigh thought of himself as an individual, but understood the importance of ceding to the team. For him, people can give of themselves as an investor or as a sacrifice.

"Sacrifice means that I am giving without expecting anything back. Shaun Hart, who played for us with the Lions, was very much like this. On the other hand, I was an individual that knew you had to act it. I am more what I think most people are, which is investors. We understand investment so we give something to the team because we believe we are going to get the rewards through our team. That is the way you have to act as a person within a team sport. You have to always be seen to put the team first, even when sometimes your individualism or your own personal ambition can make that difficult."

High performers' investment instincts lead them to seek the environment that best meets their needs. This environment adds to the attractiveness of a team and, when successful, builds mystique in the minds of your competitors. In a 16-team competition in such a competitive recruitment environment an advantage like this is much sought after.

No match: Leigh in his 300th game for Hawthorn at the Western Oval, 1984.
Photo: Geoff Ampt

"I believe in that play on words for TEAM: Together Everyone Achieves More. Ultimately, the individuals are only part of a group because we believe we achieve more within this group than we can by ourselves or with another group. You need to convince everyone that they can achieve what they need to in our organisation and get their emotional needs fulfilled. Part of meeting a person's emotional needs is through financial rewards, but that is only part of it. You also want to get the 'feelgoods' from being part of a good organisation, the belief that the medical attention they get is as good as there is, the coaching they get, the conditions they have – all those things in the club that they believe are superior to the opposition."

Part of maintaining the elite environment is getting your selection right and specifically the complex decisions around when to bring people through and when to move people on. Leigh unapologetically subscribes to the theme of his former coach, Allan Jeans, that you would go and get the worst murderer out of Pentridge if you thought it was going to help your footy team. The question becomes problematic, though, when confronted with the high-performing inconsiderate. In this instance, Leigh backs his instincts to make a judgement about whether the team gains, or does not gain, from the package of qualities of the individual. The Lions made just such a call letting go star player Jason Akermanis.

Letting go of anyone is hard, but emotionally it is often harder, though just as important, to be able to retire the great player near the end of his career. Leigh agrees with the wisdom that it is generally better to do so a year earlier than a year later.

"We all know that experienced, high-profile players who are physically struggling still have that emotional status. Players will give them the ball when they are not necessarily in the right position to get the ball. So while it seems they are playing well on some of the statistics it doesn't mean they are actually playing well. Rather, they are using their experience to their own advantage and not the team's."

For a man who does repent but does not apologise for playing so brutally and damaging opposition players on occasion, Leigh is remarkably measured. When I happen across him in a lift on the morning of the Lions' first grand final victory, over Essendon in 2001, he is smiling and totally at ease.

"How ya feeling, mate?" I ask.

"Just looking forward to it. There is nothing more that we can do – it's up to the players on the field now."

Their victory was clinical, running away in the final quarter with perfect execution after perfect execution. For Leigh, success on the day was about winning a marathon over the season and not a 100-metre sprint on the final day. "On match days, the coaches in AFL are in much less control than people think they are. You can interfere with the game a bit by interchanging a player or changing positions, but there is not nearly as much that you can influence in the two hours of the game as what most spectators think. It is more about what is done during the week to set up the performance above and beyond the talents of your individual players."

Further, team success is not achieved through a peak of emotion but rather

"We all know that experienced, high-profile players who are physically struggling still have that emotional status. Players will give them the ball when they are not necessarily in the right position to get the ball."

the ability of his players to focus on their specific tasks throughout the game, ignoring the consequences of winning and losing. Leigh's clinical coaching rationale is the product of years of gradual temperance of his personal nature.

"The mistake you make as a coach is to act out of frustration, disappointment and blame, which is what fans do – but that is all right for fans; they are over the other side of the fence. As a coach, you have to resist the temptation of letting your emotions take over. I have been better in Brisbane, but there have been times when I was a bit abusive after the game and I acted out of frustration and disappointment.

"What I have tried to do now is say very little after the game. I might talk to players briefly to wind up the match before they do their cool-down. Then a day or two later, when the emotions have subsided, we do a review of the game. Otherwise, out of great joy or great disappointment, you can say things that are too extreme."

As a coach Leigh is composed and focused, knowing that people look to him for strength and confidence in their environment. His commitment is the total devotion of his mind and soul to his pursuit of excellence for his team, and it delivers results.

"I try not to have too many other things in my life that I need to give a lot of attention to so that I can give my total focus to this particular part of my life. The total focus means that you have less emotional time for your family and your friends. Playing is the commitment of mind, body and soul. Coaching is mind and soul – there is no body to coaching, it is not a physical thing.

"I feel like I have lived my last 35 years in one-week cycles. I had trouble planning ahead and thinking a year ahead. I am more in this week. Then, once I play this weekend's game, I focus on next week …"

LAWS OF LEADERSHIP

- Put the team before the individual

- Make the most of the opportunities you are given

- Create the belief that everyone can achieve from the team

- Fulfill the emotional needs of each individual

- Have self-belief

- Trust between team members

- Maintain composure

- Coaching is mind and soul, playing is body, mind and soul

- Enjoy what you do

- Anything that is in your control, do it right

BRUCE McAVANEY

"My weakness sometimes in my calling is that I perhaps think that everything I am seeing is the best thing of all time and experience tells you it's not."

BRUCE McAVANEY *Sports Broadcaster*

Sound advice: Bruce prepares to call the Melbourne Cup, 1986.

Carl Lewis is regarded as one of the greatest athletes of all time, winning nine Olympic and eight world championship gold medals during his decorated career. For his 100-metres world championship triumph in Tokyo in 1991, the only race where six men stopped the clock at under 10 seconds, he was a vision of composure.

At the halfway mark of the race, Lewis was almost last, but he finished first and broke the world record. After the race, a reporter hit him with the obvious question: "Carl, what did you do differently at the halfway mark?"

He responded instantly, "I didn't try to run any faster."

Most great performances are steeped in composure, and it would have been easy, when all was looking poorly at the halfway mark, to panic, but he stuck to what he knew; he had faith in himself, in his preparation, and in the plan he had for the race, and he ran to that plan.

Just as the 100-metres final is the most intense 10 seconds of activity on the track, it is also the most intense in the commentary box. Invariably, Bruce McAvaney is a picture of composure as he heads the telecast of any major sporting event. He is as comfortable hosting or calling the Melbourne Cup Carnival, the Olympic Games, the Australian Open Tennis or a Rugby World Cup final. But it is the 100-metres men's Olympic final that really tests him.

GREAT MOMENTS

- The first and third Ali v Frazier fights.
- Rugby World Cup 2003 final.
- 1988 Ben Johnson v Carl Lewis. "The biggest Olympic race of all time."
- Cathy Freeman's race in the 2000 Olympics. "My most important call because the whole of Australia was watching."
- Michael Johnson breaking the 200-metres record in Atlanta.
- Hicham El Guerrouj. "The race at Athens in 2004 decided whether he would be the greatest 1500-metres runner or the best never to win gold at the Olympics."
- Carl Lewis's performance at the 1991 World Championships, Tokyo. "A magic moment."

"The biggest challenge for any broadcaster is the 100-metres men's final because the pressure is on. It's the biggest title, 'Fastest Man on Earth'. You see the heats, the semis and the quarters. You look for the fast starters, you look for the major players, and then invariably there is a shock halfway through the race and a close finish. You really just have to go with it, but it is a great challenge and good fun."

Success for Bruce comes down to four factors: knowing his subject; passion for what he does; responsibility for his output; and belief in himself. His subject is sport, and he knows it better than just about anyone, so interviewing him was intimidating. Where to start? Let's just see how good he is.

Who won the Melbourne Cup in 1968? Without breath the answer comes: "Rain Lover, it was the first of his two Melbourne Cups and he was one of five horses to win more than one. He won by eight lengths, which was a massive amount. Archer won the second Melbourne Cup by about the same margin. As a race, it reflects the mood of the country. When Carbine won in 1890, Melbourne was going through a boom at the time. When Phar Lap won in 1930 they were going through a depression. Carbine won more money in 1890 than Phar Lap did in 1930. When Phar Lap won in 1930 they had 70,000 at the track and 30,000 on the hill that couldn't afford to get into the track. So what was your question? Rain Lover won the cup in 1968."

I thought as much. No more examination needed.

For Bruce, as a leader in sports journalism, it is unforgivable to get facts wrong – you can make an error of judgement, but don't state an inaccurate fact. When calling the 1991 AFL grand final, he commented that Hawthorn had kicked the most goals in the last quarter of a grand final. They hadn't. It was Essendon, in 1985. The number-crunching, retentive fans of the AFL, and particularly the Bomber faithful, have never let him forget. His failing was that he had been only 97 per cent certain of his information. Lesson learnt.

In calling, however, it is more important to understand the relevance of the particular number than it is the number itself. Our greatest cricketer, Sir Donald Bradman, is a great example. "There are three layers of statistics with Bradman," Bruce says. "He scored 6996 Test runs but we have had three or four players over 10,000 runs, so the amount of runs he scored is irrelevant. His average, though, of 99.94 stacks up beautifully against all great players of all generations who comparably have averages in the 50s.

"But the statistic with Bradman that interests me more than any other is the amount of times he made 50 compared to the amount of times he made 100. Now, most great Test players, let's say they made 25 Test 100s, would have made about 60 half-centuries to get those 25 hundreds. Bradman made thirteen 50s and then 29 hundreds. When Bradman got to 50, he almost

always went on to make 100. A good broadcaster knows the difference between a real statistic and one that is not relevant."

So Bruce knows his numbers and their relevance, but what about his wedding anniversary … "It was Easter Monday, April 4, 1994, when we got married. I was supposed to be calling Collingwood and Carlton that day, and Annie and I got married instead. I can relate it to a sporting event. It's one I remember, and it has been 12 very lovely years."

Thought so.

Another important aspect to his job is knowing where to look when calling a race or an event. Bruce doesn't go in with preconceived lines or ideas about what he is going to say; though he will have ideas about where to look. He gains these insights from knowing the form of the competitors, if they are fast starters or fast finishers. Seeing a great runner in eighth place with one lap to go means different things for different runners – and Bruce has to know the difference and describe that in his call.

At age five, Bruce's passion was sport and sporting heroes, and he lived in no doubt that he would one day call the Melbourne Cup. He was so obsessed that at

**Box draw:
Bruce leads the commentary team at the MCG during the AFL grand final between Essendon and Brisbane, 2001.**
Photo: John Donegan

What's your number?

"If you were a cricket fan you might say 99.94. In AFL, you might say 1360: goals [Tony] Lockett kicked, and before Lockett came along it was 1299 because that is what Gordon Coventry kicked and he held that record for 60 years. If the Melbourne Cup was the most important event in my life, I would say 11 – Bart Cummings. The next best trainer is five. Or you might say three: Makybe Diva, because she is the only horse to win more than two Melbourne Cups. There are a lot of important numbers. For me, 11. I think it is remarkable what Cummings has done. I think he is a genius. Eleven. Etienne De Mestre trained five winners for the first 20 Melbourne Cups, and that was 120 years ago. There are only two trainers who had more than three winners in the Melbourne Cup in the past 100 years; Lee Freedman has trained five and Bart Cummings 11. There have been eight quinellas in Melbourne Cup history; Bart supplied five of those eight. On five occasions, Bart had the first and second over the line. Only on three other occasions has the same trainer had the same first and second, in 145 years, and Bart's done that. Eleven is my favourite number because I love the event and I love what he's done."

10 he would shut his bedroom door, sit on his bed, put the form guide on his brother's bed, get out his horse whip, whip the bed and call the race.

He has never stopped dreaming, and even during this interview he acknowledged he would love to be calling the World Cup, as two mornings earlier the Socceroos' draw with Croatia advanced them to the round of 16 for the first time in history. "Two-all. Just about the most famous scoreline in Australian soccer. It was two-all when Iran put Australia out in 1997 after we led two-nil, and Johnny Warren cried on camera. It was two-all when we beat Croatia into the next round. Can't two-all make a difference? Two-all sent a nation into mourning, and yet two-all sent a nation into celebration. They are both draws but the difference in terms of the feeling of the Australian public between one and the other was like the difference between sea level and Mount Everest. That is the line I would love to have used."

The combination of his passion, his fastidiousness and his position instil in Bruce an acute sense of his responsibility, but not so much to Australian sport as to himself. "I call for only one person and that is me. When I say that, it sounds like I am really selfish and insular. I'm not, but that is the way I operate in a call. I make sure every time I go there I can do my best. My responsibility is for me to do the best I possibly can because, if I do that, then I feel I am showing leadership with the group around me. My anticipation and my expectation and pressure comes from me, for me, to produce for me, and that's the way I have always operated. If I let myself down, I know I will let others down, and if I can produce a really good performance, host well, call well, interview well, then I am going to make the program better."

Over 30 years at the microphone, Bruce has developed great faith in his ability, and a composure not unlike that exhibited by Carl Lewis back in 1991. But Bruce didn't always have confidence. Until the age of 13, the blind faith of youth left him in no doubt that he would become a race caller. There are no barriers, and there is no intimidation for the young. From 13 to 22, though, his dream seemed a bridge too far, as the pressures and constraints of society ate at his confidence and created limitations in his mind. At 23, he so lacked confidence that he knocked back his first chance to call a race. Pursued for the next six months, he gave it a go and has never looked back. And yet he still gets nervous almost every time he calls.

"There are two types of nerves in my job: there are the normal adrenaline nerves that come with the occasion, and I don't care if it is being watched by 10 people or 100,000 people: it is important to me that I do a good job. I don't mind those nerves. The other nerves are the worst ones: when you are not prepared for some reason and you have to produce a performance in front of a camera without the background knowledge. That makes me extremely nervous."

Listening to Bruce actually makes me slightly nervous; maybe that's Pavlovian conditioning linking his voice to so many of our greatest, yet most tense, sporting memories. He seems as much a part of those events as the athletes themselves. He may not be calling with any of us specifically in mind, but he is recording history every time he gets behind the microphone, and it is a history of sport that is so important to our society.

"I don't think that sport is any more important to Australia than it is to most other countries. When Diego Maradona first went to Napoli, 90,000 people watched him train. Is soccer important to the Italians? Sport is universally important. Great music, wonderful literature, your first love, and sport can take you to places that most things cannot. It is the extraordinary buzz that you get when you are able to watch someone do something out of the ordinary and achieve. It inspires us all and gives us the hope that in our own normal, mundane existence we can aspire to higher and better things in life."

LAWS OF LEADERSHIP

- Consider the big picture

- Maintain confidence

- Nerves are OK, but be prepared

- Skills and preparation are timeless

- Know how to tell the story

- Don't have preconceived ideas

- Take personal responsibility

- Get your facts right

- Know the power of statistics and their relevance

- Maintain respect for the history of the sport

177

EDDIE McGUIRE

"As dear old Dad said, 'Square your shoulders and keep your head up, look people in the eye and walk through,' and that's what I'd like to think; that in 10 years' time I'll still be able to walk around Melbourne or Sydney or any other town in Australia and feel that I've achieved something, and that people recognise that you have made a contribution."

EDDIE McGUIRE *Collingwood AFL Club President and Channel Nine CEO*

Making his mark: Eddie on the set of *Who Wants to be a Millionaire*, 1999.

Photo: Vince Caligiuri

The black jellybean polarises people. You either love them or you hate them. Most people seem to hate them. Eddie McGuire also polarises people. They either love him or they hate him. If you don't support Collingwood, you probably prefer black jellybeans to Eddie, and he wouldn't have it any other way. Collingwood supporters and their president are comfortable being different, as long as they are standing for something – that is the Collingwood way and it is richly echoed in one of their beliefs. "If you don't stand for something, you stand for nothing."

Eddie himself is a remarkable man. For a start, it is remarkable that when you mention the reasonably common first name of Eddie, people know who you are talking about. It's a bit like Shane from the world of sport or Johnny from politics; even out of context there is a reasonable chance someone will know who you are talking about. Eddie's life has been anything but common. It is a rare and interesting story that the five-year-old fanatical Collingwood supporter became the president of his club by age 32. Or that the 17-year-old news cadet, who wore a suit to work every day in case the newsreader had a heart attack, became the head of Australia's most powerful television brand, Channel Nine. While he has yet to stamp his mark commercially at Nine, he has made a massive difference at Collingwood.

Eddie is the first to deflect credit for improvements at Collingwood during his reign as president to fans, players and supporters. He is just as ready to be frank about the state of the Nine Network, but this time he shoulders the responsibility himself. That in itself is a product of a team sport mentality – share the wins and share the losses, put your head over the ball and be prepared to cop one for the team.

Collingwood is by a few measures one of the greatest clubs in Australian sport. Take the Lexus Centre or their crowd numbers or their membership base or their sponsorship income – no other club can match the overall clout of their package. Because of this, their supporters are like no other – fanatical beyond belief, the magpie proudly on their chest. Since taking over as president in September 1998, Eddie has personally instigated a lot of this change, but it has required much soul-searching from both him and the club.

"We had lost our way as a club and I went back to the future, if you like. I actually went back into our history and thought, 'How did this club, from the worst area in Melbourne, from the poorest area, how did it become such a huge club that everyone either loves passionately or hates passionately. What was it that pulled this disparate community together?' I went back to the Depression when Collingwood won a record four premierships in a row from 1927-30, and we won Brownlow medals and Gordon Coventry was the goal-kicking machine, and I was able to find out that Collingwood stood for something. We were the only club that offered sustenance workers, those who were receiving handouts for work during the Great Depression, the opportunity to go to games for free. We also ran the soup kitchens of the area. For those people, Collingwood was the bright light in the desperate world they lived in."

His personal mandate as president was to make decisions through the eyes of a supporter – a position for which he was well qualified. It wasn't an easy task, though, as the club had an exceptionally bad reputation. Whereas they had grown as an institution inclusive of all socioeconomic and racial backgrounds, they had become the antithesis, drawing a crowd with the worst record for racial, religious and sexual vilification.

First, Eddie spoke to the supporters, and specifically to a guy by the name of Joffa. Now Joffa was the Happy Jack of the Gabba in Brisbane or Yabba from the Hill at the SCG. He was the maddest and at times baddest supporter the club had, and he had hardly seen the end of a game in 10 years because he was forever getting ejected for his bad behaviour. But Joffa turned out to be a revelation, a full-time Salvation Army worker, no less, who had some wonderful ideas for the club. Most importantly, for the first time, he and others began to feel that their voices, for so long ignored, were finally being heard.

Armed with the insight of the past and the present, Eddie made

Collingwood stand for something again. "We started running the soup kitchens again in Collingwood, and we had no money at that stage, so we're proud our philanthropy began when we didn't have much to give. We also put on a very strict policy as far as racial vilification was concerned. If we heard anybody at a football match racially vilifying, then they were out, and out for good.

"Now, in the Collingwood Social Club area, which used to be the most rabid crowd in world sport, there is no tolerance for intolerance, and don't worry, they still give the opposition merry hell, and they give the umpires the same as well, but we've been able to change the whole way of thinking. As a result, we have become a very successful corporate club because we now stand for something, and people like our values in the community. It wasn't about winning premierships first day, it was actually about repositioning Collingwood to once again have relevance in the community."

With change there are casualties and survivors. One of the casualties was Victoria Park, their home ground, but one of the survivors was the jersey, as Eddie believed that Collingwood supporters would never compromise on

Mr President: Eddie with Collingwood fans after victory over St Kilda, 2003.
Photo: Vince Calgiuri

What Australia means to me ...

"You get the opportunity to be the person you want to be and can be, and it's up to you. I think sports is still the personification of what the ideal of Australia is to all of us, and I think it's great that we don't have ridiculous nationalism, but all of us still dream of one day wearing green and gold. Regardless of how old you are, you still dream."

that piece of history. It wasn't easy, though, as Victoria Park was special, even Eddie's first experience there is etched in his brain. His father, an Essendon supporter, brought him along to a Collingwood game at Victoria Park. When they arrived at Victoria Park Station his first thoughts were, "Wow, how big is this club – they even have a train station named after the ground." For Eddie, it was bigger than Disneyland, and it only got bigger and better as Collingwood kicked the first goal. As the sea of black-and-white supporters leapt to their feet and roared, he knew that he belonged, that he was an integral part of this huge community.

"We wanted to make Collingwood financially strong again, independent of where we finished on the ladder, and we've been able to do that. I wanted to get to the MCG and make that our home ground, the biggest and best for the people's club, so that every Collingwood supporter, regardless of their socioeconomic situation could get a seat at the MCG for the lowest possible entry fee. We could have gone the other way, down to Telstra Dome, and have the classic supply-demand situation, but we decided that we wanted to be big. Our average crowd this year is 63,000 people, and that's not bad for a suburban club from struggle town. We are very proud of what Collingwood's become over its 114 years of history."

Eddie has taken a lot of criticism in his time, none more so than with his first CEO role at Nine and, while he is used to it, it still takes a chip off him every time. This, though, is the Australian way, and the way of the media, a format with which he is very familiar. Though frustrating and at times distracting, he is not about to complain because he likes the fact that, while we tend to cut down our tall poppies, we keep them accountable, and that is not a bad thing at all. Eddie admires people who have a go, take a risk and

"You must enjoy the victories, because in life there are more defeats than there are victories, and that's why we should celebrate and enjoy the good times when they do come around."

stick to the task, not letting the knocks stop them from getting to where they want to be. Passion, dedication and a willingness to try new things are critical.

"If you are not making mistakes you are not trying hard enough to do new things. Nine became 'The One' because we took risks. Graham Kennedy was the King when he was 23. He wasn't 73 or 63 or anything else, he was a young bloke. Bert Newton – I remember seeing a photo of his 21st birthday on television. You have to get people who are exciting and who are excited to have a go, and give them direction and let them have their head."

Even Eddie himself started hosting *The Footy Show* when he was just 28. Time will dictate his success as a CEO, but failure would not be due to lack of courage. "The major thing is to have courage. Not foolhardy courage, but courage to do things that will ultimately bring about the result that is required. Invariably, there are no short cuts, but don't be disappointed when you see some people fluking a win along the way even though you think they may not deserve it, just keep sticking to it. Also, you must enjoy the victories, because in life there are more defeats than there are victories, and that's why we should celebrate and enjoy the good times when they do come around."

And which ambition sits highest in Eddie's hierarchy between Nine and Collingwood? "I've been involved for a long period of time with Channel Nine, and have had record ratings and things like that, but I haven't seen blokes holding up the cup yet. It's a bit like choosing between children in some ways. We have some challenges in front of us at Channel Nine, remaining No.1 and putting a distance between us and everybody else, and that is paramount in my mind, but it doesn't mean you can't chew and walk at the same time.

"As a culmination of so many people's hopes and aspirations and sweat and tears, it would be fantastic to stand there on the last Saturday in September and see Nathan Buckley hold up that premiership cup with Mick Malthouse. I think that would be a moment that I would never forget."

LAWS OF LEADERSHIP

- Learn how to lose as well as how to win

- Be competitive

- Have passion for all you do

- Value the importance of history

- Provide direction to those around you

- Don't let people down

- Ensure a strong team spirit

- Accept that everyone makes mistakes

- Possess an ability to listen to people

- Go with your heart and your gut

PAUL McNAMEE

"Skill sets are important, and at the end of the day, if you haven't got the skill sets, try and find a way. Be creative, go lateral. It's not necessarily in front of you."

PAUL McNAMEE *Former World No.1 Doubles Player and Sports Administrator*

Have you seen the Woody Allen movie *Match Point?* It starts with the ball hitting the net and wobbling, slow motion kicks in, it can either go over the net or fall back on camera side. The implication is that, depending which way it falls, your life will move in a certain direction. We all have poignant moments in our lives, forks in the road that, depending on what happens, take us in one direction or another. Well, that really happened to Paul McNamee. "I had match point in the semi-final of the Australian Open singles in 1982, and I hit a shot that hit the net on my match point and, of course, if it had dropped over I would have won, but it fell the other way and I went on to lose the semi. And I thought I had a good chance if I got to the final. But my wife said, 'Thank God that ball didn't go over. Imagine what a pain you would have been to live with if it had.' "

The experience was neither a dead-end nor an inspiration for Paul, but another opportunity in what has been an interesting, life. His journey has taken him to all parts of the globe, through his years as a budding junior, ascending the ladder of professional tennis, becoming the No.1 doubles player, to become the CEO of the Australian Open, one of the four premier tennis events in the world.

As we speak, he has taken the lessons he learnt from sport and business

Net gains: Paul McNamee, 2005.

Photo: Marina Oliphant

to his new role at Golf Australia as the executive chairman of the Australian Open and the Women's Australian Open.

At 11, Paul was exceptionally talented at most sports. His mother Pixie was also good at sport and her brother, his uncle Dick Reynolds, was a triple Brownlow medallist for Essendon and an AFL legend. It was at this age he first had to choose between the two sports that he most loved – tennis and golf. Back then, tennis won. You can't be a jack of all trades, his mother had told him, you have to be a little bit of a specialist. "Mum was never pushy, but that's the way she saw it. She thought that I needed to prioritise a little bit. I liked all sports, but I couldn't choose between tennis and golf, which were my two favourite sports. In the end, I decided that because I loved running around so much I had to go for tennis. Having a love for a sport is a very important ingredient to making the sacrifices required later on to try and be a champion."

A victory over his mate Ernie Ewert to win the state under-12 championship put Paul on the tennis treadmill. The trappings of success were quick to follow, with a half-priced racquet – replete with sponsor's stencils – and discounts on strings; they were important symbols initiating him into the ranks of "pro in the making". Years later, living his dream on the circuit, life wasn't so simple and glamorous. He lived by a basic rule of thumb: he had to "keep his nose in front". For Paul, this was relevant on two levels. First, it was about how well he was going; was he living up to his potential? Second, it was about the money; was he able to break even? "If you can make a living, you are good enough to be on the tour. If you can't make a living and you need sponsors and other people to invest in you to supplement your income, I suspect you are not good enough. Funnily enough, I believed that, just like in business, if you play tennis for a career you should be able to make a profit out of it."

Scratching enough wins, and staying in $1-a-night accommodation in places like Spain, helped Paul spin a profit, but his younger brother Brian wasn't so fortunate. He was a good player, but ultimately gave up the tour because he realised that he was never going to profit. "My brother gave up tennis because he was broke. That was the reality. I could have helped bail him out as I was the 'banker' back then, but it wouldn't have been right. I knew deep down he wasn't going to make it. But it wasn't for me to tell him that; you have to find that out yourself. I might be able to see that someone is not going to make it, but that is a crushing blow to deliver to somebody. I think that you should let them find their own way, they will figure it out eventually. Being broke is a good way to figure it out. My brother is now CEO of CSL, one of Australia's biggest companies. He could bail me out now."

At 24, ranked about 80 in the world, Paul's tennis career stalled. He surmised the root of his problem was his lack of a two-handed backhand. This was the weapon missing from his armoury. Flying back to his home base at the Harry Hopman tennis camp in Florida after winning tournaments in Cairo and Nice with doubles partner Peter McNamara, he decided it was time to change. In an unprecedented mid-career move, he was going to change from being a one-handed backhander to a two-hander.

"I was flying back and I thought, 'I'm just going to switch. That's it, and if it doesn't work out, I'll quit. I'll go back, finish my law degree and see what happens because I've got to be better than the 80th best lawyer. I mean, come on.' At that point, I made a pact with myself that I was not going back to the one-handed backhand, this was it. If it didn't work, I was quitting." He announced his intention to "Mr Hopman", who, while knowing it was an unusual decision, backed his student with a coach for five hours a day and any other support that he needed. For the next four months

Game plan: Paul in action, 1982.

through the Florida swelter Paul worked seven days a week between eight and 10 hours a day. Finally, he chose Boston as the stage to unleash his weapon on the tennis world, but ingloriously the first backhand he hit flew over the fence. "I'm thinking, 'People paid money to come and watch this.' I couldn't even look at the crowd I was so embarrassed. Players started to watch my matches because I was so bad. I could do it in practice, but lost confidence in the match. I'd become a joke and could hear the taunts, 'Come out and see this guy whose backhand is so bad.'

Paul found himself in Palermo, Sicily, drawn to play against his mate from years ago, Ernie Ewert. "I'm ranked 70-something and he's ranked 370-something, and it's a match that I have to win. You don't want to lose to someone you played in juniors … He was the guy I beat to win the state championship when I was 12, and I knew I could be a good player when I beat Ernie. Now I'm playing on the tour, when I have made it and he hasn't, and I have to win this match. But … I lose to Ernie … I lose to him. It's an unthinkable result and I'm destroyed." Distraught, Paul headed to the back of the club and started hitting balls against the wall and, like an alcoholic who falls off the wagon, he hit a one-handed backhand … then another … and some more. Another professional walks by. "You know you could have beaten Ernie with a one-handed backhand, what are you doing? You're a pro, you're supposed to try to win the match."

He confided in a mate, Brazilian Carlos Kirmayr, who later became Gabriela Sabatini's coach. "I'm a mess, Carlos, I just hit some one-handed backhands against the wall and I feel like Judas because I made a pact that I wouldn't change back." Carlos grabbed him. "You need to stick with this, and you must follow through. If you need strength, I'm going to give you that strength. I know that you want this, so you have got to hold on." He steered Paul through his darkest hour, the hour he almost quit on himself, and the next week they went to Barcelona. "I play a guy from the US, Terry Moor, and he is ranked 50 in the world and I beat him playing my two-handed backhand. Second round, I play Jose-Louis Clerc, who's ranked 6th in the world and a terrific player on clay, and I lose to him 6-4 in the third set. I won a set off Jose-Louis Clerc on clay! I would never have won a set off him with a one-hand backhand.

"We come back to Australia, Mac [Peter McNamara] and I win the NSW and Australian Open doubles. The next year I win my first ATP singles tournament, I go to the French Open and beat John McEnroe on centre court. I get to the third round at Wimbledon and win the doubles. Suddenly, I'm top-30 singles and No.1 in the world in doubles. All this happened after losing to Ernie and nearly bailing out. It's a long story, but I nearly blinked, and my God that was a great lesson for me to see it out." The other lesson for Paul was that, if you haven't got the skill set, then find a way, be creative and lateral in your thinking. If the answer is not in front of you at the time, then you may have to do something radical.

In his role as CEO of the Australian Open tennis tournament, he is credited with creating a unique and outstanding tournament that sits proudly on the world tour. The essence of his success has been focusing on the dual initiatives of vision and brand. "Firstly, you have to have an idea of where you want to be five and 10 years down the road. With the Australian Open, our vision was to one day be treated on the same level as the other three grand slams – Wimbledon, the US Open and the French Open – and this has been achieved. The second goal was engagement with Asia, to play a leadership role and be part of Australia moving in that direction.

"Secondly, and I don't care what business you are in, is building a brand – the process of popularisation. You must be able to say this club or this event means this and these are its brand values. Are you innovative? Are you prestigious or are you exclusive? Wimbledon, for example, is a very prestigious brand. The Australian Open brand is not the Wimbledon brand, and unashamedly not the Wimbledon brand because we are about being open, accessible and affordable. Understand who you are and what you are about, and once you've got your brand values it's very easy to make decisions."

Paul's challenge in his role as executive chairman of the Australian Open golf championship is similar but different. "We know now that we want to be one of the biggest golf events in Asia-Pacific and now we are on that road. We don't aim to be the fifth major – I don't believe that I will live to see a fifth major in golf or tennis. But if we are the biggest in Asia, that gives you global cachet and global cut-through, and that is a fantastic goal for events like the Australian Open golf championships."

Vital to the success of the golf tournament is what Paul describes as the administrators' ability to "create and build atmosphere, because the better the atmosphere the luckier you get". But while he sees many opportunities to improve the atmosphere at the golf, he will not do anything that compromises the integrity of the sport itself. "As an administrator, the integrity of the core product is the most important thing, but then you have got to remember that you are also in the entertainment industry."

So this year the Australian Open is moving back to the future, where spectators will be able to walk the fairways behind the golfers and watch the flight of the ball.

"If you can't have atmosphere on the course, you can't rate on TV, because it doesn't jump across the screen. You have to create that buzz and the buzz will jump across the TV screen into the home so the viewer can feel it."

Paul will do everything in his control to create a successful event but, as far as he is concerned, the result can look after itself. For, as a cabbie once told him, and as he discovered in that Australian Open semi-final, "You can't script the result, mate."

LAWS OF LEADERSHIP

- Be committed with everything you do

- Continuously develop your skills

- Create a vision and share it with your team

- Value your credibility – consider the promises you make and always deliver

- Understand and utilise the importance of branding

MICHAEL **MILTON**

"It is about performing, not only on the hill, but getting your equipment right, spending time at the gym and doing everything well. When younger members of the team expect me to do all the right things, it motivates me as well."

MICHAEL MILTON *Paralympic Downhill Skier*

Try for a moment standing on one leg. Now close your eyes. Don't put the leg back down, keep it up. Now imagine you are standing in the back of a ute travelling at 100kmh. Now double it. You're almost at the speed that Michael Milton travels on skis. Or I should say ski.

Some people lead through inspirational speeches, some through the ability to create a high-performance environment, some through incentives and some through fear, but some lead purely by example. Michael Milton is one of those. "For me, the most important aspect of being a leader is leading by example. That's where I feel my strength lies when I'm working within that team environment with the younger athletes. It is about performing, not only on the hill, but getting your equipment right, spending time at the gym and doing everything well. When younger members of the team expect me to do all the right things, it motivates me as well."

Michael's example is there for all to see. With a world record of 213.65 kilometres an hour, he is Australia's fastest ever speed skier. This in itself is an extraordinary feat, but his achievement is even more spectacular for the fact that he has done it all on just one leg – his right one.

Michael lost his left leg to cancer at the age of nine. Born into a family who lived and worked around sport, Michael was passionate about an active life

Inspiration: Michael just after winning the Pro Mondial in Les Arcs, France, 2006.

Picture: Jennie Milton

CAREER STATS

Winter paralympics

- 1992 slalom gold, first Australian winter gold
- Super G, silver
- 1994 giant slalom, gold; slalom, silver
- 2002 slalom, gold; giant slalom, gold; Super G, gold; downhill, gold
- 2006 downhill, silver

World championships

- 1996 giant slalom, gold
- 2000 slalom, gold; Super G, gold; downhill, gold
- 2004 slalom, gold; giant slalom, gold

- Four world speed skiing records (one-leg)
- Australian open speed skiing record
- Medal of the Order of Australia 1993
- Australian Sports Medal 2000
- Laureus World Sportsperson of the Year with a Disability 2003

from his earliest memories, and it seems he was destined for a life on the snow. His parents had what he describes as the perfect honeymoon – snowed-in at a ski resort – and the year Michael was born they started a retail ski outlet. In the summer, they sold sailboards. The moment it became his passion, however, was at the start of his darker days in hospital as a boy.

"I'd just been diagnosed with cancer, and I was in a room with the oncologist, a psychiatrist and my parents, and they were explaining what was happening. They were going to amputate my leg, and I was going to have to undergo chemotherapy. I was thinking, 'What's life going to be like with one leg? What will I be able to do and what won't I be able to do?' The thing I asked was, 'Will I be able to go skiing with my family?' because that was the thing that I loved in my life up 'til then." Two days later, Michael's parents arrived with a video of a guy skiing with one leg, and it was the perfect tonic. "I saw a guy skiing with one leg, and it was like, 'That's what I want to do'. From then on that was the tape I'd pick out when I was at my lowest ebb, going through chemo. I'd sit there and watch and dream about what was going to happen at the end. After everything got better I was going skiing, and that's where my passion fully developed."

As he dealt with his new life, his dream remained his dual interests of sailboarding and skiing. In the summer, he imagined himself on a sailboard on the water. In the winter, he lived for the thought of snow on the mountain. His school books were replete with drawings of ski race courses, the kind he dreamed of skiing himself. They would not remain dreams for long.

Michael's lowest ebb came after the cancer had cleared and he was rebuilding his life, a 10 year old learning to become comfortable in a body with just one leg. He threw his $3000 prosthesis out the second-storey window, screaming, "I want a real one! I want a real one!" The words echoed through the house.

The attitude and support of not only his parents but also his social environment were important to his rehabilitation. Interestingly, it was more what people didn't do for him than what they did that helped to make him the success he has become. "Australian people have a pretty good attitude towards people with a disability in terms of just letting you have a go. They are not smothering and not over-helping, which can be a dangerous trap to fall into. It was key in my childhood and has been for a lot of people that I know with a disability. The ones who are successful and are able to achieve on the sporting field and in life are the ones whose parents gave them enough rope to go out and ride skateboards and knock their elbows and knees."

Sport initially was a hobby for Michael, but it continued to build his self-esteem and his belief that he could achieve significant things. Hobbies, though, don't often pay the bills, and after winning his first Paralympic gold medal his father was on his back, "Get a real job. You can't ski forever – you won't

be able to make a living out of it. You must have something to back yourself up." His father's fears were realistic. At the time no Australian athletes with disabilities were able to make a living out of their sport.

"I was a professional athlete in some ways and I was achieving at high levels, but at the same time I was working my guts out with two or three jobs all Australian winter to fund the overseas season. There have been a lot of tough times in the past in terms of funding for athletes with disabilities, so making ends meet was difficult. There are now only about three or four athletes with disabilities in Australia who are able to make a living out of what they do. After I won four gold medals in Salt Lake, the response wasn't really what I expected, and I came to the realisation that I need to be more creative to earn a living out of my sport. That was a real awakening for me."

Doing things creatively for Michael meant changing the paradigm. No longer would he just compete against disabled skiers, he would compete against all-comers in the extreme sport of speed skiing. It was a new direction,

Full speed ahead: Michael races to victory in his record-breaking run (213.65km/h) at the Pro Mondial, 2006.
Picture: Jennie Milton

a new challenge that made use of his existing skills, and the idea of skiing at over 200kmh really resonated with people.

"I'd like to see what I have done in sport to inspire people with disabilities to look for something different and perhaps something more. I hope I have challenged people's perceptions about the abilities of people with disabilities and what is possible, and I'd like to think it has encouraged other athletes to step outside the sphere of Paralympic competition."

Not only has Michael gone outside that sphere of Paralympic competition, but also he has gone outside the realms of human endeavour. Upon meeting him, what strikes you is the development of his right leg, sturdy like the trunk of an established gum tree as it supports his solid frame. It doesn't look overworked, but the reality stretches the imagination to consider how it supports his body travelling at 213.65km/h downhill.

The process has been demanding. Steve Graham, his junior coach, sensing that he had an extremely talented yet lazy teenager on his hands, systematically drilled this lethargy out of him. Away with the junior ski team in Colorado, they would go on one-kilometre runs at 7am every day in -15 degrees. After a couple of mornings when Michael turned up with his crutches Steve handed him a pair of ski poles and told him he could go running with those. Every morning for the next week Michael was out on the snow hopping, while his teammates ran, building his leg, and his character. "It was over the top in terms of toughness, but there were many, many things that he did with me that would overload me, that toughened me up and taught me a lot, and we still work together to this day."

Perhaps Michael's greatest legacy is his courage, the way he faces the fear of travelling at more than 200kmh on one leg. What would it be like moving at that speed? What's the fastest you have ever been in a car? On the slopes, he accelerates from 0 to 100kmh in about three seconds, which is not much slower than a formula one racing car. And he does all this on one ski, with little more than his suit to shield him from a fall. It's very hard to fathom.

"Skiing fast is what you'd expect it to be in many ways – it's scary. The best speed-ski track is in a place called Les Arcs in France. It's about two kilometres long from start to finish. You start at about 67 degrees gradient, which is practically a cliff face. You wear a red rubber suit with an aerodynamic faring behind the leg, to reduce drag. The helmet is shaped down your back and over your shoulders and it has quite a narrow lens in it which cuts out peripheral vision, because one of the ways our brain senses speed is through peripheral vision. You go from zero to 100 in 3.2 seconds, and as you accelerate you start to feel the buffeting of the wind at about 150. At around 180, the ski starts to become noticeably less stable. It's a bit like death wobbles on a skateboard, really.

"At this speed, you have the opportunity to back out – you can stand up and

"Skiing fast is what you'd expect it to be in many ways – it's scary."

lose your aerodynamics and slow down, or you can grit your teeth and go through that rough stage. Once you are over 200, it actually feels a fraction smoother than it does at 180. Then you look ahead and you see two red lines drawn in the snow 100 metres apart. That's the timing zone, and they record your average speed over that 100 metres."

To protect himself from fear, Michael has a set routine. He has to get four key areas ready for a successful run. First, his equipment – his skis must be waxed so they will be as fast as possible, and all his gear must be at hand. Second, he prepares by stretching, staying warm and getting the heart rate up. Third, he mentally runs through and pictures his tactics. Lastly, he focuses on a key word that echoes in his mind all the way down the mountain, distracting him from the fear. At the bottom of the mountain, he checks his time.

"When I saw 213.65 it was an amazing feeling, partly because it is physical – you have scared the wits out of yourself and you've got all the adrenaline going through your body and you're on that natural high. But when you combine that with reading that number and knowing that you've achieved your goal and everything you've worked for, well that's a feeling I'm addicted to."

Michael's has been a journey of breaking new ground with wonderful success. "My environment changed at age nine when I was put in a totally different place, physically and mentally. It's hard to know what sort of person I'd be if I had two legs. It's an unanswerable question because there's no way of knowing what would have happened. I've always thought that you are much better off enjoying the life that you are living than thinking about the life that you could have had. The life I'm living now is 200 days on the snow, it's following my passion, it's skiing, it's now having a family and having a wonderful partner to share my life. I can't ask for any more than that."

LAWS OF LEADERSHIP

- Maintain your motivation

- Preparation is the key to success

- Know your goals and work towards them

- Get the basics right and the rest will follow

- Have passion and enjoy your sport

- Know your strengths

- Lead by example

JOHN **NEWCOMBE**

"I'm a legend because I won some great tennis matches, but what you are like as a person, that's the real key."

JOHN NEWCOMBE *Tennis Legend and Former Davis Cup Captain*

There is a natural cycle to most things in life, including the learning journey. We are taught a skill, we learn it and we apply it, first consciously and then unconsciously. Then we are expert, and we teach the skill to someone else. They apply it and the cycle begins again. Sometimes the learning cycle plays out over a short space of time and sometimes it can play out over years – even half a century – but when that circle is complete the satisfaction is enormous.

John Newcombe's contribution to Australian sport has been enormous and there is much for which he can be admired. Above all, though, Newk is known for his never-say-die Aussie spirit and his larrikin nature.

Newk was a fiery young boy, often at odds with the world around him and with those closest to him. It was in these early years that his education began, and a lot of that education is due to Newk's mother, Lilian, who never missed an opportunity to take him aside and teach him a lesson.

"Mum recognised that there was some sort of extreme fire inside of me, and if that fire could be controlled in a positive direction it could be a tremendous force. Alternatively, if it was not controlled and it went in a negative direction, it could tear you apart." Through his mother's message, then, John began to understand that he had the power to choose and, ultimately, use his own attitude.

Grand slam: John in action against Chuck McKinley at the Davis Cup in Adelaide, 1963.

Photo: Alan Lambert

INFLUENTIAL PEOPLE
• Lew Hoad
• Ken Rosewall
• Don Bradman
• Dawn Fraser
• Herb Elliott

The victory secured and the lesson taught, Lleyton ran over and hugged his mentor, exhausting his last energy with the words that said it all, "Thanks mate, thanks."

In the under-14 state championship final, 12-year-old John was losing and it showed. His body language told the story: shoulders drooping, feet dragging, racquet dropping. Changing ends at a particularly low point, his mum piped up, "Why don't you start playing tennis and stop feeling sorry for yourself." His initial reaction was to deny it, but quickly enough he knew she was right. He chose his attitude and won the championship.

Just 14 years later, John was on his preferred surface of grass at his favourite tournament, Wimbledon, in the final against one of the players he most admired, Ken Rosewall.

He seemed well on the way to a comfortable victory with a two sets to one advantage and leading 3-1 in the fourth, but easy it wasn't to be. Rosewall, through the weight of crowd support and a distracted competitor in Newcombe, won the next five games.

"I was 3-1 up in the fourth and I had always had a good rapport with the Wimbledon crowd, but the crowd just got 100 per cent behind Ken. I let this get to me and I started fretting about it and got into a kind of sulk, and from 3-1 he won five games in a row and the fourth set 6-3.

"In 1970, you didn't have a chair to sit down on at the change of ends, you just stood there and you got your own drink, and I said to myself, 'Right, you've got 60 seconds now to pull yourself together. How badly do you want to win this?' I said, 'I really want to win this bad, so I thought 'All right, you've got to stop all of this rubbish going on in your head. Your whole body's filled with negativity; you've got to push that negativity out and replace it with good solid energy and go out on the court'.

"After that 60 seconds, I walked out on the court. There was a player at the other end of the court and there was a tennis ball, and nothing else existed for me. I beat Ken 6-1 in the fifth. I just put myself into a zone where I knew what Ken was going to do before he did it."

It was as proud as John has been of himself. He chose his attitude and had Wimbledon No.2 in the bag.

Not all great players make great coaches or captains, so there was trepidation in 1994 when Tennis Australia decided that John, as captain, would team up with Tony Roche, as coach, to lead Australia's Davis Cup

CAREER STATS
• Australian Championships/ Australian Open Singles 1973, 1975; Doubles 1965, 1967, 1971, 1973, 1976
• Wimbledon Singles 1967, 1970, 1971; Doubles 1965, 1966, 1968, 1969, 1970, 1974
• US Championships/ US Open Singles 1967, 1973; Doubles 1967, 1971, 1973

challenge. Davis Cup was the tinder that lit the tennis fire in John's belly. In 1953 at Kooyong and '54 at White City, he watched the likes of Lew Hoad and Rosewall, and they stirred his initial tennis ambition.

Not too many years later, he revelled in playing in the cup. It wasn't so much the opportunity to represent his country, but to do so in a team, that was the greater thrill. While Australia eventually realised glory in his time as captain, the six years before his appointment were relatively lean.

"We found that we had a bunch of young guys who were just starting. They were new guys who'd come in, and at that stage, to get to a quarter-final of a grand slam tournament, an Australian bloke thought he'd done real well. We had to re-educate them in their thinking. We said, 'No, that bar's down there, our bar is up here. We are going to win Grand Slams and we are going to become the best team in the world.' "

Seven years later, their tenure over, they had reclaimed the Davis Cup; they were the best tennis team in the world. It was a job well done.

A Davis Cup moment ...

"There's a time to be quiet, there's a time to say something. I suppose in my first match I learned a little bit. The Woodies (Todd Woodbridge, Mark Woodforde) were playing doubles, we were playing Russia, their first match together, and they'd just won Wimbledon the year before. I said to them: 'Guys, you know what you've got to do out there. I'll watch the opposition and see if there's anything I can pick up on that they're doing that'll be good.' They were going through a bit of a low spell at this time, so they lost the first set 6-4, and they lost the second set 6-0, and it just happened so quickly, the second set, and they were beaten, and they came down to the chair to sit down. I stood up and I said, 'Where do you blokes think you're going? You're not going to sit down here, you're the Wimbledon bloody champions, you get out on that bloody court and show these Russians who you are. Don't ask me to figure it out for you, you figure it out.' They won the next two sets but lost in five. However, we had established a rapport and the Woodies won their next 11 matches, never losing again in Davis Cup competition."

Throughout this new era in Australian tennis, it wasn't just the victories that gave John pride, it was the imparting of his knowledge that satisfied him most. The learning cycle continued in 2000 in Spain, when some of his mother's wisdom was passed on to Lleyton Hewitt.

"With one match in Spain in 2000, I knew Lleyton Hewitt was going to be tired, after about two hours of play." Hewitt had suffered from a breathing problem all week, which meant that he hadn't been able to do all of his training, and this worried John, particularly in the hostile and fiercely parochial atmosphere that is Spain.

He said to Lleyton, "Mate, every point is going to be war out there, and you've got 13,000 Spaniards you've got to try to kid. After two hours, I reckon you're going to be stuffed, and you've got to tell me as soon as you feel it."

About two hours and 10 minutes later, with Hewitt at one set all and 3-2 down in the third, he was beginning to struggle. "At the change of ends, we had a little routine where I'd pass him the water. This time as he took the water his hand was shaking and spilling the water, and he looked at me and said, 'I'm stuffed', and I looked at his body and his body was just shaking, and he's looking at me, and I thought, 'Oh, geez, here we go.' "

John knew what he wanted to do, but didn't know how Lleyton would respond. "Immediately, I got him to just sit back in his chair and close his eyes, and I explained to him that his body was full of negative energy and he had to get rid of it. I had him taking deep breaths, breathing out all of that impurity inside of him and, with his eyes closed, he imagined this clear blue sky up above him, and that he was breathing that clear energy down into his body, and we only had time to do it about three times, but by this time I'm talking him through it and he's sitting there with his eyes closed, he's almost hypnotised, and I thought, 'He's responding.' "

The process was facilitated by the trust that existed between the two men, a trust built up over years, even before they had met. "He was trusting me and he got up off the chair and I said, 'Mate, you're the strongest bastard that ever lived. You're going to be able to run forever.' "

Lleyton went back out onto the court and at every change of ends they went through the same routine. Four hours and 20 minutes in to the contest, the score was 5-4. Serving for the match in the fifth, he won 6-4.

The victory secured and the lesson taught, Lleyton ran over and hugged his mentor, exhausting his last energy with the words that said it all, "Thanks mate, thanks."

The learning cycle isn't complete, though, until the student can practise the skill unaided.

Two years later, John sat at home while, in Shanghai, Lleyton was up against Juan Carlos Ferrero in a final after beating Roger Federer in a huge match in the semi. "The final was not looking good, as Hewitt was down a break in the fifth, and he came back with one and won the match. He called me afterwards and he said, 'Mate, I did it by myself.' He did that whole exercise of replenishing his energy at the change of ends by himself."

The cycle complete, Newk put down the phone, content in the knowledge that his job, like his mother's before him, was done.

"You learn more from every time you lose a match than when you win a match."

LAWS OF LEADERSHIP

• Know your opponents

• Recognise the fire inside you and use it as a force

• Leadership is knowing something needs to be done and organising that to happen

• Vision

• Big picture (the match itself) – small picture (one step at a time)

• Aim high

JOHN O'NEILL

"Great captains are remembered for leading great teams, and it's the same in business … you've got to feel sorry for people whose timing was just not right … if you're fortunate enough to be there at the right time, grab the opportunity with both hands."

JOHN O'NEILL *Socceroos CEO and Former Australian Rugby CEO*

I write about John O'Neill from a very personal perspective, as he has had as indelible impact on me as he has on Australian sport. When I was first appointed Wallabies captain in 1996, John, then in his first 12 months of a nine-year tenure as CEO and MD of Australian Rugby, was a valuable confidant. When I sought his counsel upon my retirement some six years later, his advice was invaluable. It was my great fortune that at these two critical junctures in my adult development I was able to turn to one of the greatest change agents Australian sport has seen.

Change is one of the most confronting challenges that people face in life. Few deal with it well, even fewer lead it well. John has led change projects within Australian sport like no other.He has successfully managed two transitions in two of our highest-profile professional sports over the past 10 years. He has taken rugby and football (formerly known as soccer) from amateur and, at times, amateurish sports in Australia to serious international competitors on the world stage.

Success has many routes, and unlike Michael Hawker, who took the lessons he learned in sport to much success in business, John has used basic business skills to bring about change in sport. In light of this, it is rather ironic that it was actually rugby union that fast-tracked John's business career at what

Agent of change: John O'Neill, 2005.
Photo: Tim Clayton.

And now for something really big ...

"The greatest achievement (for football in Australia) is the move in to Asia. As important as the creation of the A-League has been, and as wonderful as qualification for the World Cup for the first time in 32 years was, the positioning of Australia into Asia is the most important achievement. It moves us out of a very small domestic economy of Oceania – ourselves, New Zealand and 10 other Pacific Island nations – into the biggest and fastest-growing football economy in the world. And it gives us competition.

When I looked at the sport that I inherited, and it had all sorts of problems, but its perennial, year-in, year-out one was that it had no competition. We beat Uruguay last November and they were the fifth-placed South American team. To finish fifth in South America, they played 18 home and away games, against Brazil, Argentina, Colombia, Chile, Paraguay and others. We played the Solomon Islands, home and away, and then we went and played Uruguay.

Moving into Asia, we have year-in, year-out competition: 2006 we're playing in the World Cup; 2007 we'll be playing in the Asian Cup; 2008, with a bit of luck, we'll be in the Beijing Olympics; 2009 we'll be playing World Cup qualification games; 2010 we'll be in South Africa. I mean, that's the repertoire. The transaction that will transform football is the move in to Asia."

was then the Rural Bank (later to become the State Bank of NSW). The year was 1981, and Nick Whitlam, who had just taken over as CEO, was walking the floors of the bank at about 6pm looking for dedicated employees working back late. After much wandering through empty desks, Whitlam found a young John O'Neill, and the two of them struck up a conversation.

John, as coach of Sydney University third grade, was still at the office only because training that night didn't start until 6.30pm. "We introduced each other and chatted away, and as a result of that conversation he offered me a job as his personal assistant, and seven years later I succeeded him. The truth of the matter was that I was waiting to go to rugby training, but I quickly hid my bag under the table."

After years of success with the bank John applied, unsuccessfully, for the role to run the Olympic Games in Sydney. Finally, the opportunity to lead the Australian Rugby Union became available. By early 2004, with the most successful ever Rugby World Cup under his belt, John found himself unwanted by the code so he moved on to football. Success in that realm has been marked by the formation of the Hyundai A-League national competition, our first World Cup qualification since 1974 and the achievement he ranks the highest, the move into Asia – the biggest and fastest growing football economy in the world.

The two codes of football are very different, but John saw the fundamentals of each challenge as essentially the same. "Each has a professional component and a community component all in the one envelope. The challenges have not been dissimilar: turning a bankrupt organisation into a solvent organisation,

**Business of leading:
John in his State
Bank days, 1991.**
Photo: Elizabeth Dobbie

producing an iconic national team, creating a professional league and then engaging the community."

Many expected the political environment in football to be untenable, but the man who hired him, Frank Lowy, in conjunction with Football Australia's main backer, the Australian Government, orchestrated a three-year moratorium where politics had to be parked. "Frank promised he'd take care of the politics, and he's been able to do so."

Rugby was a great education on the politics of sport, but it was also a commercial environment with none of the rules respected by traditional businesses. "Corporate entities should be, and mostly are, well structured, well governed, well managed, have lots of checks and balances and have an environment where once a decision is made – by whoever is empowered to make that decision – everyone gets on with it ... if you're the managing director of a major corporate you bring with you a lot of authority and a lot of delegated power from the board."

These structures weren't present in rugby because it had been an amateur sport, and the business side of the ARU was retarded essentially by a lack of cash. Consequently, the latest and best-positioned political opinion usually held sway. In one particular eye-opener, John rebuked the players' representative on the ARU Board, Rod McCall, for what he perceived as inappropriate behaviour. The formal response came back from McCall that, in sport, opinions were like arseholes – everyone had one.

"I quickly realised that the fact I was called the managing director of the ARU didn't bring with it that spontaneous respect or regard for decisions. I had to earn that respect and build from scratch, structures and arrangements, and management techniques that clearly the sport was completely unfamiliar with." But change was going to happen, and as far as O'Neill was concerned there would be no sacred cows. Even the jersey – possibly more as a result of ARU finances – was sacrificed, the traditional gold bulleted for a multicoloured version positioned for success at the cash register rather than for the traditionalists. This decision in particular drew enormous criticism from the rugby faithful and was reversed after two years when finances had improved. Says John: "Am I apologetic about it? No, I'm not. Would I prefer to have had other options? Yes, I would have, but I didn't."

He saw these decisions as easier than many he had faced in his banking days, and he used that experience to guide his judgment. "You take advice, but ultimately leadership is what you're paid to do – to make the judgment call. Judgment is something that you refine and get better at as you get older. If you've been through some difficult moments in your life, personally and professionally, your computer-like memory or instincts, store them away until they come to the fore again at some moment in time."

Central to John's success is the strong leadership team he assembles around him. "They are genuinely one of the best management teams in sport, and the common denominator is they all love a challenge, and I think they see football as one of the last frontiers."

John's own leadership style is a product of his upbringing and what he has learnt. "I came from a large family, nine children, seven girls and two boys, and when my mother died at a young age I had a father who was a very dominant person in my upbringing." Leadership was thrust upon him by his family. "The expectations were always that John would do well, or John would make the speech at the birthday party or at the wedding. The public persona side of me very much came out of my upbringing."

These experiences have enabled John to get about his business of leading, a task he enjoys and that drives his ambition. "Unless you're ambitious, you won't strive for that extra yard or strive to achieve something that might normally be out of your reach."

And, in driving his ambitious agenda, John suggests a few absolute requirements for leaders. "You must be yourself, don't try and manufacture a persona that's not your own soul. At times that has exposed me … but you get more benefit out of being yourself and crafting your leadership style to suit your own personality.

"Always be grateful that you have had the opportunity and the privilege to lead, and also understand that you don't always get it right. If you get somewhere between 75 per cent and 80 per cent of your decisions right, that's a fantastic record. Rod Macqueen is a legendary coach because he won 82 per cent of the games he coached the Wallabies.

"Reading people is very important, and sometimes in life you see people in stressful situations that expose a character flaw, and then after the event that character flaw gets covered up. There will come a time again when the pressure is on and that character flaw will re-emerge. You have got to be aware of that because in tough times you need very good people around you who you can rely on.

"There are also times in your leadership that you have to be aloof, circumspect or distant (though not arrogant) but that is the loneliness of leadership. You can't always be one of the boys."

Oh, yes, the advice is starting to sound familiar now …

Life rewards courage, and John's hard-driving agenda for change has reaped his two greatest moments in sport: the Wallabies' Rugby World Cup win in 1999 and the Socceroos qualifying for the 2006 World Cup in Germany.

"The Socceroos' win against Uruguay was a uniquely unifying moment. For a sport that had been so dysfunctional and so dislocated with ethnicity, that audience of 82,000 people and the four to five million people around Australia that watched the game, absolutely united, non-denominational, absolutely ecumenical, and the feelgood factor for days and weeks and months later, was extraordinary."

"Overall, leadership is a combination of your own make-up and your own character, together with your training and development."

LAWS OF LEADERSHIP

- Be professional

- Once a decision is made, do your best to implement it

- Always look at the big picture

- Consult widely

- Develop sound judgement

- Remain calm

- Ensure you have good training and opportunity

- Be yourself

- Credibility and reputation is everything

- Conduct yourself with the highest standards

RICKY **PONTING**

"The baggy green to us, I think, is the whole reason that we play. It is the symbol of Australian cricket. I aspired to wear the baggy green … It is almost like when you have it on you have a cape on or you are bulletproof."

RICKY PONTING *Australian Cricket Captain*

"There have only ever been 42 captains of Australia, I am No. 42." Ricky at the Gabba, 2003.
Photo: Andy Zakeli

S port turns on a dime, a pivotal moment that dictates the fortune of an innings, a match or a series. Such a moment occurred in the fourth Test of the 2005 Ashes, the most monumental Test series of our time. In the second innings, with the Australians beginning to edge their noses in front of England, Australian captain Ricky Ponting was run out by a substitute fieldsman for 48. Throughout the series, England had employed the tactic of replacing members of their XI, predominantly to rest them but under the guise of injury, with specialist fieldsmen. Australia thought the strategy, while within the laws of cricket, against the spirit of the game, and it was playing on their minds.

As Ricky made his long and demoralising walk back to the pavilion, he was given a send-off by many of the England fieldsmen, bringing him to boiling point. So when the smug England coach hung over the balcony, laughing and mocking him, Ricky sprayed him with a string of invective. Ricky was docked 75 per cent of his match fee, but far more damning were the images of a captain under siege, a captain who was anything but composed. The Australians fought on manfully, with Ricky at the forefront, but the momentum had shifted and the Ashes were all but gone.

Short of a prime minister, there is not a leader in Australia under more scrutiny than our Test cricket captain. Imagine that your most intense

INFLUENTIAL PEOPLE

- Kim Hughes, *cricketer*
- David Boon, *cricketer*
- Dennis Lillee, *cricketer*
- Rod Marsh, *cricketer*
- Greg Chappell, *cricketer*

moments in the office or at home with your family were scrutinised, sometimes to obsession, by most Australians. The analysis would be confronting: he should have been sterner there; he had plenty of time to make that decision and it was so obvious; how could he let them get away with that; he lost his cool far too quickly. And then they would get out of your home and observe you at the office.

Leading is hard enough, let alone learning your craft in front of the nation. Effectively, that is what Ricky has done. Due to his age, before captaining Tasmania and leading Australia, leadership roles had passed him by. He was 14 playing in the under-17s, 15 playing in the under-19s and 12 when he made his debut for his club team. Nonetheless, as that 12-year-old boy drank Coke in the dressing rooms till 11 o'clock in the evening, and that 17-year-old Tasmanian debutant watched every move David Boon made, he was absorbing the lessons of leadership from those around him.

"I always looked at myself as a leader around any team I was in. Even if I was one of the young guys, I felt I could be a leader around the group through my energy and my body language, and I always took on that role. When I was in the Tasmanian team and not captain, I would always try and think as a captain on the field, think about what I would do in a given situation, and think what fields I would set for certain bowlers. Then, when in the Australian team, I would just sit back and closely watch the captains that I played under. I learnt a lot from Mark Taylor and Steve Waugh, and there is probably a little bit of their style in what I do today."

Still, just because you observe it doesn't mean that you are able to do it yourself.

And so it is with captaincy. The perfect ones are so long retired that romantic notions of their performances blind the reality. It is a privilege of the retired sportsman that the distance of time camouflages many a fault. Ricky's poor reaction upon his dismissal in England exposed the pressure of leadership, but his reaction that evening revealed his measure as a man. The mark of a leader is not how many mistakes you make, but how quickly you realise that you have made them and how quickly you reconcile for them. "I was at absolute boiling point. Walking off the field, I had their coach sticking his nose out over the balcony, smiling and laughing at me as I walked off,

Reputation: Ricky celebrates his 100 in the Boxing Day Test against South Africa at the MCG, 2005.
Photo: Vince Caligiuri

"If someone has done something wrong by me, or by someone else in the team, then it is up to me to get on top of it there and then, and not just expect it to go away over time."

CAREER STATS
- Test cap No. 366
- ODI cap No. 123
- Test Debut December 8, 1995
- One-Day Debut February 15, 1995
- Led Australia to victory in 2003 World Cup when the side won all 11 matches played
- Made an unbeaten 140 against India to lead Australia to a 125-run win in final of 2003 World Cup
- Player of the Series in Australia's 3-1 Test win in the West Indies in 2003, scoring 523 runs at an average of 130.75, including two centuries and his maiden double hundred, 206, at Port of Spain
- Led one-day side for tour of South Africa in 2002 to a 5-1 success
- Took over captaincy of Test side for tour of Sri Lanka in 2004, winning series 3-0

knowing how much it would have got under my skin. That night I wrote an apology to everyone, to the fans and everyone watching back in Australia and to my team mates as well, letting them know that my behaviour was not acceptable, and I was regretful for what I had done. I made sure that I got across to the rest of the team that that wasn't the way to play cricket."

Ricky was remorseful because, in taking over as captain of the most successful Test side in history, a side that had set standards of excellence in performance, one of his goals was to set exceptional standards in behaviour. In his previous two years as captain, he had personally set very high standards in on-field behaviour. Within an hour of his indiscretion, Simon Katich followed suit, and was reported for an inappropriate reaction to a contentious LBW decision.

"We were always going to be remembered as being a very good cricket team, but at the end of the day you want to walk away from the game knowing, and having the public know, you are a good person to go with it. I really want this team I captain to be remembered for having a good reputation in the public

Captain's blazer ...

"There have only ever been 42 captains of Australia, I am No.42. The tradition I have tried to start is to have a captain's blazer, a blazer you go out and toss in every morning, the first morning of the Test match. Traditionally, there is only a striped green and gold one, there is only a tour blazer, I think it was England in 1989, and it never had any significance at all with captains, or even the team. I went back through the history books and looked at blazers that Bradman wore, and designed one that is pretty much exactly the same as they wore back then, except that is has the coat of arms on the pocket with the No. 42 underneath. So that signifies that this is my captaincy jacket and whoever takes over from me will have their own with 43 on it. The start of a tradition. Forty-two people to ever have captained Australia is obviously a great honour, a great thrill. For that reason, and for even the reason that there have been less than 400 players to play, it makes you determined to make every post a winner and not ever take anything for granted from the game."

eye. Instead of the ICC coming down on us or Cricket Australia coming down on us, it is up to myself and the senior members of the group to really put the foot down if anyone goes outside the boundaries of the spirit of Australian cricket."

While it can be tough taking over a great team, the upside for Ricky was learning from some exceptional leaders. He sought out Steve Waugh, who reinforced the importance of concentrating on his own game. He was to prepare himself as a batsman first and foremost and not worry too much about the other guys, as they would get themselves prepared.

Steve's words resonated and, although Ricky didn't score a century in his first year as skipper, amid claims that he couldn't handle the pressure of leadership, he still averaged in the 50s with the bat. Finally, he broke through with a double century against Pakistan in Sydney in January 2005, and he hasn't looked back. Before he was captain, Ricky's Test batting average was 55.97. As captain, it stands at 63.21.

As Steve Waugh advised, Ricky has been able to separate the tasks of captaincy and batting so that when he heads to the crease he is doing so as the No.3 batsman for Australia, not as the captain. There is never a time where he has to bat differently as the captain than if he weren't. Either way, his mental approach is paramount and it is his routine that protects him. If thoughts creep into his mind while in the middle, be they about captaincy or whatever, he must shut them out. "I have always tried to keep the game as simple as I can, breaking things down ball by ball. It is important for me to have little key words that I say to myself and repeat over and over in my head every ball. When the bowler is halfway in his run-up, I say to myself, 'Watch the ball', and then just as he is about to deliver the ball I say, 'Watch the ball' again. That routine focuses me on the ball and keeps other thoughts out of my mind."

It is a credit to Ricky that he has stamped his own influence on this Australian side, remaining true to himself yet demanding the respect of all his team. "I have tried to create a really open environment around our team and to open up the lines of communication as much as possible. I am really honest with the guys, and I expect honesty from them in return. If someone has done something wrong by me, or by someone else in the team, then it is up to me to get on top of it there and then, and not just expect it to go away over time. One thing I have learnt along the way is to deal with issues as quickly as you can and get them over and done with so they don't linger any longer than they have to."

Possibly Ricky's greatest moment to date was when he led the Australian side to World Cup victory in South Africa in 2003. In spite of losing Shane Warne through suspension and Jason Gillespie through injury, the team was undefeated through the 11 matches of the tournament, and it culminated with Ricky scoring 140 not out in the final against a threatening Indian side.

Personal milestones mean little to him, though, with the exception of playing his 100th Test, appropriately marked with a century in each innings. "I would be the most unstatistically orientated person you could come across. One thing I am pretty proud of, though, is that I have been able to play 100 Test matches; that was a really special game for me. I will probably hold that up more than how many runs or how many 100s I have scored. I wouldn't know within 500 or 1000 how many runs I have scored in either form of the game. Records or stats don't really mean anything to me. I am out there trying to do the best I can for my team in the different situations I am confronted with."

Whether or not he cares himself, history and statistics will judge Ricky Ponting kindly, as a player and as a leader. "In five years' time I would like cricket to be Australia's No.1 game and for all of us to be remembered and recognised as good or great players and, importantly, for being good people in society as well."

LAWS OF LEADERSHIP

- Understand the environment you are working in and how to change it to suit different requirements

- Back your instincts

- Ensure your own preparation is complete before you worry about your teammates'

- Take on advice but make your own decisions

- Remain composed in the heat of the moment

- Learn from your mistakes

- Deal with issues quickly

- Keep focused on the task

- Tell someone what to do, rather than what NOT to do

- Be a leader in everything that you do

PAT **RAFTER**

"I think there are times when your words can empower, calm someone, console someone or pep them up. I like to think at times my words did that."

PAT RAFTER *Former US Open Tennis Champion*

It is arguable that Pat Rafter is not a leader. After all, tennis is predominantly an individual sport and, while he has won numerous tournaments including the US Open, twice, he has never led or coached a team. In sport, though, there are many ways to lead that do not require the little (c) beside your name, and that's where Pat fits the bill. It is inarguable that Pat Rafter has led Australia through his sportsmanship.

In Australia, it is not enough to be a winner. In Australian eyes, how you win matters as much as what you win. We call it sportsmanship. If the greatest measure of a person is that he confronts the demons of defeat as evenly as he does the spoils of victory, then Pat passes with the highest grade. There has been no better example in Australian sport of how someone should behave before, during and after a contest.

One of nine children, Pat's junior years in tennis were unspectacular. While those around him were fast becoming men, he wasn't, at least physically, and it showed in his results with early exit after early exit. Some years he couldn't even make the Queensland team for his age group.

Through those years the only consistency among his inconsistency was his family and their support – particularly that of his mother Jocelyn. "My mother would travel with me from tournament to tournament, and there she'd stand

A very boyish Patrick Rafter playing in Queensland in 1991.
Picture: Jim Hooper

214

INFLUENTIAL PEOPLE

- Jocelyn Rafter, *mother*
- John Newcombe
- Bjorn Borg
- John McEnroe
- Pat Cash
- Mal Meninga
- Allan Border

CAREER STATS

- Pro 1991-2002
- ATP singles titles 11; 2 grand slams
- US Open winner 1997, 1998
- Wimbldeon finalist 2000, 2001
- Ranked No. 1 in the world July, 1999
- ATP doubles titles 10
- Davis Cup 1994-2001
- Played 32 games for Australia, won 21, lost 11
- Finalist 2000, 2001
- Australian Sports Medal 2000
- Sport Australia Hall of Fame 2001
- Australian of the Year 2002

on the other side of the net, hitting balls back to me. By the time I turned 17 or 18 I was actually starting to play a bit better, holding my own with some of the better kids in Australia around that age group."

As much as he liked working and touring with his mother, he disliked doing the same with his father, Jim. "I didn't like being coached by my father. There was a real pressure when I went away for tournaments with him, and I didn't enjoy it. I loved my father and respected him, but when it came to tennis I didn't give him enough respect. At the end of a match, dad would give me some constructive criticism, but I would take it as a personal attack. He did know, though. I would go to a coach and the coach would say, 'Do this', and dad would say, 'That's what I just told him. You could have saved yourself $50'. With my mother I never felt the same tension – I enjoyed travelling with her."

Jim Rafter was persistent, though, and while he didn't help Pat's serve he gave him the odd one for his behaviour. Pat's extreme competitive drive often saw him lose his cool on court. At one tournament, he drop-kicked his racquet over the fence, and Jim immediately dragged him from the court and out of the game. It didn't change Pat overnight, but the seeds of sportsmanship were sown.

As Pat's tennis improved, so his ambition increased, but not wildly. For the first time, he started to believe that he may be able to eke a living out of being a professional on the circuit. His goal was to make the top 50 in the world, and at the end of his career to be able to buy his own house from the proceeds. Even that wasn't looking too likely, as he wavered on the periphery of the Open tour. The pressure mounted, with first-round exits the norm.

"The pressure really hit me in 1992. My mum and I were travelling through Asia for six to seven weeks; I was ranked about 250-300 in the world and playing in qualifying tournaments here and there. After another first- or second-round loss, this time in Tokyo, mum and I made our way down to McDonald's for dinner. I was two or three years out of school, almost 20 years old, and watching others in the 19-20 year age groups that had made it. I had the expectation that that's where I should have been. At this dinner, I turned to mum and said, 'I don't know if I can deal with this pressure – I don't know if I have what it takes.' With her response, mum took all the pressure off me, 'Pat, you don't need to be a great tennis player, you don't need it. If this is not

" 'Pat, you don't need to be a great tennis player, you don't need it. If this is not what you want then that's OK.' It was the greatest thing that Mum ever said to me. It took all the pressure away."

Great, sport: Pat
after receiving his
**Australian of the Year
Award at Kirribilli
House, 2002.**
Photo: Penny Bradfield

what you want then that's OK.' It was the greatest thing that mum ever said
to me. It took all the pressure away."

His brother Geoff was also a big influence. Geoff had been a player and was
Pat's coach for some time. He worked on relieving Pat of pressure, and he had
a theory to which Pat related. Geoff always thought that no one dealt well
with pressure, and those who could take the pressure off themselves, put it
aside, look at life in a different way and focus on something else, would be the
ones to really succeed.

Almost cruelly, Geoff became a victim of his own advice. At the Australian
Open in 1997, Pat stopped using him as his coach. He loved his brother,
and Geoff was good for him, but he felt at this point in his career he needed
someone different. "I had planned to work with my brother Geoff in
1997, but sometimes we bumped heads really hard. We parted ways at the
Australian Open, and I was very emotional. I don't regret it because it was
the best thing for my career, but I regret hurting my brother. It hurt mum and

> *"I remember running around the university tennis courts, talking to a couple of mates, just talking about how great it would be to play Davis Cup for Australia. We were 12, 13 and 14 at that stage. It was always in the back of my mind ... it was the pinnacle of our game."*

dad, too – I think they still have a bit of pain over it, and Geoff wished it was different as well, but everyone understands it was what I had to do for myself. It was a selfish thing I was doing at that stage of my career, but it was the best move for me to have made. I don't think I've sat down and cried with my brother like that before. It was very tough, but it was an experience that I felt lifted a whole weight off me, and it was another important step in my becoming a man and becoming a better tennis player."

With a new coach and a US Open victory just eight months later, Pat's career quickly exceeded everyone's expectations, especially his own. The nation loved his results, but they loved him more. Over the next few years, it was the combination of his sense of fair play, his never-say-die attitude and his graciousness in both victory and defeat that Australians loved.

However, his greater success didn't come without angst. Pat found that sportsmanship was not something you could turn on and off like a light switch. You were either a sportsman or you were not, and if you faltered it could affect your performance. "There was one occasion with a big point in the Davis Cup final against France in 2001, which I sometimes think about. We were up 3-1 or 4-2 in a tie break and Lleyton [Hewitt] hit a shot over my head and I felt it go over my hat. Now I don't know if it hit my hat or if I felt the wind, but I didn't own up to it. It stayed on my mind the whole time – I think that maybe I should have brought it up. We all played on and I think we lost the point. That always stuck on my mind."

I think Pat can continue to sleep the sleep of the just.

As well as his untiring ethic of fair play, Pat always left a piece of himself on the court, whether at training or in a match. Gary Stickler, one of his most significant coaches in Queensland, instilled in Pat the belief that urgency in his training would pay back many times over in the match. Their fitness schedule was conducted on court in very physical four-hour sessions made up of sets of 15 minutes hard at it with a couple of minutes off in between. Pat became a fighter, never giving up, outlasting his competitors through sheer will and stamina.

Sportsmanship is also about team and, although tennis presents few opportunities, Pat is a team player. His all-time sporting hero was Queensland rugby league legend Mal Meninga, and Pat envied the camaraderie that team sport allowed. Tennis's only answer was Davis Cup, and at the start of every year, when plotting his calendar, he first marked down the four majors and then the Davis Cup.

Pat's defining moment, however, came in one of his darkest hours. Like all tennis fanatics, he dreamed of winning Wimbledon. Unlike most, he had two opportunities to do so.

The first was against Pete Sampras, in 2000, when to no one's surprise, including himself, he was beaten. The Goran Ivanisevic match the following year was a different story. "In this match, I could see this win coming. I just didn't think I was going to lose to Goran. I had beaten him the last few times we played, I had the experience of the year before, and I just thought it was my time. I didn't see the loss coming."

Although devastated, he immediately went to Goran, shook his hand and didn't skip a beat of graciousness. That morning, his father echoed the thoughts of the nation when interviewed on ABC Radio. "We know that he's a good tennis player, but every time we see him losing something that he had his heart so set on, I'm so proud of him the way he handles it." And then later, accepting the Sports Australia Hall of Fame's "The Don" award for the athlete whose example most inspired the nation, his dad said, "The way Pat handled losing made me feel, 'You are a very great man, my son'."

And so say all of us.

"Sportsmanship is largely learned. We are brought up as Australians on the sportsmanship of people like Fitzy, Newk and Roachey. These lessons have filtered down, and it became my responsibility. I also had a responsibility to my father, to my family and, more importantly, to myself."

LAWS OF LEADERSHIP

- It's about process, not end result

- Surround yourself with a good support team

- Smart preparation and efficiency – training and fitness in one

- Take the pressure off

- Know how to deal with losses and victories

- Maintain respect, sportsmanship

- Give your best at all times

- Learn to fight

- Keep it simple

- Believe in yourself

- Never take a situation for granted – it may not come around again

LOUISE **SAUVAGE**

"You have to be kind of obsessive to a certain extent. I know I was, and am, about many things. Being a perfectionist, and wanting to make sure that I've done everything that I possibly can and be satisfied within myself to know that I couldn't have done any more."

LOUISE SAUVAGE *Former Paralympic Athlete*

Many think sportspeople look at the world from a skewed perspective. For starters, they read the newspaper starting at the back and only sometimes get to the front page. If they feature on the back page, they've probably made it; if they feature on the front page, they have probably done something wrong. Anywhere in between is more likely to be a human interest story rather than a celebration of their mastery – and in the ambitious mind of an athlete that is a "nice to have" rather than a necessity.

For Louise Sauvage, one of Australia's most successful and versatile athletes – who has won internationally in events as short and sharp as the 100 metres and as long and exhaustive as the marathon – it took too long to get onto the back page. "The biggest obstacle for me has been acceptance – acceptance that my sport is real and that it deserves recognition and sponsorship and the attention of the media. It's always tough for any athlete to get that.

"When I first started off I was in the human interest pages of the paper – the fact that I did a sport and the article was about my sport didn't matter – I had a disability and it was warm and fuzzy. It wasn't until I made it to where everyone else was, in the sports pages, where any elite athlete deserves to be, that I thought, 'OK they're taking me seriously now, this is good.'"

To Louise, it was important. She hated being patronised, and she yearned to

Clout: Louise at an early childhood intervention conference, 2004.
Photo: Adam McLean

INFLUENTIAL PEOPLE

- Heinz Frei, *Swiss paralympian*
- Bono, *lead singer U2*

CAREER STATS

Paralympics

- Athens 2004 silver 800m, 400m
- Sydney 2000 gold 1500m, 5000m, silver 800m
- Atlanta 1996 gold 400m, 800m, 1500m, 5000m
- Barcelona 1992 gold 100m, 200m, 400m, silver 800m

Olympics

- (800m women's wheelchair)
- Athens 2004 bronze 800m
- Sydney 2000 gold 800m
- Atlanta 1996 gold 800m

"You have to be accessible to people, open-minded, good at communicating, a very good listener, tolerant, not judgemental, be willing to make your own assessment of things ..."

be recognised for what she achieved. She wasn't out there six days a week, in all weathers and at times most of us are not yet brewing the morning coffee, to be simply thought of as a "really nice" story.

To meet Louise, there is no question that she is an athlete. Her muscular and athletic upper torso and arms – her tools of trade in sport and life – impressively dominate her appearance. Speak with her, however, and her softly spoken, self-effacing manner belies the fact she is one of Australia's most successful and most competitive sportspeople. For someone who has achieved so much, Louise could also win gold medals for humility. She is aware of her success, but it takes some cajoling to extract the detail. When she does get talking, and recounts some of her special triumphs, glimpses of her steely eyes speak of an uncommon resolve and a love of competition and winning.

Louise was born with myelodysplasia, a severe spinal disability that inhibits the function of the lower half of the body, giving limited control over the legs. The condition required her to have 21 operations by the time she was 10 years old. Sport, then, initially through swimming, formed an important part of her life, keeping her upper body strong through rehabilitation. At age eight, her graduation to wheelchair sport opened up a whole new world of opportunity.

"I did sport at school, but because of my disability it was not really the same, as I couldn't compete against the other children. When I started wheelchair sport it was like, 'Cool, this is awesome', and I just loved doing everything and anything that I could get my hands on.

"From then on it was a lifestyle for me, it wasn't an option, and I was going to do it no matter what. At wheelchair sports there were lots of other children who were similar ages and with similar disabilities, so I could compete on an equal level, and that was great."

Compete and win she did, from Barcelona to Boston and Atlanta to Sydney, the wins kept coming. A total of nine Paralympic gold and four silver medals, gold in the 800-metres women's wheelchair demonstration race at the Olympic Games in Atlanta and Sydney, and bronze in Athens, as well as victories in some of the world's most prestigious road races, including the Boston, Los Angeles and Honolulu marathons.

Louise, though thrilled with her success, has never been satisfied, and ambition drives her on. While comfortably considered a leader with her

Golden moment: Louise wins the women's 5000m T54 final at the Sydney Paralympics, 2000.
Photo: Julian Andrews

own athletic prowess, she has in more recent times turned her attention to coaching – a natural progression where, unsurprisingly, she has used her leadership skills for the benefit of others.

She has been coaching for just less than two years, and is the first to admit that she is learning, but indications thus far are positive. Her first athlete is Angie Ballard, a 400- and 800-metres track racer who won gold in the 400 metres and silver in the 100, 200, 800 and 1500 metres at the 2005 Summer Down Under Series.

"The responsibility of being a coach is vast. There are so many different things that I have to think of now, and there's way more responsibility than being an athlete. I've got to try and manage and take care of the overall picture from not only the sessions that I give, but the athlete's mental state, diet and recovery and trying to match everything up."

Matching everything up for Louise is about knowing her athlete as a person as much as a competitor. More than anyone, she understands how the world turns from a track racer's perspective, and without this knowledge she would only be doing half a job and thus risk getting half the results.

"I'm trying to know the overall picture, what they're trying to achieve, not only on the track, but in their life. I don't believe in sport being everything in life – I don't think that is healthy at all. They need to have something else. My athlete

"I love winning. It's a phenomenal feeling. If anyone's ever won anything, they know what kind of feeling it gives them, and to want to continue doing that probably spurs me on more than anything, just to see how far I can push myself, both physically and mentally, and trying to get to that next level. I think one of the hardest things is to stay on top once you're there, so to continue proving is really, really tough."

goes to university, so mixing it up so that her life balances out is important."

Knowledge of your athlete is essential for effective communication, and it has reached the point now that when Angie is having a bad day Louise knows almost instantly how she is feeling. This knowledge helps her to decide not only how she may need to adjust her next session, but also what she may need to say to remedy any anxieties. Positive reinforcement at appropriate times can make all the difference.

"Sportspeople are often your average person that has had great success at something they are really good at, and they have worked bloody hard to get there as well, so they deserve the recognition that they get. It's not always given to a lot of sportspeople, unfortunately, depending on what sport they are in."

Louise's thoughts on leadership have been framed from the challenges of her life and the combination of experiences as both a competitor and now as a coach, so she is very clear on what it takes for her to be successful. "You have to be accessible to people, open-minded, good at communicating, a very good listener, tolerant, not judgemental, be willing to make your own assessment of things, and be willing to get out there and speak out about what you believe in."

And, on that last point, Sauvage has been particularly active spreading her influence far beyond the race track. Earlier this year she was happily back in the "in-between" pages of the newspapers railing against discriminatory practices in the travel industry. Using her considerable clout and faultless reputation, she was standing up and leading a crusade not for athletes with a disability but for people with a disability, and she was taking on some of the biggest players in Australian business – Qantas and Virgin airlines.

Sauvage, along with fellow wheelchair athlete Paul Nunnari, has been campaigning against Virgin Blue's requirement that a carer must accompany a disabled passenger on a flight. They were also opposing Qantas' limitation of carrying a maximum of only two electric wheelchair users on 737s domestically, a restriction still in force due to legal obligations surrounding occupational health and safety for ground crew.

However, since they have spoken, their words have been heard and Qantas invited them to assist in educating their staff on how to better meet the needs of customers with disabilities.

It is amazing to think that a shy, retiring girl has developed the confidence and strength of character to take such a stance and command both the attention and respect of seasoned corporate executives, resulting in better treatment of people with disabilities. If that were the only reward for her dedication to her craft, then it would be reward enough.

Make no mistake, though, Louise's greatest moment to date has been the merging of her two, at times competing, agitations: the pursuit for appropriate recognition of her sport and the athletes in it and her personal journey for elite performance. Her worlds collided in Sydney 2000 when the demonstration sport at the Olympics was chosen to be the 800-metres wheelchair race, and Louise was competing, in her own country, in the prime of her career, in front of family and friends. Could it get any better than this? Yes it could. She could, and in fact would, win the gold medal.

"If I had to pick my greatest moment, it would be winning the demonstration event at the 2000 Games and coming back later that evening and having my medal presented to me by Juan Antonio Samaranch, who was head of the IOC. I was on the dais in the No.1 position, and the flag was being raised and the anthem was being played because you're No.1. You have got 110,000 people singing the anthem with you, it's just unbelievable. There was no time to be emotional, I just couldn't stop smiling, it was just awesome."

LAWS OF LEADERSHIP

- Commit to everything you do

- Remember the big picture

- Provide feedback

- Continue to learn

- Don't judge people or situations

- Know the strengths and weaknesses of your opponents

MARK SCHWARZER

"Leaders must be well respected as a player and as a person, and experience is important as well in being a leader. I don't think leadership is something that can be taught. I think it comes naturally, and some people either have those qualities or they don't, and I think it can take some people time to develop. You also need to lead by example, not only just talk about what should be done on the pitch or what should be done off the pitch, you have to lead by example."

MARK SCHWARZER *Australian Soccer Goalkeeper and Former Australian Soccer Captain*

Leadership is about coping with pressure, and pressure moments don't come any bigger than November 16, 2005. More specifically, at 10.30pm when Mark Schwarzer stood in front of goals as our nation's last line of defence against the Uruguayan challenge. The prize that evening for the Socceroos – a ticket to Germany and entry into the World Cup finals for the first time since 1974. "I didn't feel that much pressure. In penalty shoot-outs, the pressure is predominantly on the kickers and not as much on the goal-keeper. The kickers are expected to score, whereas the goal-keepers are not expected to save." I find that hard to believe ... In fact, I don't believe it.

That day in November, Australia's nominated kickers lined up and, one by one, they stood front and centre and waited their turn. In between each Australian attempt, Mark had to defend the best the Uruguayans had to offer. Harry Kewell converts first for Australia, to huge cheers. Stage call, Mark Schwarzer. As Uruguayan Dario Rodriguez strikes the ball, Mark dives to his left and strikes it away to the massive roars of the crowd. 1-0 Australia.

Next, man-of-the-match Lucas Neill kicks the ball into the back of the net, as do Uruguay's Gustavo Varela, Australia's Tony Vidmar and Uruguay's Fabian Estoyanoff. Australia 3 Uruguay 2. "During the penalty shoot-out, there was not one ounce of nervousness in me. I was nervous before the game, I

Focus: Mark Schwarzer, 2006.
Photo: Vince Caligiuri

226

"There are defining moments in the game and there are split second decisions that are made in the game. Those split seconds at times become defining moments."

was nervous a little bit at the beginning of the game and even a little bit at the start of extra time, but not at the penalty shoot-out. I felt more nervous watching the World Cup final from a bar in Spain than being out there in the qualifiers against Uruguay. When you are out there in the middle of it all, it's different to sitting here. On the sidelines, you can't dictate what happens in the game because you're not involved."

The suspension builds as Australian captain Mark Viduka lines up the goal that will give Australia an unbeatable lead. In the most unlikely scenario, he misses, sending his shot wide to the right of the post. It's still Australia 3 Uruguay 2, but Australia have had four kicks to Uruguay's three. Schwarzer must save again. He has to stay composed in the heat of the moment. "I was just saying to myself, 'Stay on my feet and don't move, make sure the kicker has all the pressure'. A lot of goalkeepers make a first move and go a particular way, and that makes the mind up for the kicker. At this level, you've got a lot of unbelievable players who are very experienced, and they are able to wait until that last split second before making up their mind as to where they are going to kick the ball. I was just saying to myself, 'Stay on your feet as long as possible, don't make any movement, let him make the first move', and hopefully, with him making the first move, he's going to struggle, because he's waiting for me to move, and then in that last split second he's in a position where he's got to make a decision whereas he is probably thinking most of the time, 'The keeper's going to move, and I'm going to find it easier to slot the ball whichever way in the opposite direction.' "

It's the old double bluff ... guns at 20 paces ... who blinks first ... and Mark doesn't blink. As Marcelo Zaleyeta lines up for Uruguay, Mark stands his ground to the last, trusts himself and ... SAVES! The score remains Australia 3 Uruguay 2. John Aloisi then calmly pots the final goal: 4-2 Australia. Australia are through, Mark is the hero, the crowd goes berserk, and Australia has another favourite sporting team. Mark's saves and John Aloisi's goal sparked a contagion that raged uncontrollably throughout the nation, peaking as the Socceroos progressed through to the round of 16 of the World Cup for the first time in history. It was a fever that Mark never believed would infect Australia.

Football was always Mark's game, but it wasn't until age 10 that he ended

**Finders keepers:
Mark during a team
training session
at St George
Stadium, 1993.**
Photo: Tim Clayton

up in goals. Mark was coached by his father, Hans, in his local club side in
north-western Sydney. Now, fathers coaching sons are either too harsh and
unfair on them or too soft and favour them. Mr Schwarzer was the former.
When no one wanted to be goal-keeper, his father made the decision, "OK, no
one else wants to go into goal – my son's going in goal. You go in goal."

"No one really wanted to be goal-keeper in those days, as you either won
the game 5-0 or you lost it 5-0 – it wasn't the most pleasant position to play.
You either had a lot to do but you let the goals in and you lost or you had very
little to do and you stood around being bored. Dad claims that I used to trip
over my own feet, and that's why he put me in goal, though I like to argue
that point with him."

Mark progressed through the ranks all the way to the under-16 World Cup
in Scotland, where he played against East Germany, US and Brazil, giving him
a taste of world-class opposition. At the same tournament, he met the greatest
footballer of all time, Pele. It was an inspiring moment, energising him with
the drive and the recognition that, "Yes I want to be a professional footballer."

His initial stint as a professional in Germany, though, was not enjoyable. As
a foreigner, he wasn't respected as a player or made to feel welcome until he
had an opportunity to play in the first team. He played well, but even then
it was veiled respect at best. Mark was downcast and found himself thinking

Head high ...

"I played in a [League] Cup final in 2004 at Cardiff in front of 75,000 people. I let one of the tamest shots in history go in, and after the initial frustration, I turned around and kicked lumps out of the goal post and walked off towards the crowd in disgust. From that point on, something clicked in my head and I just reverted back to saying, 'Forget about it, that's it.' And from that point, I went on to make quite a few considerable saves and good saves to keep us in the game, and to win the game in the end 2-1. I think what I learnt was that you can swing things around and then you can go and pick yourself up after making such a horrendous mistake and go on to perform and make a difference and help your team win the game."

there must be more to life than feeling demoralised; packing up and going home was becoming a very real option. When he was selected in the Australian team to take the place of the injured Mark Bosnich, one of the other goal-keepers quipped, "What has he been called up for, the basketball team? Can't be football."

Through this time he realised the importance of support, and his most ardent supporter, his then girlfriend and wife to be, Paloma, held him together. "Listen,' she said, "You know this is not what you want, you know you want to stay. You'll only regret going home so you have got to stick it out. Let's make a move, let's move from here and try something different." And so they did. They moved to England.

The change was good for Mark, who discovered an environment that was encouraging and positive, something he thought was created partly by the pay structure. In England, all your contract money was guaranteed whereas in Germany only about 40 per cent of your contract was guaranteed and the rest was dependent on how many games you played and where the team finished. In Germany, for example, this didn't encourage the No.1 or No.2 goal-keeper to go out of their way to help the No.3 keeper, whereas in England it was more about the team first then about the individual.

Mark thrived in the new environment as it was more typical of the Australian way and one of the reasons he felt the Socceroos did so well in Germany. "There has been a very good team spirit for the last six years I've been involved full-time with the national team. There's a younger generation and an older generation, and most of the older generation all grew up around the same time or played in the same league and against each other in representative football, and same with the younger generation. First and foremost, however, everyone is Australian, and everyone follows each other in some way or another through their careers, and you feel that natural bonding towards each other."

This Aussie bonding fortified the squad throughout the World Cup, but all was not smooth sailing. Mark's frustration was around selection and not being recognised earlier as the No.1 goalkeeper, with Socceroos coach Guus Hiddink often not deciding until a couple of hours before kick-off which of his keepers would play. The battle was between Mark and his teammate Zeljko Kalac. Mark chose to let his performances on the field and in training tell the story. Ultimately, Mark won through.

Guus brought a strong sense of discipline and focus into the team. "The discipline side of things was one of the key ingredients missing, and Guus brought that in. He also had the ability to get everyone pulling in the right direction and understanding how we wanted to play." Guus understood his players, reading their mood and their confidence in their body language and using this to drive them as a team.

He demanded everyone eat together at meal time. "Nine times out of 10, he would be the first one in the room and position himself so he could watch every player come in. He would watch how you sat down, who you'd sit with, what you'd do, and how much you'd eat. Nobody was allowed to eat until everyone was present and the captain or the coach gave the go-ahead, and no one could leave the table until the OK was given. "There were certain things he instilled in us, even in those early weeks in the job, that everybody came away thinking, 'Shit, we train a lot' or 'We train hard', but they also came away with an unbelievable confidence and self-belief that, this time, we were going to qualify for the World Cup." And so they did, eventually bowing out to future champions Italy in the dying seconds of their sudden-death round of the final 16.

Mark was the keeper again that day, this time failing to stop the penalty goal that Lucas Neill surrendered moments before full-time. It was through no fault of his nor of Lucas', but it was the end of a wonderful rollercoaster ride where the Socceroos sat as equals to all other teams in Australian sport, and that to Mark was the biggest prize. "My first dream, playing for Australia, came true when I was 19. My second dream came true when we qualified to play in the World Cup. My third one came true when the atmosphere and the people of Australia got behind football the way they did."

LAWS OF LEADERSHIP

- Take the opportunity when it presents itself

- Follow your ambition and be passionate about it

- Put the pressure on your opposition not yourself

- Focus on the big picture, not on a single moment

- Contribute to the team

- Lead by example and help others along the way

- Don't make the same mistake twice

- Keep your mind focused on the job

- Set achievable goals

- Believe in your own ability

KEVIN **SHEEDY**

"I dreamt of being a footballer. I dreamt of being a coach.
And I always felt there's nothing wrong with dreaming.
Just try to achieve."

KEVIN SHEEDY *Essendon Football Club Coach*

**Genuinely excited:
Kevin and James
Hird after winning
the annual Anzac
Day clash against
Collingwood, 2005.**
Photo: Vince Caligiuri

I arrange to meet Kevin Sheedy at 5pm in his "office", but I am a little early. His office is on the corner of Clarendon Street and Wellington Parade in Melbourne, where it overlooks the verdant Fitzroy Gardens, a haven in a busy and expanding city. I'm finding it difficult to locate. Then I realise it's in the Hilton Hotel … Actually, in the brasserie on the left-hand side and, by the way, it's the table in the back corner. His "staff" welcome me and, although it's obvious they weren't expecting me, politely lead me to my seat. "He's not here yet. Would you like a drink?" I get the feeling I'm not the first person to find themselves in this situation.

About five after five, I receive a call on my mobile. Kevin may be 10 minutes late. Half an hour later, I have my second drink. Maybe I should order some fries with this one, as it's almost dinner time and a few tables are starting to fill. After an hour, I'm wondering if I'm in the right place. The staff, I'm sure, are starting to feel sorry for me, as they again assure me that this is where he meets people. Earlier that day, no less than John Bertrand, that master of yachting precision, assured me this is where Kevin meets people … I hope he doesn't mention punctuality as an essential leadership quality.

Finally, he arrives, but before I see him I hear him talking to his "staff", "What? One hour! Oh, no!"

"Sorry mate, got held up … you know how it is in a footy club …"

Kevin Sheedy certainly knows what it's like in a footy club. In Aussie Rules, his name is synonymous with longevity, likewise success. As an uncompromising player, he was dubbed the "back pocket plumber" by his coach Tommy Hafey and appeared in 251 games for Richmond, winning three premierships. In his 26 years as coach of Essendon, he has won four premierships and finished runner-up on three occasions. If you were born after 1975, you wouldn't remember any other Essendon coach.

As I write, times are tough for Kevin and his team. Two days before our meeting, 50,000 people watched Essendon tie with Carlton in a game to establish which of the teams would sit last on the ladder. It's the sign of a healthy sport when 50,000 people watch the two bottom teams slug it out, but is it also a sign that the Essendon club is unhealthy? The circumstances don't faze him. "I look at our results and compare them to the American gridiron system. You can't compare us to league and rugby, as they don't have a draft like we do. San Francisco won five Superbowls in 25 years. I don't think anyone in Australia has done any better.

"In our game, you're looking to get the four- to five-year period right. Have you got the people that are going to take you there? Some you will and some you won't. Are they worth keeping or will they restrict the opportunity for the club to go on? And you've always got to keep an eye on yourself to make sure that you're not the person holding the club back. Hopefully, you're not. Our club has been quite capable of making very good changes in the last decade or so."

At least for Essendon, the tie with Carlton was an improvement on their previous 14 games, which all ended in losses, equalling their worst losing streak ever. Never flustered, though, and keen to display the foundation behind his faith, Kevin pulls out some stats he intends to present that evening to a Redenblacks function, a group of about 15 people who form one of the many coteries around the football club. "See this," he says, "We are last on the ladder but second in the league in this stat … and that is important. Look here … once again, third on this one and we are the fourth here. In getting the ball into the opposition's 50-metre zone, we are the only team in the bottom four on the ladder in the top six."

"I've driven home 200 times a loser, but there's a lot of people who lose 200 games and go nowhere. I'm prepared to lose 200 on my way to try and get somewhere."

He shifts my focus to another sheet. "Have a look at this," he says, pointing to a team sheet that looks very impressive, Lloyd, Laycock, Rioli, Hird, Watson, Henneman, etc. These are the guys unavailable for selection at the moment, and the young guys taking their place are having a go and giving me these stats. They're actually running teams in the top eight to one kick or two kicks. Some of these matches, we've led the whole game and lost it in the last few minutes – we're running these teams to the end."

Kevin is genuinely excited about the team's potential and genuinely not worried about the future. Experience is a good thing. "I've lost 200 matches in my life as a coach; most coaches have never coached 200 games. That means I've driven home 200 times a loser, but there's a lot of people who lose 200 games and go nowhere. I'm prepared to lose 200 on my way to try and get somewhere. We might be last at the moment, but we are just around the corner from getting somewhere."

Kevin has led his club in developing a truly national brand and fan base, and through it all kept an unwaveringly balanced perspective. "Life's pretty good for us, but it's not great for other people sometimes. It's a huge challenge, and they're going through some terrible times in their lives. Essendon stands for the

CAREER STATS

Player
- Richmond (1967-1979)
- 251 games, 91 goals, 3 premierships

Coach
- Essendon (1981-)
- 613 games
- 376 wins
- 230 losses
- 7 draws (at end of 2006)
- 4 premierships
- 3 runners-up

common man, the real honest person that's in between Liberal and Labor, that could be of any religion or ethnicity – it's an amazing collective of people."

Success on the field is but a chapter in the Kevin Sheedy story. He is also a clever marketer and a champion of indigenous footballers in the league. It is this latter achievement for which he is roundly respected. Initially, his endeavours into indigenous Australian culture were specifically about encouraging young Aboriginal children to play the game and supporting anti-racial vilification laws in the AFL. His influence has touched many people far beyond his original ambit, broadening horizons for all Australians.

"Where I grew up you just never met an Aboriginal kid. You read comic strips about Aboriginal kids ... standing there with a spear or a boomerang, and you're thinking, as an eight-year-old kid in 1954, 'What the hell is this?' You never got to know that part of Australia, 'cause in the '50s no one had a car and no one went anywhere. Then in the '60s they only went 100 miles further, which is still nowhere. When we changed from VFL to AFL, our club needed to look outside its own thought patterns and try to embrace Australia and not just be a suburb in Melbourne – have team, have club, will travel. That's what we did, and we've got a great supporter base in just about every city now because of it."

A change in the rules of recruiting helped the cause of indigenous footballers, and Essendon was one of the first clubs to capitalise. Previously, teams were only allowed to recruit a maximum of two players from outside Victoria, but the introduction of the draft removed any limit. "The old rule in the VFL probably restricted indigenous players' entry into the clubs, as your two picks generally came from Western Australia or South Australia. The draft opened all of Australia and our connections and supporter base that we had created meant that we recruited terrific players."

He points to a map of Australia replete with Essendon's colours; the background is black and a red sash drapes the continent from Bunbury in the south-west corner up to Cooktown in the north-east. Scattered around the map are the names of the indigenous players who have worn that famous red sash and the towns from which they originated. "Our first three draft choices for last year were Patrick Ryder, an Aboriginal boy from Geraldton, Courtenay Dempsey from Cairns and Richard Cole in Alice Springs." His pride is evident as his finger moves to all quarters of Australia. He goes on to speak about Gavin Wanganeen, an indigenous player he recruited from Adelaide who became a legend at Essendon and then returned to Adelaide and captained Port Power. "He's probably one of the greatest superstars our game has seen and the first indigenous player to get a million-dollar contract. That's fantastic for him."

Kevin wanted to make a difference, and his influence didn't end with recruitment. It continued with building the confidence of his new players and integrating them as part of the Essendon team. "The Aboriginal kids are sometimes more nervy and lacking in inner confidence and belief. Why wouldn't you be after all the rotten things that non-indigenous Australians have probably done to Aboriginal people over 200 years. There has to be mistrust there. I don't know who's done what to whom, but there is one thing that you can do and that is build your own bridge. Start now. That's what this country needs to do."

Kevin always takes responsibility for his team's performance and that of his staff, a result of a lesson that he learnt early on. "I reckon in the early days I would delegate work and not actually check to make sure it was getting done. I was taught early on by a very smart board member that, 'Delegation does not mean abdication'. This doesn't mean that you have to go and sit on someone's shoulder, but that you simply have to make sure that things are getting done. If you want to be a leader, you need a vision as to where your group is heading. You must have a great work ethic, you must be a good liaison between people, have good timing, concentrate on your own personal development, and select your mentors well."

On the point of mentors, Kevin believes it is one of the most important ways a parent can positively influence their children's lives. You cannot always choose their friends, you can't choose their family, but you can help guide them towards people who will be good mentors. "You don't have to be too obvious, but as you go through life make mention of how good that person is at something or how impressed you were with this person for something else. Subtly, the message will get through and your children will choose the right role models and mentors."

I was fortunate to have so much time with Kevin Sheedy. He was definitely worth the wait. After a good hour of entertaining and insightful chat – and a couple of chardonnays – we finish and I pick up the bill. The staff haven't even charged me for those first few drinks – they must have felt sorry for me – and while he didn't mention punctuality, he did have a good sense of humour.

LAWS OF LEADERSHIP

- Look outside your own environment

- Ensure ongoing personal development

- Be adaptable

- Develop a strong work ethic

- Timing is everything

- Find a mentor

- Maintain an overall vision

- Ensure good communication

JAMES TOMKINS

"Respect your teammate enough to give him the best opportunity to succeed, and get really dirty on yourself if you don't."

JAMES TOMKINS *Australian Olympic Rower*

I s going to the Olympics for the sixth time a new experience or the same experience all over again? For James Tomkins, who will be 42 when the cauldron is lit in Beijing, it is potentially a sixth different experience, with a sixth different lesson, from his sixth consecutive Olympics.

James's Olympic journey began in Seoul in 1988, and one of his greatest moments ended as his most valuable lesson. "In the Seoul Olympics, we stuffed up. It was a missed opportunity. It was like one of those flashbacks in a movie. I remember watching the flame slowly extinguishing and thinking, 'It will now be four years until I have another opportunity to get the right colour medal.' As the flame slowly dwindled, that was my realisation. We get a world championships every year, but it's four years between Olympic Games – the opportunities are so limited."

When talking to younger teammates, which is actually all of the team nowadays, it is no surprise that one of James' key messages is to grab opportunities because they may never occur again.

With the lesson of Seoul, the colour of James's Olympic experiences improved markedly, as did his reservoir of knowledge and confidence.

"Seoul in 1988 was about taking ownership of our performance. Barcelona in 1992 was about understanding that there are no absolutes. Atlanta in

Crew: James Tomkins and cox Dale Caterson leaving Sydney for the Seoul Olympics, 1988.

Picture: Robert Pearce

"To succeed in rowing, you have to be very dedicated and very clear on where you are going, and you must have the ability to see something through to its conclusion. "

1996 was about trusting each other. Sydney 2000, I was dealing with the unexpected, including the loss through injury of my boat partner Drew Ginn. Athens, then, was the culmination of everything, with a particular emphasis on attention to detail. There are no five easy steps from a textbook on management that could possibly replace these experiences. Living through them counts for so much more."

One of the most powerful forces for learning is feedback, and early feedback about James as an athlete, and specifically as a rower, was exceptional. As a six-year-old, he watched all sport on television and then imagined himself in the competition. In the early '70s, there was a cycling show called *Flashing Pedals*. At the end of the hour, he would be out on his Malvern Star, his block the velodrome, his imagination running wild.

From early on, James's first high school and Australian rowing coach, Noel Donaldson, saw his potential. He was a highly respected coach, so James was struck when word circulated that Donaldson had said, "If he isn't rowing for Australia in five years' time, then there is something wrong with him." It was James's first feedback, albeit indirectly, about his potential. Initially disbelieving, it did however, build his confidence and an ambition to go further in rowing.

Amid the challenge to test himself, James particularly liked the team aspect of rowing and the support network his crew could provide. "Rowing is physically and technically such a demanding and precise sport that if someone is slightly off it will directly affect the way everyone else performs and, of course, the result. In Aussie rules, you can have someone out on the wing who has zero possessions and yet the team still win. That would be disastrous in rowing.

"Our race is incredibly intensive, but you can always remember every move, stroke by stroke. When you look back it is all in slow motion, so you know exactly what has happened. There is so much detail so that every split second you could describe in five minutes. In a team, everyone will feel that same thing, and it is great sharing that experience."

Every sport has its fear that must be overcome. For rowing, it is the fear of exhaustion, knowing that in the six or seven minutes of a race there will be a

point where you will be physically smashed with seemingly no more to give. At that point, your mental strength must take you further. This strength is fortified by your personal preparation and your preparation as a team.

"To succeed in rowing, you have to be very dedicated and very clear on where you are going, and you must have the ability to see something through to its conclusion. Leading into Athens, Drew and I went three years with four international regattas, so there is a long time in between competitions and huge amounts of preparation for each of those competitions.

"You have to be very patient and understanding that improvement in your performance will only be incremental. A lot of work goes into a small increase. Also in the team environment you will require a lot of empathy. Empathy to understand that what you do and how you do it will have a direct bearing on everyone else. You must respect your teammate enough to give him the best opportunity to succeed, and get really dirty on yourself if you don't."

James is a composed rower, just as he is a composed person – nothing

Stroke of fortune: James trains on the Yarra, 2004.
Photo: Wayne Taylor

CAREER STATS

Olympics

- Athens 2004: men's coxless pair, gold
- James and Mike McKay become first Australian rowers to compete at five Olympic Games
- Sydney 2000: men's coxless pair, bronze
- Atlanta 1996: men's coxless four, gold
- Barcelona 1992: men's coxless four, gold

World championships

- Milan 2003: men's coxless pairs, gold
- St Catharines 1999: men's coxless pair, gold
- Cologne 1998: men's coxed four, gold; men's coxed pair, gold
- Vienna 1991: men's coxless four, gold
- Lake Barrington 1990: men's coxless four, gold
- Nottingham 1986: men's eight, gold

seems to faze him in good times or bad. One of those tough times was in qualification for Sydney 2000. Six weeks out from the games and all was looking wonderful for an opportunity to win a hat-trick of gold medals – all he and Drew Ginn had left to do was qualify, and that was about to happen. At least, that was the plan.

In the pre-race warm-up, Drew, who had been managing a lower-back injury, broke down, rupturing two discs in his back. What to do? Panic never entered the equation. With Drew unable to row, James single-handedly led them back to shore where reserve Matthew Long jumped in the boat.

There were numerous problems: James had never rowed with Matthew; they both usually rowed stroke side, the left side of the boat, and there was no bank of trust between them.

"Longy came in and he also rowed stroke side, which is the equivalent of writing right-handed. He had to learn to write left-handed in 15 minutes. Understanding the importance of the regatta, I just tried to make it as comfortable as possible for him by allowing all the pressure to come to my side. Ideally, you want the boat balanced, but typically if you have someone in that situation, the boat is going to be heavily down on their side, which makes it incredibly hard for them to row."

But row they did, winning the whole regatta, qualifying for the Olympics and training for the next six weeks to get Matthew up to speed with the basics of working together as a pair. Whereas with Drew they would have spent the time finetuning, here they needed to build up a bank of trust. The result was a bronze medal, a remarkable achievement in the circumstances.

If there were lessons from all his Olympics, Athens was the graduation, and with Drew back in the boat their goal was to row the perfect race. This time the preparation was over a three-year period, with few races but a lot of kilometres over the water, and a lot of sweat in the Yarra.

Two years out from the event, their final was scheduled for August 21 at 10.30 in the morning. A broad training focus served them in the early days before finetuning had them attaining all their goals along the way. They had the journey perfectly planned, and this time there were to be no hiccups. The race day itself was almost a formality.

"Just prior to the race, our coach's pre-game address was, 'Thirty minutes to go, we better get going.' We knew exactly what we had to do and how each of us would respond. Drew and I did not have a conversation until we had crossed the finish line.

"We didn't speak over breakfast, and it wasn't until the warm-up that he said a couple of key words and then a couple of key things during the race and we both responded physically. We didn't need a conversation – I knew exactly what he was going to do and he knew exactly what I was going to do.

"At the 250 metre mark, he said, 'stride', indicating that we would relax and stretch out a little. At 500 metres, it was 'arms'. In the middle of the race, where we needed a really big effort, it was 'legs'. With just one or two key words down the course, the whole race plan came together. That is what was missing with Longy. That is what came naturally with that bank of experiences with Drew."

So where to from here, at 41 years of age, with three gold, one bronze and nothing more to prove? Does the flame still flicker and does Beijing await. Could there be a seventh Olympics in London?

"The only goal I have is what's next. That is the only goal I have ever set myself, the next one. In one of [cyclist] Lance Armstrong's books he says, 'The athlete that starts to look back on their career is the one who is about to retire.'

"I haven't done that yet."

"Seoul in 1988 was about taking ownership of our performance. Barcelona in 1992 was about understanding that there are no absolutes. Atlanta in 1996 was about trusting each other. Sydney 2000, I was dealing with the unexpected, including the loss through injury of my boat partner Drew Ginn. Athens, then, was the culmination of everything"

LAWS OF LEADERSHIP

- Composure

- Have a say in the direction of your training

- Trust

- Understand your position as a leader

- Make the most of every opportunity

- Lead by example

- Dedication – see something through right to the end

- Learn not to make assumptions

- In a team, know your aspirations and those of your teammates

- Attention to detail

GAI WATERHOUSE

"I often relate my role to being a football coach. I have a team of footballers, but they are four-legged, and I have to get them fit, and we have a grand final on … I've got to be able to get them to peak on that day."

GAI WATERHOUSE *Horse Trainer*

Winning streak: Gai cheers the field during the Golden Slipper at Rosehill, 1988.

In an industry ruled by genetics and lineage, you may be forgiven for thinking that the progeny of a genius has a short cut to success. You may have to think again. Advantage, yes. Short cut, NO. Gai Waterhouse may have some natural advantages in her genetics and in her environment, and while it may seem obvious that one of Australia's greatest horse trainers should produce another of our greatest trainers it has been anything but a short journey, and Gai has been anything but an overnight success. Hers has been a lifelong journey that continues to this day.

There have been obstacles. Gai is a woman in a male-dominated field and she always had her heart set on becoming an actress. At the same time, she also had to fight her father to even let her become a trainer, and then, when he relented, she endured a 2½-year legal battle against the Australian Jockey Club, with only a change in the law allowing her to proceed. And that was just to get her licence. Then she had to get about her business of training winners. In hindsight, that was probably the easy part.

The seeds of success are planted when you find something you love doing. This love may just creep up on you; maybe you won't even realise it's happening, but it is. Gai's success on the track is the result of a lifelong love affair with the people, the sport and, most importantly, with the horses.

But it all began with the people. "I'm sure a lot of successful people are the same, where they are influenced from a very young age by someone they admire greatly. My father was that person. He was the most famous race horse trainer Australia's ever known, and he broke every single record in his lifetime of 60 years as a horse trainer."

The home environment was very important for Tommy J. Smith, and while he never exerted any undue pressure on Gai he insisted the family eat together, especially at breakfast. "If I was in bed when Dad came home from the track at seven o'clock, he would be asking Mum, 'Where's Madam?' and Mum would say, 'Look, she's just having a little rest in, Tom.' 'THE SUN WILL BURN HER EYES OUT!' and he'd rush up the stairs, and you'd think, 'Ah, here he comes.' It was good training, I was always up early."

Not as good as the training she received around the breakfast table, where Gai would hear her dad talking to the owners, the jockeys and the press. The chatter would wash around her, some of it sticking, surreptitiously building her knowledge and her interest in the track.

Gai may have liked horse racing at this time, but she loved acting and was so determined that she applied to NIDA. She was accepted, but her dad wouldn't let her attend. As an olive branch after completing her university studies, her parents took her on a world tour for three months, at the end of which she stayed in Britain, Europe and Canada for another three years.

The time wasn't wasted – she pursued acting, earning roles in *Dr Who* among other shows. At the same time she stayed up to speed at the track.

"In that time, I kept going to the races because the one bond I had with dad back home was to talk to him about how I'd been to Newmarket, I'd been to York, I'd been to this and that."

Back in Australia, Gai focused seriously on her acting, but also went to work in the family business. The horses quickly took over. "Clocking the horses and supervising and looking and learning, and all of a sudden the more I was around the stables the more I thought, 'Gosh, I really like this.' I became like a pig in mud – I couldn't get enough of it, I couldn't learn enough, I was asking things, I was looking and watching." Gai was in love.

"I was consumed with being a success. From the moment I got my licence I made up my mind that I wouldn't fail. It was that absolute determination not to fail, and to make my father proud of me, that drove me forward."

But love sometimes is unrequited, and when she spoke about getting her racing licence Tommy was incensed at the suggestion. "We had a most dreadful fight … almost a stand-up."

But love, as it does, found a way and Tommy rang her the next day with his blessing. It was all Gai needed, she was on the move. "I was consumed with being a success. From the moment I got my licence I made up my mind that I wouldn't fail. It was that absolute determination not to fail, and to make my father proud of me, that drove me forward."

Her ambition required a strong belief in herself, a belief partly developed through the competition she faced against the thousands of girls casting for roles at BBC TV in London. This belief solidified her self-fortitude, enabling her to be tough as she drove both her staff and her stables. Sometimes they even incurred her wrath. "I can give them a rev like nobody; they could rocket to Bondi and back the way I rev, but then it's gone. Once I've said it, it's finished."

Soon after the "rev" she would return and explain exactly why they were

Perceptive: Gai during an early morning training session at Randwick, 1995.
Photo: Belinda Pratten:

247

About T.J. ...

T.J. Smith began training horses in 1941 and won his first race with Bragger at Rosehill in 1942. He set the tone for his successful career when 100-1 chance Playboy won the 1949 AJC Derby, the first of his 35 derby winners. T.J. won his first Sydney trainer's premiership in the 1952-53 season, and went on to win the premiership for the next 32 years, setting a world record and firmly establishing his place in racing folklore.

the recipient of her wrath. Her warm manner and the respect she has built up over the years ensure her relationships remained rock solid.

Respect, though, only builds up through consistency, and it did so for Gai through her behaviour, her performance and her approach to her team.

"I often relate my role to being a football coach. I have a team of footballers, but they are four-legged, and I have to get them fit for the grand finals, which are the carnivals – spring and autumn carnivals in Melbourne and Sydney, and then you've got winter carnivals. "Every two months I am at a carnival with my horses, and I've got to get them to peak on that day. They miss by a day, I might have done a hundred thousand [dollars]. I might have done a million, I can't miss a beat. I've got to make the horse peak at the right time."

One of the contributing factors to Gai's success has been what many thought may be a disadvantage – the fact that she is a woman. "I think a woman is far more perceptive – she is far more aware of people's moods and subtleties. I think I've got patience with the horses that wouldn't be with a man. Because of my trained eye, I can tell by just looking at my horses if they're happy or if they are not."

This subtlety around the animal is all the more important because, in an industry where the speed of the horses hasn't changed as it has with runners and other athletes, and a lot of the equipment such as the saddles and bridles are as they have been for decades, Gai's sensitivities can make all the difference.

Gai is the dominant figure in her stable's success, but she is quick to share the praise with her people. "I have around me a team of young men and women who are very receptive to the horses and very communicative with me."

"I'm the person who puts racing onto the front cover, not the back page. And I think that's important."

Yet while life at Tulloch Lodge is team-orientated, final decisions and responsibility for results clearly sit with Gai. She looks after 130 horses in the stable now. She has had more, but this is the optimum number because it allows her to personally be on top of each of the animal's programs. Everyday she gleans from her staff how the horses slept, what they ate, how they ran, how it felt to ride them, and she changes aspects of their program accordingly.

"I never tie the rider to the horse. I am constantly trying to find the rider that suits the horse, the conditions that suit the horse, that make the horse happy, to get him to work at a higher level."

Through her trials and tribulations, success has been sweet and satisfying. If the best revenge is to live well, any such instincts Gai has must have been sated by her success.

"I'm the person who puts racing onto the front cover, not the back page. And I think that's important. I work in a very male-dominated sphere, and the boys' club is there right down to your knickers and who gets the horses – sometimes the lady trainer with the red lipstick might be fifth on the rank or 10th on the rank. You've got to put up with that all the time – it just drives you insane – but I cop it on the chin."

After 14 years as a trainer, and most of those with major success, it is unfortunate that it remains so hard to change people's ingrained belief, but that is something that Gai has dealt with in her own competitive way. "I think, 'Oh, well, if they're not going to back me, they won't be in the winner's circle.' "

And that she has proved time and time again. And she has loved every minute of it.

LAWS OF LEADERSHIP

- Have passion for what you do

- Determination is important to success

- Be innovative

- Handle the pressure

- Manage your timing

- Communicate clearly with your team

- Don't let people down

- Stand by what you believe

- Be practical and realistic

- Believe in yourself

- Listen to those around you and be patient

STEVE **WAUGH**

"Leaders do need people to talk to them as well, often they are going through the same emotions. All of a sudden you are expected to be immune to pressure and your intelligence doubles."

STEVE WAUGH *Former Australian Cricket Captain*

Common thinking: mental toughness is the ability to stay focused in the heat of battle when the contest is in the balance.

Uncommon thinking: mental toughness is the ability to stay focused at practice, when there is nothing at stake.

It may sound counter-intuitive, but this was the simple revelation that transformed Steve Waugh from being a very good cricketer to one of the greatest. It was the legendary Bob Simpson who instilled in Steve the attitude that it actually matters most when it doesn't really matter.

"After I was dropped [from the Test side in the 1991 Ashes series] and came back, I tried to analyse what I changed, and I didn't really change that much. The biggest influence was Bob Simpson.

He told me that I didn't train the right way. 'You make mistakes at training, so you are going to make them in the game,' he said. So I really changed my routine with both batting and bowling. In the nets, I put myself into a game situation every time. I didn't want to get out. I played the ball according to its merits, and I tried to simulate match conditions so that when I was under pressure I could duplicate it later. I knew in my mind I was building up that reservoir of mental toughness that I could call upon during the tough times."

Perfect practice leads to perfect performance. Steve knew that if he could

Quad scoop and mullet: Steve with twin Mark, 1981.

CAREER STATS

Tests 1985-2004

- Played 168 matches, 10,927 runs (ave 51.06), including 32 centuries (highest score 200)

- Retired with second highest runs and centuries in Test history

- Took 92 wickets (best 5/28) and 112 catches

- Captain 1999 -2004

- Most successful captain in Test history, winning 41 of 57 Tests

One-Day Internationals 1986-2002

- Played 325 matches, 7569 runs (highest 120no, strike rate 75.82)

- 195 wickets, 111 catches

- Captain in 106 matches 1997- 2004

- World Cup wins 1987, 1999

- Scored 24,052 first-class runs (ave 51.94)

- Allan Border Medal 2001

- Australian of the Year 2004

do it at training in the nets when there was nothing at stake, when there were no selectors or crowd, and when it didn't get recorded against you, then that was mental toughness. Simpson's chestnut was the seed of an idea that sprouted a routine that inspired our toughest and most stubborn Test cricketer. Mental toughness was Steve's mantra, and so it will remain.

Steve's appetite for runs was whet as a seven-year-old playing in the under-10s. "I hit a straight drive and the sensation of the ball coming off the middle of the bat, running past the fieldsman for four runs, was the best ever. I thought, 'It won't get any better than this'."

Some seven-year-olds would be correct in these sentiments. Steve wasn't. Soon, as he and twin brother Mark arrived at games, they heard the murmurings of opposition parents, players and coaches, 'It's going to be tough, we're playing the Waugh brothers today'. Steve liked that.

In the Test side years later, he kept building his resource of mental toughness, learning from his teammates, one of the toughest of whom was Allan Border. It was Border's toughness that helped turn an ordinary Australian team into one on the verge of greatness. "I learnt a lot from Allan in the middle. He would say, 'Let's practise some mental disintegration on these guys, let's wear them down'. He was always big on mentally buggering the opposition, so they were out of the game. For mine it was mental interrogation – asking the searching questions of the opposition."

Those early Test years were good practice for Steve because the team struggled, losing a lot of matches in both the one-day and Test match arenas. Each loss was less a regret than a lesson. A regret would indicate that you looked back on the moment constantly. Steve's style was to learn the lesson and move forward, and as the good times rolled around, those memories burned, and he vowed never to return to the bad times.

Towards the end of Steve's time in the Baggy Green, it was this bank of mental toughness that saved his career with a century in an Ashes afternoon at the SCG in 2003. Although Steve made it look so easy, a battle waged.

"I was under massive pressure and had all these negative thoughts before I went out to bat. It was like a boxing match in my head, with negative and positive belting each other up. It would have been my last game if I didn't score runs – I would have been dropped, no doubt about it. I was stretching before the match, waiting to bat, thinking, 'Don't embarrass yourself ... This could be your last dig ... I hope I get some runs' ... all negative stuff.

"Then all of a sudden, walking out to bat, it just hit me, 'You have nothing to prove, you have played 18 years, 160-odd Tests, what are you worried about? Just go out and let it happen. Don't think about anything except the ball you face.' "

He did that right to the last, scoring a four off the last ball of the day to bring up his century amid the hysteria of the crowd.

When Steve was chosen to captain Australian in 1999, it was foreign territory for him. At 33, he had hardly captained a senior team, and initial reviews were not great. Keith Stackpole, in his newspaper column, slammed one of Steve's early performances as captain. He said that at any stage in the field, there were half a dozen traffic cops out in the middle, with no one person in charge. Steve, who led very much by consensus, was jolted by these words.

Not long after, he was jolted by a collision with Jason Gillespie in Sri Lanka. Australia lost that Test and Waugh lay in hospital with a broken nose, the critics calling for his head and for Shane Warne to be installed as captain.

"When I was in hospital, I thought, 'If I don't get back onto the field for the second Test match, Shane may become captain and I may never get the chance again'. So I made a pact with myself in hospital. From now on I was going to captain my way, go on gut instinct and not lead by consensus. I would

Trust: Steve Waugh, 2003.

Photo: Jon Reid

The baggy green ...

"It is a massive advantage, a massive thing we have on our side, and we weren't really utilising it as much as we could. It is a powerful symbol, it's a bit like the All Blacks and the haka. It gives them almost a power and a mystique. I think the baggy green was the same for us. I used to turn around as captain and see 10 guys walking in behind me with the baggy green in different shades of green, different wear and tear. Walking out on the field, if two batsmen saw 11 of us wearing that cap, it just gave us that symbol of unity and strength. It was like you would have to take us all on. Someone wrote in an article that it was like there were 11 prizefighters entering the ring, and that is how I wanted it to be. We would take them on if they were going to try to take us apart. We would protect each other. It gave us a link to the past, to the 380 other players. So there was that history element to it. It made it more special to play for Australia. You only get one cap these days, so it is something special, something to pass on to the grandkids."

still take input, but I would make the tough decisions myself. Up until that point, I wasn't being true to myself in the way I was captaining."

And so he went about captaining Steve Waugh-style. Not as an amalgam of those who had gone before, but as his own man, with his own imprint on his own Australian side.

As his reputation for mental toughness grew, he became calculated about its benefits for himself and, of course, for his team. "I always tried to use it to my advantage. I don't think I was tougher than anyone else, but if they gave me that tag then I would try and use it. I used it in the press against our opposition to try to build up the mystique and the myth, and all of a sudden they felt intimidated."

His ambition for the team was unambiguous – he wanted it to be the best side in world cricket in both forms of the game for a sustained period of time, not three to four years but for 10 to 15 years. Not in one Churchillian address, but more over time, he etched the essence of how they were going to play the game on his mates.

"We are going to be aggressive; we are going to try and disorientate the opposition; we are going to be in their face all the time; we are going to be together as a unit; we are going to enjoy each other's company; we are going to fight to the death, and opposition are going to know they are in a battle against us."

It was a hardened attitude he instilled in his team, and he did so through his own credo. "Attitudes are contagious. Is yours worth catching?" The contagion created an environment where players backed themselves and their teammates – no one was restrained.

Every man has a limit, though, and part of mental toughness is realising when the end is nigh, when your time is up, when you have pushed, prodded and cajoled all you can.

For Steve, that time came in Barbados in 2003, needing a Test win to clinch the series. It was the flattest of tracks, and his team had just bowled the Windies out in 128 overs and held a 314-run lead. If he were to enforce the follow-on, his bowlers would have to bowl up to another 100-plus overs in hot conditions on the slowest, flattest wicket ever.

He trusted them, but would it be the right decision? He sent them in.

"I asked for a huge effort, that we keep going on every ball, that we get stuck in and give it everything. When we won that Test, I thought, 'That is as far as I can come as a captain.' I couldn't ask any more. My time was up.

"I sat on the beach with Lynette in Barbados and said, 'I won't tour again, my time as a captain is just about up. I have gone full circle.'

"I asked more than I probably should have. I put our bowlers under stress and mentally and physically pushed our team beyond the boundaries of what was acceptable. They didn't ask any questions. That was one of my proudest moments."

Waugh never toured again and, fittingly, played his last Test in Sydney eight months later, against India. Opposition worldwide breathed a sigh of relief.

Australians breathed a sigh.

It was a hardened attitude he instilled in his team, and he did so through his own credo. "Attitudes are contagious. Is yours worth catching?"

LAWS OF LEADERSHIP

- Lead in your own way

- Don't forget about your own game

- Make decisions for the benefit of the team, not the individual

- Remember that your attitude affects the result

- Think of the big picture

- Respect the history of the game but create your own history

- Challenge your opposition

- Be prepared to fail in order to succeed

- Praise in public, criticise in private

APOLOGIES

Writing this book has been a wonderful journey – one where I've spent time with a lot of interesting people, and learnt a lot about them and about myself. It hasn't been such a wonderful journey for all those around me. So instead of the customary acknowledgements page I have written my apologies page.

First, and most sincerely, I apologise to my family, as Lara, Elijah, Sophia and Lily have endured closed doors at home from which only emerged a tapping keyboard and the sounds of Bizet's The Pearl Fishers, my background music of choice. Granted, most of this was done after 8pm and before 8am, so it was Lara who copped the brunt…very sympathetically.

Next I would like to apologise to all my work colleagues for the same closed door policy that applied at times in the office. Particularly I defer to Jen Hampshire my tenacious researcher and organiser, and Adam Jacoby, who has directed traffic from a commercial perspective.

For the same reason, I would like to apologise to all those passengers I sat next to on aeroplanes, both domestically and internationally, over the four months where I was either researching, writing or refining this project.

Now I would like to apologise for these next lot of thankyous.

Importantly there are no apologies if there are no legends. This is by no means a definitive list of leaders in Australian sport – that debate would go on forever – but everyone here has a story to tell. Thankyou to all the contributors for indulging me with your time, your trust, and your stories.

Interestingly, US Professor and friend of mine Joe Macdoniels, read through some of the interviews and stories for this book and was stunned by the candour of the contributors – his observation was that US sportspeople are so much more contrived in their responses.

I would also like to thank Michael Johnston and his team at Fairfax Books for their willingness to listen and provide advice right to the last minute.

I would like to thank wholeheartedly our Prime Minister, Mr John Howard, without whose passion for and support of, sport in Australia - which I have experienced first hand - we would not be so successful.

From a personal perspective I thank my mother, Rosa, and sisters Berny, Antoinette and Rosaleen, business partners Chris White (International Quarterback) and Ian Basser (Mettle Group) for their support, and my brother Damian, Rob Coombe and John Murphy for their continued interest in my endeavours.

Finally I would also like to thank Sir Robert Jones (Bob), for advising me that if you want to write fiction, first you must write non-fiction…well there is certainly no fiction in these pages…